Other Books and Series by Jeff Bowen

Cherokee Intermarried White 1906 Volume I thru X

Applications for Enrollment of Creek Newborn Act of 1905
Volumes I thru XIV

Applications for Enrollment of Choctaw Newborn Act of 1905 Volumes I thru XX

Choctaw By Blood Enrollment Cards 1898-1914 Volumes I thru XX

Oglala Sioux Indians Pine Ridge Reservation 1932 Census Book I
Oglala Sioux Indians Pine Ridge Reservation Birth and Death Rolls 1924-1932
Book II

Census of the Sioux and Cheyenne Indians of Pine Ridge Agency
1896 - 1897 Book I
Census of the Sioux and Cheyenne Indians of Pine Ridge Agency
1898 - 1899 Book II

Northern Cheyenne Tongue River, Montana 1904 - 1932 Census
1904-1916 Volume I

Identified Mississippi Choctaw Enrollment Cards 1902-1909 Volumes I, II & III

Northern Cheyenne Tongue River, Montana 1904 - 1932 Census
1917-1926 Volume II

Visit our website at **www.nativestudy.com** to learn more about these
and other books and series by Jeff Bowen

Portrait of Tecumseh from Lossing's
The Pictorial Field-Book of the War of 1812
is a pencil sketch drawn by Pierre Le Dru,
a young French trader at Vincennes, circa 1808.

SAC & FOX - SHAWNEE ESTATES 1885-1910

(UNDER SAC & FOX AGENCY)

VOLUME I

TRANSCRIBED BY

JEFF BOWEN

NATIVE STUDY
Gallipolis, Ohio
USA

Copyright © 2022
by Jeff Bowen

ALL RIGHTS RESERVED
No part of this publication can be reproduced
in any form or manner whatsoever
without previous written permission from the
Copyright holder or Publisher.

Originally published:
Santa Maria, California
2018

Reprinted by:

Native Study LLC
Gallipolis, OH
www.nativestudy.com

Library of Congress Control Number: 2022900261

ISBN: 978-1-64968-125-6

Made in the United States of America.

This series is dedicated to
Tanner Tackett
the Constant Gardner
and Friend
and
In memory of
Raina Mae Fulks.

Ab·sen·tee

noun: **absentee**; plural noun: **absentees**

       1. a person who is expected or required to be present at a place or event but is not.

(According to Webster)

Shawnee

noun, plural Shaw-nees, (especially collectively) Shaw-nee.

       1. a member of an Algonquian-speaking tribe formerly in the east-central U.S., now in Oklahoma.

(According to Dictionary.com)

Shawnee Teaching

"Tagi nsi walr mvci-lutvwi mr-pvyaci-grlahkv, xvga mytv inv gi mvci-lutvwv, gi mvci-ludr-geiv. Walv uwas-panvsi inv, wa-ciganv-hi gi gol-utvwv u kvgesakv-namv manwi-lanvwawewa yasi golutv-mvni geyrgi.

"Tagi bemi-lutvwi walr segalami mr-pvyaci-grlahkv, xvga mvtv inv gi bemi-lutvwv, gi bemi-ludr-geiv gelv. Wakv vhqalami inv, xvga nahfrpi Moneto ut vhqalamrli nili yasi vhqalamahgi gelv!"

Translation:

"Do not kill or injure your neighbor, for it is not him that you injure, you injure yourself. But do good to him, therefore add to his days of happiness as you add to your own.

"Do not wrong or hate your neighbor, for it is not him that you wrong, you wrong yourself. But love him, for Moneto loves him also as He loves you!"

Thomas Wildcat Alford
circa 1936

Special Note

You will notice throughout these volumes the author has attempted to duplicate from the original documents places on the page that were destroyed due to water damage. Whole sections of a page could be missing or torn into multiple pieces. In order to duplicate the damage you will find various shapes with a white format to try to represent the damage and the loss of the ability to completely transcribe many of the pages.

INTRODUCTION

The history of the Shawnee is fascinating. Naturally the most famous Shawnee known would be Tecumseh, born circa. 1768, after four other siblings before him. His father was Puckeshinwa, a Shawnee war chief from Ohio. Puckeshinwa crossed the Ohio close to what is now Gallipolis with his fourteen year son Chiksika by his side. As they followed the lead of Chief Cornstalk during the fall of 1774. Tecumseh's famous father was mortally wounded during the fight they would soon encounter. The Shawnees were unexpectedly discovered by a couple of early morning turkey hunters from the settlement called Point Pleasant. These hunters ran as fast as possible back to where the Ohio and Kanawha Rivers meet and sounded the alarm that the Shawnees were coming, the fight lasted most of the day but not without loss to both sides. The Shawnees were badly outnumbered. Pucheshinwa was carried back across the Ohio or as the Shawnees called it the *Spaylaywitheepi*, with the intention to take him back to his village. He must have known his time was short as he laid there telling Chiksika to make sure he devoted his time not only to Tecumseh's but also his younger brothers training in becoming warriors. Pucheshinwa succumbed to his wounds shortly after that request and was secretly buried deep in the forest that day. Chiksika saw his father mortally wounded while defending their home. He had a reverence for his father as a great warrior. He wanted to follow his father's path and not die an average death. In his heart, it had to be on the battlefield as a warrior. Tecumseh followed his brother's every step and planned to die defending his land as his father and brother had. There was no surrendering or giving in to the Americans.

There are several descriptions out there of Tecumseh from his contemporaries, but David Edmunds found one during his research that seems to be the most commanding of any found. "Captain John B. Glegg, Brock's aide-de-camp, who was present at the meetings between Brock and Tecumseh, recorded one of the most vivid descriptions of the Shawnee. According to Glegg, in August 1812 Tecumseh still was in the prime of his life, giving the impression of a man ten years younger. Tecumseh's appearance was very prepossessing; his figure light and finely proportioned; his age I imagined to be about five and thirty [he actually was forty four]; in height, five feet nine or ten inches; his complexion, light copper; countenance, oval, with bright hazle eyes, beaming cheerfulness, energy, and decision. Three small silver crowns, or coronets were suspended from the lower cartilage of his aquiline nose; and a large silver medallion of George the Third, which I believe his ancestor had received from Lord Dorchester, when governor-general of Canada, was attached to a mixed coloured wampum string, and hung around his neck. His dress consisted of a plain, neat uniform, tanned deer-skin jacket, with long trousers of the same material, the seams of both being covered with neatly cut fringe; and he had on his feet leather moccasins, much ornamented with work made from the dyed quills of the porcupine."[1]

There were approximately 39 years that passed between Tecumseh's and his father's deaths.

It is hard to believe that the Shawnee's history being as extensive as it was during the early stages of the United States that their descendants' records were so closely guarded under the care of a vegetable bind in an leaky attic. Not only the Shawnee's but also the Sac & Fox, the Pottawatomie and the Kickapoo. There are also many other tribal affiliates to be found in this series, not to mention someone like Jim Thorpe and his family members of the Sac and Fox tribe. Not only was he a gold metal Olympian and multiple sport competitor, but at the time one of America's favorite sons. Thank goodness someone was finally conscious of the situation. The description in the next paragraph explains the neglect of these important documents as given by the Oklahoma Historical Societies Microfilm Catalog.

"In 1933 a survey of Indian tribal records in Oklahoma revealed that the files of the Shawnee and the old Sac and Fox agencies had been sadly neglected, and the lack of space for storing them properly had resulted in much loss. Charles Eggers, Superintendent of the Shawnee Agency, reported that most of the non-current records of his agency were boxed in a storehouse. The papers of the old Sac and Fox Agency were in the loft of a warehouse which was also used for storing vegetables. The roof of the building leaked and the papers were in danger of destruction from moisture. Following the passage of the Congressional Act of March 27, 1934 (H.R. 5631 Public No. 133) which placed the tribal records in the custody of the Oklahoma Historical Society."

As described above the history of the Shawnee people isn't an ordinary history but an extraordinary time in all of our ancestors' lives. Reading Allen W. Eckert's extensive studies taken from what is known as the Draper Papers, a historical record meticulously documented beginning circa 1830. Though Draper covered an approximate time between the 1740's to the 1810's, his collection covered documents and transcriptions concerning Boone, Kenton, Rogers Clark and Joseph Brant, not to mention a considerable amount of Shawnee history from the entirety of the Ohio and Mississippi Valley's. Other authors such as Colin G. Calloway and R. David Edmunds provide an in depth study of the Shawnee people as well as Tecumseh and his life leaving no rock unturned in their research.

As you read different references you find diverse opinions on Tecumseh's mother as to what tribe she came from. Eckert through Draper's work says, "This was

---

[1] Tecumseh, R. David Edmunds Pg. 162-163, Para. 3-4

when Pucksinwah, then twenty-six, led the war party against the Cherokees that had resulted in the capture of Methotasa."[2] Indicating Tecumseh's mother might have been Cherokee. Yet, R. David Edmunds writes, "In 1768, while the Iroquois were selling Shawnee lands at the Treaty of Fort Stanwix, a Creek woman married to a Shawnee man gave birth to a son at Old Piqua, a Shawnee village on the Mad River in Western Ohio. The woman had a difficult labor before giving birth in the small lodge especially constructed for that purpose, some distance from the family's wigwam. The mother, Methoataske (Turtle Laying Its Eggs), had grown up among the Creek villages in Alabama and had met her husband when some of the Shawnee sought refuge among the Creeks during the 1750s. The father Puckeshinwa, remained with his wife's people until about 1760, when the family left Alabama and migrated to Ohio."[3]

You also will find different opinions on how they dressed back then or wore their hair. In Edmunds' book *Tecumseh*, his brother the Prophet Tenskwatawa states, "Warriors should again shave their heads and wear the scalp locks worn by their ancestors." And yet in Thomas Wildcat Alford's *Civilization,* he says, "We boys wore our hair short, very much as the girls of today wear their hair bobbed. This is the way Shawnee men always have worn their hair. Never did they braid it, as some other tribes do."

Alford's book *Civilization* out of the many resources read was likely one of the most informative and enjoyable references in the study. Thomas Wildcat Alford was born in 1860 and belonged to the Absentee Shawnee tribe. He states that he was a descendant of Tecumseh. He spoke about when his family slept under the stars each night and that he never had an English name until his father had him go to school at a Quaker mission. Mr. Alford also talks about two things with real clarity. Alford educates us about clans in the sixth chapter, expounding upon the active history of the Shawnees and the different responsibilities of each as well as divisions among the clans that created tribal changes. These dissensions were nothing new. Anyone that has read extensively about the Shawnee will realize that Alford understood his people and their history. When he wrote about tribal clashes or divisions during the early days, he managed to translate on paper their strength and character. He showed for generations they literally believed they were given an ability to make themselves self-reliant when it came to survival. They traveled far and wide following their own path while installing their own way of life that made them powerful adversaries whether it be against the British, the French or the Americans moving west. Other tribes found them to be awful enemies or potent allies. Then he compares their tribal government

---

[2] A Sorrow in Our Heart, Allen W. Eckert Pg. 22, Para. 3

[3] Tecumseh, R. David Edmunds, Pg. 17 Para. 1

and the clan leaders to being quite similar to the U.S. Presidency and the different government entities. Alford also brings up business committees for the tribe.

He starts with a concise description of the clans, "Originally there were five clans composing the Shawnee tribe, including the two principle clans, Tha-we-gi-la and Cha-lah-kaw-tha, from one of which came the national or principal chief. The remaining three, the Pec-ku-we, the Kis-pu-go, and the May-ku-jay, each had its own chief who was subordinate to the principal chief in national matters, but independent in matters pertaining to the duties of his clan. Each clan had a certain duty to perform for the whole tribe. For instance the Pec-ku-we clan, or its chief, had charge of the maintenance of order and looked after the celebration of things pertaining to religion or faith; the Kis-pu-go clan had charge of matters pertaining to war and the preparation and training of warriors; the May-ku-jay clan had charge of things relating to health and medicine and food for the whole tribe. But the two powerful clans, the Tha-we-gi-la and the Cha-lah-kaw-tha, had charge of political affairs and all matters that affected the tribe as a whole. Indeed, the tribal government may be likened to the government of the United States, in which each state (clan), with it governor (chief), is sovereign in local matters, but subordinate to the president of the United States (principal chief) in national matters. The difference is that the president of the United States must be elected, and may be changed with each election, while the principal chief came to his office by heritage and held it for life, or during good behavior.

At the time of which I write the Shawnee tribe had been divided for many years, and only the Tha-we-gi-la, the Pec-ku-we, and the Kis-pu-go clans were represented in the Absentee Shawnee band. These three clans always had been closely related, while the Cha-lah-kaw-tha and the May-ku-jay had always stood together, and were represented in the group that I have mentioned as living in Kansas at the time of the Civil War."[4]

As referenced earlier Thomas Wildcat Alford brought up their present Indian agent, Thomas, on September 13, 1893, wanting him to present a list of prominent men in their tribe to hold positions on a business committee. This presented a whole new world for the tribe with new pressures through white change so to speak. The government was instilling in their world the destruction of their heritage in tribal customs and culture all to control Indian land through allotment. When he was being told to help form this committee, he was actually being told, what we are doing is we are wiping out your way of life forever. The Congress of the United States was presenting the abolition of all tribal governments so the land could be manipulated through the Curtis Act of 1898. They said, we are splitting the land up. They were allotting so many acres to each tribal member. How much they got depended on

---

[4] Civilization, Alford; Pg. 44, Para. 1-2

whether they planned to farm or raise cattle. If they were building herds they were given double the land for grazing. Alford said, "It was on the thirteenth day of September, 1893 that Agent Thomas informed the Shawnees that he had been directed by the Commissioner of Indian Affairs to submit for approval the names of seven of the most prominent men of the tribe who would constitute a Business Committee to supersede the chiefs and councilors of the old tribal government. The Business Committee was to represent the Absentee Shawnees as a tribe in all dealings with the United States and to act in an advisory capacity to the individual members of the tribe. They were to certify to the identity of grantors of sales of land and to act for the tribe in other matters.[5]

During the study it was noticed that the Curtis Act being enacted on June 28, 1898 and Alford's mentioning its initiation during 1893 became a point of interest or at least premature. It was found that Congress had actually started working in this area of seizure approximately five years prior to the agent's notification, "In 1893 Congress began a special allotment process for the Five Tribes, enacting a number of laws that affect the governmental powers of the tribes. Some of these laws, like the 1889 and 1890 Acts, extended certain Arkansas laws over Indian Territory and expanded federal court jurisdiction; they are relevant today only insofar as they may indirectly affect tribal judicial powers."[6]

Their mention of these laws only being relevant today, though actually not spoken, plead plausible deniability while coinciding with the Indian Reorganization Act of 1934. The government was on a mission. Land and control. The allotment had to take place. They were wanting statehood. They were wanting the Native people to be under one umbrella with everyone else. Tribes were nations. Just like a foreign nation, they were their own government. Originally our constitution was modeled after the Iroquois model, had to start somewhere? So what we did was split up the land among the people that already owned it. Then we took what was left, approximately 90 million acres and sold it at a profit. Who got the money? Only the politicians at the time know? But years after taking the chiefs and councils away there was likely mass chaos like a town hall today. So the government likely was wanting out of the tribal control business. At least enough that they could just control it without being in the bullseye so to speak. Congress and the state had already achieved its goals. So this act was written with the statement that it was a model to make all think we do this for you. "The IRA was intended to provide a mechanism for the tribe as a governmental unit to interact with and adapt to a modern society, rather than to force the assimilation of individual Indians.

---

[5] Civilization, Alford; Pg. 161, Para. 2

[6] Federal Indian Law, Cohen; Pg. 781, Para. 3

The IRA was also an attempt to improve the economic situation of Indians. The Act was intended to stop the alienation of tribal land needed to support Indians, and to provide for acquisition of additional acreage for tribes. Tribes were encouraged to organize along the lines of modern business corporations; a system of financial credit was included to reach this economic objective."[7] Interestingly enough Cohen and Alford both mention this same organizational technique, only one as law and another as a tribal member.

It is disconcerting just in reading a reference from Senator Charles Curtis as he mentioned in his biography that by the time Congress finished rewriting the bill he had submitted he hardly recognized it. "Officially titled the "Act for the Protection of the People of Indian Territory", the Act is named for Charles Curtis, congressman from Kansas and its author. He was of mixed Native American and European descent: on his mother's side -Kansa, Osage, Potawatomi, and French; and on his father's - three ethnic lines of British Isles ancestry. Curtis was raised in part on the Kaw Reservation of his maternal grandparents, but also lived with his paternal grandparents and attended Topeka High School. He read law, became an attorney, and later was elected to the United States House of Representatives and Senate. He served as Vice-President under Herbert Hoover. In the usual fashion, by the time the bill HR 8581 had gone through five revisions in committees in both the House of Representatives and the Senate, there was little left of Curtis' original draft. In his hand-written autobiography, Curtis noted having been unhappy with the final version of the Curtis Act. He believed that the Five Civilized Tribes needed to make changes. He thought that the way ahead for Native Americans was through education and use of both their and the majority cultures, but he also had hoped to give more support to Native American transitions."[8]

The records within this series concern The Absentee Shawnee as well as many other people with different tribal affiliations. Also within these pages are closely related tribes that were under the same agency (The Sac & Fox Agency, Oklahoma) for many years like the Sac & Fox, the Pottawatomie and the Kickapoo. There are likely state recognized Shawnee tribes in the United States, but, "The Absentee Shawnee Tribe of Indians of Oklahoma (or Absentee Shawnee) is one of three federally recognized tribes of Shawnee people. Historically residing in the Eastern United States, the original Shawnee lived in the areas that are now Ohio, Indiana, Illinois, Kentucky, Tennessee, Pennsylvania, and other neighboring states. It is documented that they occupied and traveled through lands from Canada to Florida, from the Mississippi River to the eastern continental coast. In contemporary times, the Absentee Shawnee Tribe headquarters in Shawnee, Oklahoma; its tribal jurisdiction

---

[7] Federal Indian Law, Cohen; Pg. 147 Para. 1-2
[8] Curtis Act of 1898, Wikipedia

area includes land properties in Oklahoma in both Cleveland County and Pottawatomie County." [Today] "There are approximately 3,050 enrolled Absentee Shawnee tribal members, 2,315 of whom live in Oklahoma. Tribal membership follows blood quantum criteria, with applicants requiring a minimum of one eighth (1/8) documented Absentee-Shawnee blood to be placed on its membership rolls, as set forth by the tribal constitution. Though it is not a formal division, there is a social separation within its current tribal membership between the traditionalist Big Jim Band, which kept cultural traditions and ceremonies and has its primary populace in the Little Axe, Norman area, and the assimilationist White Turkey Band, which adopted European ways of the European majority, with many families based in the Shawnee area. Regardless of historical viewpoints, the bands cooperate for the future of the tribe."[9]

When this study was first pursued an old Xerox copy of a catalog that sat on the shelf for twenty five years was the first place searched for a viable source. It was titled, "Catalog of Microfilm Holdings in the Archives & Manuscripts Div. Oklahoma Historical Society 1976-1989". As mentioned in the description from this catalog's Introduction for the Sac and Fox Indian Agencies, it states, "In 1901 the Sac and Fox Agency was divided. The Sac and Fox Agency itself remained at the old site near Stroud with jurisdiction over the Sac and Fox and the Iowa. The Shawnee, Potawatomi and Kickapoo Agency (sometimes simply called the Shawnee Agency) was established about two miles south of Shawnee, Oklahoma. The agencies continued their separate existence until 1919 when they were merged becoming the Shawnee Agency.

Of course today in 2018, everything is digital and on the computer. You have to be thankful for having an old catalog and books on a shelf. There is nothing like the feel of holding a book in your hand. You can pick it up when you want and let your eyes travel to anywhere or any time in history. It has solid print that nobody can manipulate or change. It's just yours to wrap yourself up in without any glowing distractions as Native Americans call them, "Talking Leaves".

Jeff Bowen
Gallipolis, Ohio
NativeStudy.com

---

[9] Absentee-Shawnee Tribe of Indians Wikipedia

Sac & Fox – Shawnee Estates
1885-1910 Volume I

AFFIDAVIT AS TO LAWFUL HEIRS.
INHERITED INDIAN LANDS.

STATE OF Oklahoma,) ss:
COUNTY OF Lincoln,)

Frank Carter and Alex Connelly of lawful age, each first being duly sworn, say:

That affiants were well acquainted with Mamie Pattequa, deceased, who was the identical Indian of the Sac and Fox Tribe of Indians residing on the Sac and Fox Reservation, to whom a trust or other patent containing restrictions upon alienation was issued for her allotment, No. 133 for the following described land situate in the County of Pottawatomie, State of Oklahoma, to wit:

NW/4 of Section 33, township, 11, North of Route 4, East, I.

Affiants further say that they are well acquainted with the family history of the said Mamie Pattequa, deceased allottee: that died on or about the 5th day of February 1895, 190...., at the age of 38 years. un married and with issue, leaving as h er sole heirs at law the following named persons:

Bertha Pattequa, daughter, now aged 15, sharing a .... 1/2 int.
Addie Pattequa, daughter, now aged 13, sharing a .... 1/2 "

Said decedent [illegible] no other child or children, nor the issue of any deceased child or children.

Affiants further say that they are each well acquainted with the grantors who acknowledged a deed bearing date ...., 190......, conveying the above described land to ....; that the said grantors are the identical persons by name hereinbefore mentioned as the sole heirs of the deceased allottee.

Affiants further say that the said allottee did not reside upon h...... homestead or allotment, nor cultivate the land sold during h...... lifetime and immediately preceding h...... death.

Affiants further say, that they are each residents of Lincoln County, State of Oklahoma; and have been for over ten years last past and are members of the Sac and Fox Tribe.

Witnesses:
[Signature Illegible]   Fra [paper torn]
    [Signature Illegible]   Ale [paper torn]

Sac & Fox – Shawnee Estates
1885-1910 Volume I

Subscribed in my presence and sworn to before me this   [bottom of page torn off]
My commission expires   Jun   [paper torn]

AFFIDAVIT AS TO LAWFUL HEIRS.
INHERITED INDIAN LANDS.

STATE OF   Oklahoma,   )
) ss:
COUNTY OF   Lincoln,   )

    Ulyses S. Grant   and   Alex Connelly
of lawful age, each first being duly sworn, say:
    That affiants were well acquainted with   Lucy Black
deceased, who was the identical Indian of the   Sac and Fox   Tribe of Indians residing on the   Sac and Fox   Reservation, to whom a trust or other patent containing restrictions upon alienation was issued for her   allotment, No. 214   for the following described land situate in the County of   Lincoln   , State of   Oklahoma   , to wit:
SE/4 Sec. 7, T 16 [?], R.G.E, I.M.

    Affiants further say that they are well acquainted with the family history of the said   Lucy Black   , deceased allottee: that   she   died on or about the   2nd   day of   July   1892   , 190   , at the age of   50   years
    married and with out issue, leaving as her sole heirs at law the following named persons:
James Black, husband, inherited 1/2 interest in her estate.
Mary [Illegible], sister, inherited 1/2 interest in her estate.
James Black died Aug. 25, 1892, leaving William Parkinson, aged 75 years
[Name Illegible] [illegible], whose father, Mah-ake-na, deceased, was a brother of [Name Illegible...] He died Nov. 8, 1906, aged 75 years, leaving as his sole heir his wife, Mamie Parkinson, who then inherited the 1/2 interest in the estate of Lucy Black, [remainder illegible]

    (See sheet attached)

~~Affiants further say that they are each well acquainted with the grantors who acknowledged a deed bearing date................., 190.... conveying the above described land to........................., that the said grantors are the identical persons by name hereinbefore mentioned as the sole heirs of the deceased allottee.~~

~~Affiants further say that the said allottee did not reside upon h....-homestead or allotment, nor cultivate the land sold during h.....lifetime and immediately preceding h.....death.~~

Sac & Fox – Shawnee Estates
1885-1910 Volume I

Affiants further say, that they are each residents of **LINCOLN** County, State of _____ and have been for over ten years last past and are members of the Sac and Fox Tribe of Indians.

Witnesses:
[Illegible] RS Reeves
Charles H [Illegible]

Ulyses S Grant his X mark
Alex Connelly

Subscribed in my presence and sworn to before me this _____ day of _____, 190___.

_____
Notary Public.

OCT 11 1908
My commission expires _____ 190___

Benjamin Harrison, aged 65 years, first cousin of James Black, deceased, inherits 1/5 of 1/6, or 1/6 interest in the original estate of Lucy Black, deceased.

Fannie Randall, (Kottoe) deceased, was first cousin of James Black, deceased, and inherited an undivided 1/3 of 1/2 or 1/6 interest in the original estate of Lucy Black. Benjamin Harrison and Fannie Randall (deceased) were half-brother and sister. Their father was Am-na-ane, deceased, who was a brother of Sha-was-[??]-huck, deceased, who was the father of James Black, deceased, Fannie Randall, deceased, and Benjamin Harrison, first cousins.

Fannie Randall died May 17, 1897, leaving as her heirs, Tom Penashe, husband, sharing 1/3 of 1/3 of 1/2 or 1/18 interest; Amos Black, son, aged 25 yrs.; Leona Franklin, daughter, age 36 years; Stephen Harrison, (insane) son, aged 30 yrs.; and Paul Randall, son, aged 18 yrs., each sharing 1/4 of 2/3 of 1/3 of 1/2 or 1/36 interest each in the original estate of Lucy Black.

Mary Cuppawhe died May 1, 1895, unmarried and leaving to her sole heir Caroline Pickett, her daughter, who inherited half of the original estate of Lucy Black, deceased.

James Black, deceased, left no father, nor mother, no brother nor sister, no wife, nor children, or issue of any deceased wife or children, nor issue of any deceased brother or sister.

William Parkinson, deceased, left no children, nor issue of any deceased child or children; no brother or sister, or issue of any deceased brother or sister; no father or mother, and left as his only heir his wife, Maggie Parkinson.

Fannie Randall (Kottoe) deceased, left no other child or children than as above stated, nor the issue of any deceased child of children.

Sac & Fox – Shawnee Estates
1885-1910 Volume I

Mary Cuppawhe, left no husband nor any other child or children or issue of any deceased child or children than Caroline Pickett, her sole heir.

Recapitulation:

Maggie Parkinson	1/6 interest.
Benjamin Harrison	1/6 "
Tom Penashe	1/18 "
Amos Black	1/36 "
Leona Franklin	1/36 "
Stephen Harrison	1/36 "
Paul Randall	1/36 "
Caroline Pickett	1/2 "

AFFIDAVIT AS TO LAWFUL HEIRS.
INHERITED INDIAN LANDS.

STATE OF Oklahoma,) ss:
COUNTY OF Lincoln.)

Frank Carter and Alex Connelly of lawful age, each first being duly sworn, say:

That affiants were well acquainted with Joseph Harris deceased, who was the identical Indian of the Sac and Fox Tribe of Indians residing on the Sac and Fox Reservation, to whom a trust or other patent containing restrictions upon alienation was issued for his allotment, No. 105 for the following described land situate in the County of Pottawatomie , State of Oklahoma , to wit:

SE/4 of Section 8; township 11, North of Range 5, East, I.

Affiants further say that they are well acquainted with the family history of the said Joseph Harris , deceased allottee: that he died on or about the 5th day of September , 1906 , at the age of 42 years.

........married and with .... issue, leaving as h is sole heirs at law the following named persons: Liza Martin, wife, sharing a ....1/3 interest
Mary Harris, daughter, now age 17 sharing a ......1/3 "
Moses Harris, son, " " 15 " " ......1/3 "

4

Sac & Fox – Shawnee Estates
1885-1910 Volume I

The deceased left no other child or children, nor the issue of any deceased child or children.

Affiants further say that they are each well acquainted with the grantors who acknowledged a deed bearing date ...., 190.... conveying the above described land to ....; that the said grantors are the identical persons by name hereinbefore mentioned as the sole heirs of the deceased allottee.

Affiants further say that the said allottee did not reside upon h.... homestead or allotment, nor cultivate the land sold during h.... lifetime and immediately preceding h.... death.

Affiants further say, that they are each residents of Lincoln County, State of Oklahoma and have been for over ten years last past and are members of the Sac and Fox Tribe of Indians.

Witnesses:
   Charles F Welles   [paper torn]
   John RS Reeves   [paper torn]
Subscribed in my presence   [paper torn]

OFFICE OF
THOMAS HARRISON
Probate Judge, Montgomery County

Independence, Kansas, March 18   *188* 5

Hon Isaac A Taylor: Sir   Your letter of Feb 19 1885 in regard to the estate of abbro[sic] Goodell decd was received in due time. I expected the administrator to make a settlement about that time but he informed me that he had to sue one of its notes he took at the sale and the parties took a stay of execution which extended the time of payment to about the present time. We thought [Illegible] to delay the settlement until after the collection of that money. I expect the settlement will now be made very soon.

                Respectfully,
                Thomas Harrison
                Probate Judge

Sac & Fox – Shawnee Estates
1885-1910 Volume I

Letter 6264 '87 **Department of the Interior.**

OFFICE OF INDIAN AFFAIRS

WASHINGTON

Washington, March 12th, 1887.

Moses Neal,
    U.S. Indian Agent,
        Sac and Fox Agency, I.T.

Sir:

    A claim of heirs of Lewis Goodboo, deceased, a Miami of Indiana, for $730.56, has been presented to this Office for settlement by Frank and Thomas Goodboo and Hannah Hardin, nee Goodboo, residents of Shawneetown, I.T. The said claim was referred by this office to the Second Auditor for settlement and returned with the following objections by reason of imperfection of evidence as to identity and residence,

viz:-

    "The "claim is stated in favor of three heirs, Frank and Thomas Goodboo and Hannah Hardin, "Goodboo as half brothers and sister of the deceased. Of these, an application is filed by "Frank only; but the identity of Frank Goodboo who makes claim with the half brother "and heir of that name, is not shown by the witnesses. The claim, if perfected as to "Frank, can only be allowed for his portion in absence of an application from the other "heirs, with proof of identity and post office address in each case."

    In order to complete the evidence in this case, I have to request that you notify these claimants to appear be for[sic] you and make application in writing for their shares of this money - $242.53 each - with proof of their identity as the heirs of Lewis Goodboo, deceased, to which statements, which are to be sworn to, you will append your certificate as to your knowledge and belief as to identity and post office address.

                      Very respectfully,
                          J D C Atkins
                              Commissioner.

J.B.C.

Sac & Fox – Shawnee Estates
1885-1910 Volume I

S. J. SCOTT & CO
GROCERIES, DRY GOODS
CLOTHING, HATS, BOOTS, SHOES

General Indian Merchandise

Shawneetown, I. T. May 12th *189*0

Col S.L. Patrick US Ind Agt
    Sac and Fox Agency I.T.

Dear Sir,

    I have substituted my nephew Mr Jerome Navarre to carry out the contract of Mr Bro Isadore Navarre Dec^d he can adjust all afcs[sic] and act as tho Mr Brother Isadore was living in person – his name instead of Isadore can appear in settlement, if I properly understood the suggestions. I have arranged with Mr S J Scott Co and Mr Jerome Navarre in putting the afcs in proper shape of all parties to whom Mr Brother Isadore was indebted –

    I have authorized him (Jerome Navarre) to take charge in all property here belonging to Mr Brother Isadore. In fact he is now authorized by me to take charge of all of Isadore Navarre's effects, property.

                  Yours Very Truly
                    A. F. Navarre

          ****

          Shawneetown June 27th 190[sic]

Col. Patrick
    Sax[sic] & Fox Agency
        Ind Ter.

    When Isadore Navarre died his brother came here to get boards to make a coffin for him said the weather was too warm to keep him to send off to get a coffin. I enclose bill for lumber and will be very much obliged if you will pay it out of the money due his estate for his work, as I am informed that his work was for Government and that you settle for it.

                Very respectfully
                    Elizabeth F[illegible]

Sac & Fox – Shawnee Estates
1885-1910 Volume I

Land.
17917-1893.

Department of the Interior.
OFFICE OF INDIAN AFFAIRS
WASHINGTON,
May 22, 1893.

Samuel L. Patrick, Esq.,
   U.S. Indian Agent,
      Sac and Fox Agency,
         Oklahoma.
Sir:

    I am in receipt of a communication from D.G. Cheesman[sic], Clerk in charge of your agency, dated May 11, 1893, in which he states that Mrs Cassie Eaton (Sac and Fox) has just called upon him and requested that he inquire whether an exchange can be made in the land patented to her son, Lorenzo Dow and that of her daughter, Cassie Eaton. She claims that the northeast quarter of section 17, township 11, range 4 east, was selected for her son but by a clerical error was allotted to her daughter, Cassie, who is now dead. The mother desires the exchange of the land so that her son can have the benefit of timber of which his land is destitute. He requests if anything can be done for Mrs Eaton that your office be instructed as to what papers would be required to be drawn up in order to place the same properly before the Department.

    In reply I have to advise you that I do not consider it practicable to effect the change desired by Mrs Eaton. The child being dead, under the ruling of the Department, a patent cannot issue in the name of the deceased. The land patented to Cassie Eaton, Jr., will descend to her heirs according to the laws of the Territory of Oklahoma.

                Very respectfully,
                Franklin Armstrong
(Allen)   Acting Commissioner.
  P.

Refer in reply to the following:

Finance.
L.-33,673.-'94.

Department of the Interior.
OFFICE OF INDIAN AFFAIRS
WASHINGTON September 24, 1894

Edward L. Thomas,
   U.S. Indian Agent,
      Sac & Fox Agency, Oklahoma Territory.

Sac & Fox – Shawnee Estates
1885-1910 Volume I

Sir:-

Before any action can be taken by this Office towards paying Tecumseh and Ida Roubidoux, the alleged heirs of their sister, Bessie Lee, the money claimed to be due the estate of said Bessie Lee referred to in your letter of the 28th, ultimo, it will be necessary for this office to be informed who said Bessie Lee was, the nature and the value of her estate, and any other information which will enable this Office to act intelligently in the matter.

Very respectfully,
Franklin Armstrong
Acting Commissioner.

LETTERS OF GUARDIANSHIP

TERRITORY OF OKLAHOMACOUNTY, ss.

IN THE PROBATE COURT.

*Before*J. H. Daugherty*Probate Judge*

In the name of the Territory of Oklahoma, to all to whom these Presents shall come, Greeting:

KNOW YE, ThatCeasar Washington and James Washington having been adjudgedto minors unable to managetheirestate, by the Probate Court of saidPottawatomie County, Oklahoma Territory, on the petition ofBlue Coat is hereby appointed and commissioned by the Probate Court of said County as Guardian of the personSand property of the saidCeasar Washington and James Washington untilThey all arrive at majority or until it is otherwise ordered by a court of competent jurisdiction in accordance with the decree of this Court, dated the20thday ofOctoberA.D. 189 4

WitnessJ H Daugherty

Probate Judge
with the seal of the Probate Court ofPottawatomieCounty Oklahoma Territory, hereto affixed at his office inTecumseh in said County, this20thday ofOctoberA.D. 189 4

J H Daugherty
Judge of the Probate Court

9

Sac & Fox – Shawnee Estates
1885-1910 Volume I

Territory of Oklahoma Pottawatomie County, ss

I, **Blue Coat** do solemnly swear that I will support the Constitution of the United States and the Organic Act of the Territory of Oklahoma, and that I will discharge all and singular the duties of Guardian of the persons and estate of the above named

Ceasar Washington and James Washington

according to the tenor and effect of the accompanying bond, and according to law to the best of my knowledge and ability

his
Blue X Coat
mark
Guardian

Subscribed and sworn to before me, this 20th day of October A.D. 1894

J H Daugherty
Probate Judge

****

Territory of Oklahoma
County of Pottawatomie:

I J H Daugherty Probate Judge of said County certify that on the 20th day of October 1894 Blue Coat was appointed guardian of the persons and estates of Ceasar Washington and James Washington and that the within a true copy of his letters of guardianship and as appears from the records and files of my office

Witness my hand and the
Seal of said Court this 20th
day of October 1894
J H Daugherty
Probate Judge

BOND ADMINISTRATORS

KNOW ALL MEN BY THESE PRESENTS:

That we Bluecoat as principal and
J C King and

as sureties are held and firmly bound unto the Territory of Oklahoma in the sum of Two Hundred DOLLARS, for the payment of which well and truly to be made we do hereby bind ourselves, our heirs, executors, administrators and assigns, jointly and severalty firmly by these presents.

DATED, Signed and Sealed, by us this 29th day of September A.D. 1894

Sac & Fox – Shawnee Estates
1885-1910 Volume I

THE CONDITION of the above obligation is such, that whereas, the above bounder Bluecoat *has been duly appointed by the Probate Court in and for the County of Pottawatomie and Territory of Oklahoma, Administrator of the estate of* Nellie Washington *deceased.*

Now if said Administrator shall make and return into said Probate Court on oath, within 60 *days from this date, or sooner if ordered by the Probate Judge, a true inventory of all moneys, goods, chattels, rights and credits of said deceased, and shall administer according to law, all the moneys, goods, chattel, rights and credits of said deceased and the proceeds of all* her *real estate that may be sold for the payment of* her *debts, which shall at any time come to the possession of the administrator or to the possession of any other person for* her *and shall render upon oath a true account of* her *administration annually, and at any other times when required by said Probate Court of by the law; and shall pay any balance remaining in* his *hands upon the settlement of* his *accounts to such persons as said Probate Court or the law shall direct, and shall deliver the Letters of Administration into the Court, in case any will of said deceased shall be hereafter proved and allowed, then this obligation will be void; else in full force and effect.*

WITNESS

                       Bluecoat his X mark (SEAL)
                       J C King   (SEAL)

The above bond taken and approved by me this 1st *day of* October   *A.D 1894*

                       J H Daugherty

                       Probate Judge

VERIFICATION OF SURETIES

THE TERRITORY OF OKLAHOMA
POTTAWATOMIE COUNTY

    Bluecoat & J C King

being first duly sworn each for himself, doth depose and say he is a resident of the Territory of Oklahoma and freeholder therein; and that he is worth the sum of Two Hundred & fifty *DOLLARS over and above all debts and liabilities besides property exempt by law from execution.*

                       Bluecoat his X mark (SEAL)
                       J C King   (SEAL)

SUBSCRIBED and sworn to before me this 1st *day of* October *1894*

                       J H Daugherty
                       Probate Judge

****

Sac & Fox – Shawnee Estates
1885-1910 Volume I

Territory of Oklahoma
County of Pottawatomie

    I J H Daugherty Probate Judge of said county certify that the within is a true copy of the bond of Bluecoat as administrator of the estate of Nellie Washington, deceased.

                                Witness my hand and official seal this 20th day of October, 1894

                                J H Daugherty Probate Judge

****

LETTERS OF ADMINISTRATION.

In the Probate Court.

Of the County of Pottawatomie
Territory of Oklahoma.

In the Matter of the Estate of

Nellie Washington
                 Deceased.

LETTERS OF ADMINISTRATION

Territory of Oklahoma, County of , ss

Bluecoat is hereby appointed administrator of the Estate of Nellie Washington deceased.

Witness J H Daugherty Judge of the Probate Court of the County of Pottawatomie with the Seal thereof affixed the 2nd day of October 1894

By the Court
J H Daugherty
Judge of the Probate Court

Territory of Oklahoma, County of Pottawatomie , ss

    I, Bluecoat do solemnly swear that I will support the Constitution of the United States and the Organic Act of the Territory of Oklahoma, and that I will faithfully perform according to the law, the duties of administrator of the Estate of Nellie Washington deceased.

                                 Bluecoat X mark
Subscribed and sworn to before me the 2nd day of October 1894

                                 J H Daugherty
                                 Judge of the Probate Court

Sac & Fox – Shawnee Estates
1885-1910 Volume I

****

Territory of Oklahoma,
County of Pottawatomie

I, J H Daugherty Probate Judge of same county certify that the within is a [Illegible] copy of the letters of administration of Bluecoat as administrator of the estate of Nellie Washington, deceased as appears from the records of my office.

Witness my hand and the Seal of said
Court this 2nd day of October 1894
J H Daugherty
Probate Judge

****

Office of
KING & ASHER,
Attorneys-at-Law.

FREDERICK KING
W. R. ASHER

Tecumseh Okl. Ter., Nov. 15th 189 4

Mr Edw Thomas
   Agt

Dear Sir
   I send you papers of Blue Coat as guardian and admr. and ask that you reccommend[sic] the payment of said claims as the Litchfield payroll will disclose the fact that they are just & unpaid.

Yours truly
W.R. Asher

****

Territory of Oklahoma
Pottawatomie County ss

To Commissioner Indian Affairs

The undersigned Blue Coat a Shawnee Indian hereby makes application for the money due ~~on~~ the Estate of Nellie Washington decd. and member of the absentee Shawnee tribe of Indians from the U.S. Government. Said Blue Coat being the duly appointed Administrator of said estate

his
Blue X Coat
mark

Witnesses
   W.R. Asher
   JC King

Sac & Fox – Shawnee Estates
1885-1910 Volume I

****

Territory of Oklahoma
Pottawatomie County ss

To Hon Commissioner Indian Affairs

The undersigned Blue Coat a Shawnee Indian hereby makes application for the money due Caesar Washington and James Washington as members of the Absentee Shawnee tribe of Indians in Oklahoma from the govt. of the U.S. as shown by the pay rolls of said tribe of Indians.

Witnesses
W.R. Asher
JC King

his
Blue X Coat
mark

****

GUARDIAN'S BOND

KNOW ALL MEN BY THESE PRESENTS

That Blue Coat *as principal and* J C King *as sureties, all of the County of* Pottawatomie *in the Territory of Oklahoma are held and firmly bound in the penal sum of* Four Hundred *DOLLARS for the payment of which well and truly be made, we do bind ourselves and our legal representatives.*

Witness our hands and seals this 20 *day of* October *A.D.* 1894

The Condition of the above Obligation is such, *That if the above named* Blue Coat *who has been appointed by the Probate Court of* Pottawatomie *County, Territory of Oklahoma, Guardian*

Ceasar Washington and James Washington

*shall within three months from the date of this appointment, make a true inventory of all the real and personal estate of the ward that shall some into h*is *possession or knowledge, and return the same into court, and,*

Second, shall dispose and manage all such estate and effects according to law and for the best interest of the said minors *and shall faithfully discharge h*is *trust as such Guardian, and*

*Third, shall render an account on oath of the property in h*is *hand including the proceeds of all the real estate which may be sold by h*im *and of the management and disposition of such property within one year after the date of this appointment, and at such other times as the Court shall direct, and*

*Fourth, at the expiration of h*is *trust to settle h*er *accounts with the Court, or with the said* minors *h*is *ward or h legal representatives, and shall and do pay over and deliver all the estate and effects remaining in h hands or due from h on such settlement to the person or persons who shall be lawfully entitled thereto, then this obligation to be void, otherwise to remain in full force and virtue.*

Sac & Fox – Shawnee Estates
1885-1910 Volume I

Attest,	his
J C King	Blue X Coat
J H Daugherty	mark
	J C King

The above Bond was approved and filed, this 20 *day of* October , *A.D. 1894*

J H Daugherty

PROBATE JUDGE

****

Territory of Oklahoma
County of Pottawatomie

    I, J H Daugherty Probate Judge of said county, certify that on the 20th day of October 1894 Blue Coat was appointed guardian of Ceaser[sic] Washington and James Washington and that the within is a true copy of the bond of said guardian as appears from the records and files of my office.

    Witness my hand the Seal of said Court this 20th day of October 1894

J H Daugherty
Probate Judge

Tecumseh, O. Ty.
Oct. 30, 1894

Gen. Edward L Thomas
   U.S. Indian Agent
      Sac and Fox Agency

Sir---

    Having learned that parties are trying to get control of the allotment of Charles Warried No. 324 Abs. Shawnee All't Schedule deceased I enclose herewith a certified copy of Letter of Administration issued to me by the Probate Court of Pottawatomie County July 5th 1893 which I desire to place in receipt in your Office. Mrs Nellie Warried the surviving wife of said Chas. Warried is a sister of mine and through her I have learned of the above fact.

Respectfully
T W Alford

Sac & Fox – Shawnee Estates
1885-1910 Volume I

UNITED STATES INDIAN SERVICE

Information,
request for.

POTTAWATOMIE & OT, NEMAHA Agency

HOYT, Kas., Nov., 20th, 1894.

Major Edward L. Thomas,
    U.S. Indian Agent,
        Sac & Fox Oklahoma.

Sir:-

    This Office is advised by John Rubidoux, a member of the Sac & Fox of Mo. tribe of Indians, this Agency, that he is the adopted Father of Mah-que-quah, aged about 8 years, and child of one Pe-wah-tah, a Miss. Sac, now dead, but who in life was a member of your tribe, and Agency.

    Rubidoux wishes to know what Land, Monies, and Ect. this child may have inherited in your Agency, from her Mother, and if any, the condition same may be in?. The woman Pe-wah-tah also had two other children, who are now dead, and Rubidoux thinks the sister surviving should heir their property ?[sic]

    We would appreciate if you would carefully ascertain the exact status of the child, what she may have to her credit, and coming to her, & Ect., and advise us at an early date, and oblige[sic].

    Incidentally, with this, take great pleasure in informing you, that MR[sic]. Calvin Asbury, but lately transfered[sic] from our Agency, to your own, is a very superior gentleman, and a most intelligent, and efficient employee, and we regret exceedingly to have him leave tho' of course happy to know he has received a much deserved promotion. Any courtesy you may extend Mr. Asbury, while he is yet now with you, will be duly appreciated, by,

                Very respectfully,
                Frederick F. [Illegible]
                CLERK, in charge.

Sac & Fox – Shawnee Estates
1885-1910 Volume I

Jim Bullfrog, allottee #206, died November 25, 1894.

RECAPITULATION.

Jennie Bullfrog, 1/3-1/54-7/540-77/2160----------------2595/6480. Widow.
Ellen Hood, nee Bullfrog, 1/9-1/54-7/549-77/2160----1155/6480. Daughter.
Little Captain, --- 385/6480. Son-in-law.
Martin Little Captain, ------------------------------- 385/6480. Grand-daughter.
Betsey Little Captain, ------------------------------- 385/6480. Grand-daughter.
Charley Tyner, --- 420/6480. Son-in-law.
Thomas Bullfrog, 1/9-1/54-7/540-77/2160-----------1155/6480. Son.
          Total ----------6480/6480

Jennie Bullfrog, died December 1, 1905, and her interest 1/3 as wife and an original heir of Jim Bullfrog, 1/54 as mother of Billy Bullfrog, 7/540 as mother and heir of Ross Tyner, and 77/2160 as heir of James Bullfrog, total 2595/6480, descended as follows:

    Ellen Hood, daughter,------------ 2595/25840
    (Little Captain,--------------------- 865/25840
    (Martha Little Captain,------------ 865/25840
    (Betsy Little Captain,-------------- 865/25840
    Thomas Bullfrog, ---------------- 2595/25840

RECAPITULATION.

  Charley Tyner, son-in-law, --------------------- 1860/19440
  Ellen Hood, daughter, ------------------------- 6060/19440
  Thomas Bullfrog, son, ------------------------- 6060/19440
  Little Captain, son-in-law, --------------------- 2020/19440
  Martha Little Captain, grand-child, ----------- 2020/19440
  Betsy Little Captain, grand-child, ------------ 2020/19440
          Total, ---------- 19440/19440

Sac & Fox – Shawnee Estates
1885-1910 Volume I

[Letter below typed as given]

Dale O. T.
April 1st 1898

Mr. Edw Thomas Esq.
  Sac & Fox Agency OF

  Dear Sir [First part of letter illegible…]

  Now if the Land belongs to my family I want posession of it as such and I make the Request that you see that I do get posession of it. I wrot you some time ago about this mater but have heard nothing from you I also wrote to Mr Talbert White about the mater but he has not come. now I would like this mater attended to imidately as he is doing great damage to this timber.
  I also want posession of the E 1/2 of the N.W. 1/4 of the NE 1/4 Sec 36 Township 11 Range 2 E containing 20 acres which I hold a certificate for I want you to Notify Mrs Millie A Smith to give me posession of above Land as she is claiming it and also Notify Mr Wadle to give me posession of this place as he is the Leesor.

CERTIFICATE OF PROBATE JUDGE.

Territory of Oklahoma,
ss
County of Lincoln.

  I, W L Harvey   Judge of the Probate Court of Lincoln County, Territory of Oklahoma, do hereby certify that the records of my office show that   Joseph Fox   is the duly appointed and qualified Special Administrator of the estate of   Susan Madison, Deceased

WITNESS my hand and official seal affixed at my office in Chandler, Lincoln County, Territory of Oklahoma this   Third   day of   March   1896
W L Harvey
Probate Judge.

CERTIFICATE OF PROBATE JUDGE.

Territory of Oklahoma,
ss
County of Lincoln.

Sac & Fox – Shawnee Estates
1885-1910 Volume I

I, W L Harvey, Judge of the Probate Court of Lincoln County, Territory of Oklahoma, do hereby certify that the records of my office show that Charles Grant is the duly appointed and qualified Special Administrator of the estate of Harriet Morris, Deceased

WITNESS my hand and official seal affixed at my office in Chandler, Lincoln County, Territory of Oklahoma this Third day of March 1896

W L Harvey

Probate Judge.

CERTIFICATE OF PROBATE JUDGE.

Territory of Oklahoma,
ss
County of Lincoln.

I, W L Harvey, Judge of the Probate Court of Lincoln County, Territory of Oklahoma, do hereby certify that the records of my office show that George Washington is the duly appointed and qualified Special Administrator of the estate of Albert Washington, Deceased

WITNESS my hand and official seal affixed at my office in Chandler, Lincoln County, Territory of Oklahoma this 29th day of Feb. 1896

W L Harvey

Probate Judge.

CERTIFICATE OF PROBATE JUDGE.

Territory of Oklahoma,
ss
County of Lincoln.

I, W L Harvey, Judge of the Probate Court of Lincoln County, Territory of Oklahoma, do hereby certify that the records of my office show that Ralph Dunn is the duly appointed and qualified Special Administrator of the estate of Mary Cuppawhe, Deceased

WITNESS my hand and official seal affixed at my office in Chandler, Lincoln County, Territory of Oklahoma this Third day of March 1896

W L Harvey

Probate Judge.

Sac & Fox – Shawnee Estates
1885-1910 Volume I

CERTIFICATE OF PROBATE JUDGE.

Territory of Oklahoma,
                    ss
County of Lincoln.

I, W L Harvey   Judge of the Probate Court of Lincoln County, Territory of Oklahoma, do hereby certify that the records of my office show that   David Wah ko le   is the duly appointed and qualified Special Administrator   of the estate   of   Bessie Ingalls, Deceased

WITNESS my hand and official seal affixed at my office in Chandler, Lincoln County, Territory of Oklahoma this   Third   day of   March   1896

W L Harvey
Probate Judge.

Lexington Ok
June 23rd
1896

E D Thomas
U S Indian Agent
Sauk I.T.

Dear Sir

Miss Maggie Johnson one of the heirs of Wm Johnson deceased has brought to me the certified check that was sent to you also a letter addressed and signed by ~~you~~ nobody asking for the certified check to be made to Miss Maggie Johnson on order and Mrs Ella Scott on order   I will enclose you the letter

Please let me know by mail if this is correct and give me full instructions so I can have the bank make another

Respectfully yours
Robert McAllister

Refer in reply to the following:

Finance.   **Department of the Interior.**
31764 - '96.   OFFICE OF INDIAN AFFAIRS
1 Inclosure.   WASHINGTON   August 24, 1896.

Sac & Fox – Shawnee Estates
1885-1910 Volume I

E. L. Thomas,
    U. S. Indian Agent,
        Sac & Fox Agency, O.T.

Sir:

    I inclose herewith a sworn statement from Mah-ne-pam-dosh, that she and her daughter, Mary Matchke, are the sole surviving heirs of Matchke, her deceased husband, who was the sole and lawful heir of Mkit-ao-ko, who died in Mexico; that certain money due the said Mkit-ao-ko was paid by you to one Pe-ad-wa-dah, to which he was not entitled, but that she and her daughter as the natural descendants of the said Mkit-a-o-ko[sic] should have received the same, and requests that an investigation be made to prove her statements.

    She does not make herself very clear as to what money is referred to, but is supposed to have reference to a share of the money appropriated by act of August 19th, 1890, to pay the heirs of certain deceased Mexican Pottawatomie Indians.

    Please inquire into the matter, and if satisfied that her statements are correct, take such steps as may be necessary to recover the money which, according to her statement, has been paid to the wrong person.

                          Very respectfully,
                                Thos P Smith
A.B. (C.)   Acting Commissioner.

****

Territory of Oklahoma   } ss
Pottowatomie[sic] County }

    Personally appeared before me R.R. Bertrand a Notary Public in and for the above named County and Territory on this 14th day of August 1896, Mah-ne Paw dosh formerly Mah-ne Match-Ke of lawful age, who being duly sworn deposes and says that, she was formerly the wife of Match Ke now deceased, that she has one child by said Match Ke that said child is now living and is named Mary Match Ke that she is fourteen years of age, that said Match Ke was the sole and lawful heir of Nikit-a-o Ko, who died in the Republic of Mexico, that she Mah-ne Pawdosh and Mary Match Ke are the sole and lawful heirs of said Match-Ke. That certain monies due to the above named Nikita-o-Ko have been paid by Edward S. Thomas at the Sack[sic] and Fox Agency to one Pe-ad-wa-dah, that said Pe-ad-wa-dah was not entitled to any part of said money that there is now some of said money still in the hands of said Edward S Thomas. That she the said Mah-ne Pawdosh did not know of this money being in the

Sac & Fox – Shawnee Estates
1885-1910 Volume I

hands of said Thomas until a portion of it had been paid to said Pe-ad-wa-dah, that, if she had been cognizant of it she would have filed a claim for the same for herself and daughter, that if ~~your~~ the matter is properly investigated she and her daughter will be found to be the sole and lawful heirs of said Nikita-o-Ko. She further deposes and says that all the facts stated above can be proved, beyond a reasonable doubt, and that certain parties to wit, Me-gah, Nak nash Kuk, Mis no qua and Peter Moose residing here, and Mazhe (formerly a chief) and Keth Kinn-me-qua residing in Kansas have knowledge of the above facts and can be used as witnesses.

She further says that the said Match-Ke was paid certain money as the heir of Nikit-a-o-Ko, that while a good many of the old Duchaus[sic] were alive said Mtch-Ke[sic] was always recognized as the only heir of said Nikit-a-o-Ke, and now she the said Mah-ne Pawdosh prays that the Honorable Commissioner of Indian Affairs will order an investigation of the matter, and also instruct the Agent at Sac & Fox Agency to withhold any money now in his hands until such investigation can be had.

~~Subscribed and sworn to before me this 14th day of August A.D. 1896~~
    Attest   her
  John Bertrand   Mah-ne X Pawdosh
                                                       mark

Subscribed and sworn to before me this 14th day of August A.D. 1896
                                                 R.R. Bertrand
                                                           Notary Public

---

Territory of Oklahoma
County of Pottowatomie[sic] } ss

Before me W.A. Ruggle a Probate Judge in and for said County and Territory personally appeared Jane Delaware who being by me first duly sworn according to law doth depose and say the she is a member of the Absentee Shawnee Band of Indians. That she is the only living heir of Ellen Delaware. That Ellen Delaware was a member of said Absentee Shawnee Band of Indians. That said Ellen Delaware died on or about the 24 day of February 1890. Affiant further says that she is a full sister by Blood of Ellen Delaware [illegible] That there is now due said Ellen Delaware deceased from the United States Government in annuities the sum of 104^{\underline{00}}$

                                                           Jane Delaware

Subscribed and sworn to before me this the 4" day of Nov. 1896
W A Ruggle
Probate Judge

Also at the same time and place personally appeared Charlie Beaver and Na-Na-gra-way-he-se-Ka, who being duly sworn depose and say that they are each members of Absentee Shawnee Band of Indians. That they have heard read the foregoing affidavit and that the facts therein set forth are true as they each verily believe.

                              his
Witness to mark   Charlie X Beaver
C H Gist   mark
D.W. Spencer

                                his
                      Na-Na-gra-way- X he-se-Ka
                                mark

Subscribed and sworn to before me this the 4" day of Nov. 1896
W A Ruggle
Probate Judge

Avoca, O. T. Feb. 6, 1897

Gent. Edw. L Thomas
U.S. Indian Agent
Sac and Fox Agency O.T.
Dear Sir:

        I am requested by Joseph Ap-tas-ka who has been supporting and caring for a Pottawatomie Indian woman named Pshuck-to-qua for some time. This old Indian woman is the wife of Wa-kah-soe of North Fork, Pottawatomie Co. Oklahoma. Wah-kah-soe[sic] is the party over whom so much controversy was carried on before the Grand Jury in regard to the true heirship of some money which was therefore awarded by the Department to him.

The old lady says there was no controversy concerning her money of which in some way $450.^{00} is still under your control.

She wants some of it as she is an invalid and wants something to eat. I advised the parties that according to administrative methods you would not likely be out of office until after June 1897 is probably a month or two thereafter, before your successor would be appointed but that you are a good responsible man and that because on acct of change of Administration they need not be uneasy about the money. Your friend

Jos. Moose

Sac & Fox – Shawnee Estates
1885-1910 Volume I

P.S.
    Agent Thomas

Joseph Ap-tas-ka tells me further to be sure to tell you that the old lady requested him to get somebody to write to you for money and for you to send her some. She is unable to walk or go anywhere on business. She is perfectly helpless and money would buy her some good comforts of life. Agent Thomas, I know by experience that my wife has been paralyzed the last eighteen months and has been perfectly helpless since that time, I know how to appreciate kindness in a case of this kind.

                      Yours respectfully
                        Joseph Moose

                      Sac & Fox Agency, Oklahoma.
                      March 11th 1897

Received of Edward L. Thomas, U.S. Indian Agent for the Sac & Fox Agency, Okla. ~~DEED made by~~...
to ....dated...
for the following described land   check for disapproved deed given by Susan Morris ~~(Wall) Johnson~~   Maggie Johnson   Ellen Scott   heirs of Willie Johnson containing......................... acres, approved by the Sec'y of the Interior ...., also received the following certificate of deposit on the Bank of Norman Oklahoma Signee E F Taylor Asst Cashier   for   Five hundred and Seventy five ($575^{00}.....................................) Dollars.
       WITNESS.
    C. H. Tillman   R McAllister
    M McAllister

                      Reserve Kans Sep^{tr} 20 / 97
Geo W. James U.S. Ind Agnt
        Hoyt Kans
Dear Sir

Yours in reference to the matter of the estate of Sesaqua, Sac [sic] Fox Indian girl who died May 16 / 97 [illegible]   In reply will say that the girls[sic] father Moskochaken gave the girl when quite young to his sister Pah qua sklah. Where she made her home for several years About one year ago complaint was made to Special Agent Able that she was not treated right and Agent [Illegible] had me appointed Guardian for the child.

Sac & Fox – Shawnee Estates
1885-1910 Volume I

Pa-qua-sklah claims to be the rightful heir and Moskochaken told me that he was willing to have the property divided between himself and his sister after the rent is paid in January for 1897. There will be after paying all debts about one hundred and forty dollars

Very truly yours
W A Margrave

****

Agency
Pottawatomie [Illegible. Illegible]
Hoyt Kas.

Septbr 24th 1897

The within letter of W^m A Margrave in reference to the estate of a deceased Sac & Fox of [illegible] Indian is respectfully referred to Sac & Fox Agent Oklahoma for his information with the request that he preserve the same.

George W. James
U.S. Indian Agent

OFFICE OF J. T. McLAUGHLIN.
Dealer in REAL ESTATE, Land and
Insurance, AGENT NOTARY PUBLIC
TAXES Paid for Non-resident Rooms
No 9 & 10 over Post Office.

North Topeka, Kansas   Sept 29   1897

Lee Patrick Esq.
Sac and Fox Agcy
Oklahoma Ter.

Dear Sir

Mary Vieux is married and lives in Jackson County Ks on the Reserve I do not know what her Man's Name is I understood that there was 87 acres of land which was rented at 2\frac{50}{}$ pr[sic] acres[sic] which would make 217\frac{50}{}$. Is the rent paid in 2 payments. There is only three shars[sic] in it, which if I am correct would make 72\frac{50}{}$ pr share I have nothing to do with the other heir.

Yours TC   Angeline Watkins

Sac & Fox – Shawnee Estates
1885-1910 Volume I

Refer in reply to the following:

Land.
11267-1897

Department of the Interior.

OFFICE OF INDIAN AFFAIRS

Washington,   October 20, 1897.

Lee Patrick, Esq.,
   U.S. Indian Agent,
      Sac and Fox Agency, Oklahoma.
Sir:

    About last March, some contention arose between Mrs. Cassie Eaton and her late husband, John C. Eaton, as to the heirship of the lands allotted to Cassie Eaton, Jr., Sac and Fox allottee No. 264. The lands involved are described as the NE/4 of Section 17, Township 11 N., Range 4 E., Pottawatomie County.

    About March 19, 1897, Mr. J.D. Wood, of Shawnee, wrote this office requesting that said John C. Eaton be recognized as the sole heir, and he granted the privilege of leasing the lands. John T. Oglesby, Esq., late a Special Agent of this office, was in the city shortly after the receipt of Mr. Wood's letter, and spoke of the case. Mr. Oglesby was inclined to recognize the rights of Mrs. Eaton.

    The facts appear to be about as follows: Mrs. Eaton's maiden name was Triger; sometime before the allotments were made to the Sac and Fox Indians (the exact date of which is not given) Cassie Triger and John C. Eaton were married; it is not stated whether this marriage was simply under Indian custom or in accordance with the laws of Oklahoma; Mrs. Eaton was a recognized member of the Sac and Fox tribe -- John C. Eaton is a white man; a child was born to Mrs. Eaton on July 19, 1890, the Cassie Eaton whose allotment is now in dispute; the child died on August 15, 1890, but it appears that an allotment was given it; sometime after the death of the child Mr. and Mrs. Eaton were legally divorced.

    The disputed point appears to be in regard to the relations that existed between Mr. and Mrs. Eaton at the time of the birth of the child. According to the statements of Mr. Oglesby, Mrs. Eaton claims that her marriage to Mr. Eaton was not legal; that said John C. Eaton was not the father of Cassie Eaton Jr., and that she and Mr. Eaton were not living together as husband and wife at the time the child was born. Just what the claim of Mr. Eaton is on these controverted points is not known; it is presumed, however, that he claims that his marriage to said Cassie Triger was legal; that he is the father of the dead child, and that he and Mrs. Eaton were living together as husband and wife at the time of the birth of the child.

    The matter is submitted to you for thorough investigation and report.

    I may add that in case you find that a valid marriage existed between Mr. and Mrs. Eaton at the time of the birth of the child, and the parties were living together as husband and wife at that time, under the laws of Oklahoma, the father would become the sole heir and should be permitted to control the lands, lease the same, etc.

Your findings of fact should be reported to this office as early as practicable.

Very respectfully,
W. A. Jones
Commissioner.

McPherson. (H)

****

Refer in reply to the following:

Land.
45476-1897

Department of the Interior.
OFFICE OF INDIAN AFFAIRS
WASHINGTON, November 6, 1897.

Lee Patrick, Esq.,
   U.S. Indian Agent,
      Sac and Fox Agency,
         Oklahoma.

Sir:

I have received and considered your report of October 26, 1897, in the matter of the controversy between John C. Eaton, a white man, and Mrs. Cassie Eaton, a Sac and Fox Indian woman, relative to the heirship of the lands allotted to Cassis Eaton, Jr., and as to who has the legal right to control said lands and to lease the same.

Based upon the facts contained in your report, and other statements submitted to the office, it appears that Mrs. Eaton at least has a much more equitable claim to said lands than has said John C. Eaton, her former husband.

You are accordingly directed to recognize Mrs. Eaton's right to control said lands, and you should permit her to lease the same, on just and equitable terms, in case she so desires.

Very respectfully,
AC Tonner
Acting Commissioner.

McPherson. (H)

Sac & Fox – Shawnee Estates
1885-1910 Volume I

Shawnee Oklahoma
Dec. 7, 1897

Lee Patrick Esq
  U S Indian Agent
    Sac and Fox

Sir:

    As you told me that if I get a cerficate[sic] from Alford you will send me the share of money due my daughter Cinda Emma Spybuck from Ray the lessee of the land of Lucy Nag now deceased So I herewith send you a certificate establishing the fact that Cinda Emma Spybuck is my daughter and that she is one of the heirs of said Lucy Nag, decd.

    Please send in the money to Shawnee, Okla.

               Respectfully yours
                        her
                Maimie X Spybuck
                      mark

            ****

                Shawnee, Oklahoma

        I Thomas W Alford member of the Business Committee of the Absentee Shawnee tribe of Indians do hereby certify that Cinda Emma Spybuck No. 156 is the daughter of Maimie Spybuck No. 155 now Maimie Alford the present wife of David Alford; and I further certify that said Cinda Emma Spybuck one of the heirs of Lucy Nag No. 157 now deceased.

        In testimony whereof I hereunto subscribe my name this 7th day of Dec, 1897.

                Thos. W. Alford
            Member of the Business Committee

Sac & Fox – Shawnee Estates
1885-1910 Volume I

-Copy-

Land.
2246-1898

Department of the Interior.
OFFICE OF INDIAN AFFAIRS

WASHINGTON, February 12, 1898

H.H. Butler, Esq.,
Miami, Indian Territory.

Sir:

I am in receipt of your letter of January 1", 1898, forwarding what purports to be a copy of the will of Phoebe Keokuk, dated May 12, 1893, giving and bequeathing to her daughter Marie A. Whistler her clothing, one small gold watch and a lot of ground in the town of Chandler, O.T., to her husband, Moses Keokuk And to John Keokuk, her grandson, the allotment of land, SW1/4 of Sec. 31, T 17 N., R. 6 E., in the Sac and Fox Reservation, containing 160.67 acres patented to her with the improvements thereon.

In your letter transmitting a copy of said will you state that the alleged grandson is no relation, that, in fact, Mrs. Alice Lee formerly Alice Keokuk and Marie Whistler are the only heirs to the allotted land which is now in the possession of said Moses Keokuk and under lease from him to Jacob Puckett, at a good rental value; that said two heirs request that an order be issued to the U.S. Indian Agent at the Sac & Fox Agency to assist them in securing their rights therein.

In reply you are advised that before instructions will be issued in the matter, it will be necessary that you furnish some satisfactory legal evidence as to the relation of Alice Lee, nee Keokuk, and Marie A. Whistler to Phoebe Keokuk, the deceased Sac and Fox allottee (No. 261) and how they became sole heirs.

The will shows that Marie A. Whistler is the daughter of the devisor, but as you have attacked the relationship of the alleged <u>Grandson</u>, as a legatee, you thereby throw discredit on the statement as to the <u>daughter</u>.

If it can be legally shown that Mrs. Alice Lee, nee Keokuk and Marie A. Whistler are the daughters, or the descendants, of a son or daughter of Phoebe Keokuk, the law of succession in Oklahoma Territory would give one-third of the land to the husband and the remainder to the children in equal shares. If she left only one child and a child or children of a deceased child, then the children of said deceased child would take the part of such decease child. If only one child, and no children of a deceased child, then the husband would inherit one-half of the land and the child the other half.

Sac & Fox – Shawnee Estates
1885-1910 Volume I

The lease referred to expired by limitation January 1, 1898. As the date of the death of Phoebe Keokuk is not given, it is presumed that she was dead when the lease was made; if so, and it can be shown that there are other heirs than Moses Keokuk, the lessor should be bound to such heirs for their proportionate share of the $200 per annum lease money, for the whole term of two year under said lease.

The will is null and void so far as it relates to the land allotted and patented to the devisor, as a Sac & Fox Indian allottee inasmuch as said lands were patented with the restrictive clause that they should not be sold or otherwise disposed of during the trust period, (except that they might be leases). Moses Keokuk acquires no title to the and under the will, but by descent under the law of succession as expressed, and set for in the laws of Oklahoma Territory.

Very respectfully,
A.C. Tonner,
Acting Commissioner.

R.F.T.
L.

****

Refer in reply to the following: 3 Enclosures.

Land. **Department of the Interior.**
2246-1898   OFFICE OF INDIAN AFFAIRS
10135- "   Washington, May 4, 1898.

Lee Patrick, Esq.,
    U.S. Indian Agent,
        Sac & Fox Agency, O.T.

Sir:

I enclose herewith, two letters from H. H. Butler, of Miami, Indian Territory, one dated January 11, 1898, the other dated February 22, 1898, also a copy of office letter of February 12, 1898 to Mr. Butler respecting the land allotted and patented to Phoebe Keokuk, a deceased Sac and Fox allottee No. 261, wherein he complains that Moses Keokuk, her husband, has leased and taken possession of said land (SW1/4 of Sec. 31, T 17 N., R 6 E., in the Sac and Fox Reservation, containing 160.67 acres) to the loss and detriment of Mrs. Alice Lee formerly Keokuk and Marie Whistler the alleged sole heirs of Phoebe Keokuk, and requesting this office to direct you to adjust the matter for them.

Sac & Fox – Shawnee Estates
1885-1910 Volume I

You will at your earliest convenience consistent with your other duties, communicate with the parties interested and make such adjustment of the case as is in accordance with the laws of Oklahoma as to decent and if the statement made that Moses Keokuk has received the full amount arising from the lease of said allotment of land from Jacob Puckett, whose lease expired January 1, 1898, be found to be correct, and if you should find that Alice Lee and Marie Whistler are under the laws of Oklahoma Territory entitled each to an equal share of said rents, you should make a demand on said Moses Keokuk for an accounting of all revenue received by him for said land and require him to disburse it according to the law of the Territory.

If he has renewed said lease to said Puckett, or to any other lessee, you should require him to execute some legal papers requiring him to pay over under the terms of such lease such sums as they may be entitled to receive therefrom, and at the time specified in the lease.

When you shall have effected a settlement satisfactory to the heirs of said Phoebe Keokuk, you will make report thereof to this office. Mr. Butler will be advised of this action.

                                Very respectfully
                                AC Tonner
R.F.T   Acting Commissioner.
L.

Refer in reply to the following:

Land   **Department of the Interior.**
14653-1898   OFFICE OF INDIAN AFFAIRS
                            WASHINGTON,   April 4, 1898.

Lee Patrick, Esq.,
    U.S. Indian Agent,
        Sac and Fox Agency, O. T.
Sir:

On June 2, 1897, your predecessor, General Edward L. Thomas, submitted to this office for approval a lease from himself as U. S. Indian Agent to Ferdinand M. Stump, covering the allotment of Mrs. F. V. Powers, deceased, the S.E. 1/4 of S.E. 1/4 of Section 10; the S.W. 1/4 of the S.W. 1/4 of Section 11; the N.W. 1/4 of Section 15, all in Township 12 north, Range 4 east. The lease was made in the name of Genera Thomas upon the ground that the heirs of Mrs. Powers were unknown, and could not be ascertained; also that it was better to have the lands in charge of a careful tenant than to let them lie idle. The consideration named in the lease was $75 per annum.

You are directed to report whether or not Mr. Stump is now in possession of said lands; whether he paid the rent for 1897, to whom paid, and what disposition has been made of the same; whether any of the heirs of Mrs. Powers are now known, and whether Mrs. Stump should be permitted to continue in possession of said lands.

An early report is desired.

Very respectfully,
W.A. Jones
Commissioner.

(McPherson) Li.

COPY

Sac & Fox Agency, O.T., Oct. 28, 1898.

We, White Turkey and Walter H. Shawnee, members of the Absentee Shawnee Business Committee, do hereby certify that Ma-ta-se-mo is the identical individual to whom was originally allotted the 1/2 of the NE/4 of Sec. 23, in T. 10 N. of R. 4, E. of the Indian Meridian containing 60 acres, it being the same land mentioned in a deed dated Oct. 28, 1898 from Che-we-quay to William R. Nichols, hereto attached. We further certify that Che-we-quay, is the mother of Ma-ta-se-mo and the sole surviving heir under the laws of the Territory of Oklahoma. The father of said Ma-ta-se-mo is wholly unknown. At the time of birth of said child she was not married, and never learned who the father was. We are positive that the said child was born illegitimate, and that he died on or about Sept. 14, 1893, without issue nor[sic] wife. We further certify that Che-we-quay is about 53 years of age and is a widow. We further certify that said party retains unsold the following described land, to wit:- SW/4 of NW/4 of Sec. 82, and S/2 of NW/4 and N/2 of SW/4 of Sec. 23, and NW/4 of SE/4 of Sec. 32, all in T. 10, R. 4 E, I. M., containing 240 acres.

We further certify that $4.00 per acre is a fair and reasonable price for the above described land, it being all timbered upland, timbered with post-oak and black-jack, without improvements of any kind and is in a raw state. The said Che-we-quay desires to sell the above described land to improve her own land, and we believe it would be to her advantage to [end... no further information given]

****

Sac & Fox – Shawnee Estates
1885-1910 Volume I

COPY

Territory of Oklahoma :
                       : ss.
Lincoln County. :

"Aht-se" being first duly sworn according to law says: My name is Aht-se, my age is about 50 years. I am well acquainted with Che-we-quay, have known her from childhood to the present time. I was also acquainted with Ma-ta-se-mo, who is now deceased. I know that said Che-we-quay is the mother of said Ma-ta-se-mo. That said child was born without father; that at the time of his birth said Che-we-quay was not married, and further I have never hears or learned who the father was. Said Ma-ta-se-mo died on or about Sept. 14, 1893 without issue nor wife. I am positive that said child was born illegitimate.

                                                  Her
                                    Aht Se   x
Witnesses to mark:-   mark
    Walter H. Shawnee
    P. C. Grimm

Subscribed and sworn to before me this 28th day of October, 1898.

SEAL   Phil C. Grimm
                                      Notary Public.
My commission expires Aug. 31st, 1901.

****
COPY

Territory of Oklahoma,)
) SS.
Lincoln County.   )

William Johnson being first duly sworn according to law says: My name is William Johnson, my age is about 26 years. I am well acquainted with Che-we-quay, have known her from my childhood to the present.

I was also acquainted with Ma-ta-se-mo, who is now deceased. I know that said Che-we-quay is the mother of said Ma-ta-se-mo. That he was born without father; that at the time of his birth, his mother was not married. I have never heard or learned who his father was, as he was born illegitimate; and that the said Ma-ta-se-mo died on or about Sept. 15, 1893, without issue nor wife.

                                          William Johnson.

Sac & Fox – Shawnee Estates
1885-1910 Volume I

Subscribed and sworn to before me this 28th day of October, 1898.

         Phil C. Grimm
            Notary Public.
My commission expires Aug. 31st, 1901.

****

COPY

Territory of Oklahoma :
          : SS.
Lincoln County.   :

"Che-we-quay" being first duly sworn according to law says:

My name is Che-we-quay, my age is about 53 years. I am the mother of Ma-ta-se-mo, who died on or about Sept. 15, 1893, without issue nor wife. I was not married at the time of birth of said child, the said child was without father. I raised the said boy, and was in my custody until the time of his death. I have never made any claim whatever as to who his father was, as he was born illegitimate. I believe that my son's estate descends to me under the laws of the Territory of Oklahoma, and that I have the right to sell the same.

               her
         Che we quay x
               mark

Witnesses to mark:
Walter H. Shawnee
P. C. Grimm

  Subscribed and sworn to before me this 28th day of October, A.D., 1898.
SEAL

         Phil C. Grimm,
            Notary Public.
My Commission expires Aug. 31st, 1901.

****

COPY

Territory of Oklahoma. :
           : ss.
County of Pottawatomie. :

Sac & Fox – Shawnee Estates
1885-1910 Volume I

I, Che-we-quay, do solemnly swear that the sale of the land described in the attached deed is a bonafide transaction; and I have no agreement or understanding by which I am to pay back to the grantee any part of the consideration or purchase money. I am to receive no part of it in stock, cattle or other thing of value other than lawful money of the United States:- Nor have I the understanding or agreement to pay any part of said money to any other person for the grantee's use.

                                                     her
                                 Che we quay x
Witnesses: mark
    Walter H. Shawnee
    P. C. Grimm

        Subscribed and sworn to before me this 28th day of October, A.D., 1898.
SEAL
                                Phil C. Grimm,
                                       Notary Public.

My Commission expires Aug. 31st, 1901.

                            ****

REFER IN REPLY TO THE FOLLOWING:
    Land.   **Department of the Interior.**
   58536-98
                    OFFICE OF INDIAN AFFAIRS
                        WASHINGTON,   January 7, 1899.

Lee Patrick, Esq.,
    U. S. Indian Agent,
        Sac and Fox Agency, Oklahoma.

Sir:

        Referring to your communication dated December 24, 1898, relative to the descent of an allotment made to a child whose father and mother were never married and who never lived together, you are advised that under the circumstances stated it is believed the allotment would descend to the mother.

                                      Very respectfully,
                                            WA Jones
                                                Commissioner.

Allen (G)

Sac & Fox – Shawnee Estates
1885-1910 Volume I

REFER IN REPLY TO THE FOLLOWING:
Land.
15558-99.

Department of the Interior.

OFFICE OF INDIAN AFFAIRS

WASHINGTON, April 20, 1899.

Lee Patrick, Esq.,
   U. S. Indian Agent,
     Sac and Fox Agency, Oklahoma.

Sir:

    You will have Mr. Tanksley appraise, on his next trip, the E/2 of the NE/4 of Sec. 22, T 7 N, E 2 E, sold by James B. Quintard as sole heir of Maddie F. Quintard, to Estelle E. Kidney, for $240.

Very respectfully,
AC Tonner
Assistant

Commissioner.
R.F.T. (G)

Refer in reply to the following:
"A" 29770/99.
McC

Department of the Interior.

OFFICE OF INDIAN AFFAIRS

WASHINGTON, June 30, 1899.

Mr. Lee Patrick,
   U. S. Indian Agent,
     Sac and Fox Agency, Oklahoma.

Sir:

    Your communication of the 24th instant has been received enclosing receipts "in duplicate" from Benjamin Franklin as the father and legal heir of Susan Ward, deceased.

    You have again failed to furnish the usual certificate that Benjamin Franklin is the legal heir and is entitled to receive and receipt for the money due Susan Ward. The receipts furnished will therefore be retained until the proper certificate is furnished.

Sac & Fox – Shawnee Estates
1885-1910 Volume I

(K)

Very respectfully,
AC Tonner
Actg. Commissioner.

Shawnee Oklahoma
July 24, 1899

We the undersigned members of the Absentee Shawnee Business Committee do hereby notify on honor that we were personally acquainted with John Forman and his family during his life time and that he died June 20, 1899 at the age of about 69 years, surviving him his wife Sallie Forman age about 41 years and his children, Susie Wilson nee Forman, Frank Forman, Ellen or Tiney White Turkey nee Forman, Betsy Alford nee Forman, Eli Forman, Mary Forman and James Forman. These children were the offspring of his first and second marriages. Said John Forman, deceased, we further certify that these surviving members of the above named family are the only heirs of John Forman, deceased, and that all other members died without issue prior to his death and that he left no father nor mother.

Thomas W. Alford
John C King

Holton Kansas, July 25, 1899.

Indian Agent, Sac & Fox Agency,
Lincon[sic] County, Oklahoma Territory.

Dear Sir.---

Bazil M-Nis-Non-Se called in our office today and wanted us to write to you about the money that is coming to him from the sale of land that had belonged to Frank Pas-Ca-We. Bazil met you on the road as he was going up to the agency last winter, and you gave him one hundred dollars of the money that was coming to him. He would like to get the balance as soon as he can. If Frank Pas-Ca-We left any debts Bazil would like to have them settled, that is his part of them.

John Laracy of Sacred Heart Mission has written several letters to Bazil about the matter, and wanted Bazil to send him the power of Attorney, to collect the money and pay the debts of Frank Pas-Ca-We. But Bazil expecting to receive the money from you, did not answer his letters. He thought that you would send the money to him. We wrote some time ago to John Laracy about the matter but have not received an answer yet.

Sac & Fox – Shawnee Estates
1885-1910 Volume I

Now had we better make out the power of attorney and send it to John Laracy, or can we have the money sent so Bazil can get it here at Holton Kansas.[sic] Bazil M-Nis-Non-Se lives about ten miles from here on the Diminished Pottawatomie Reserve. He is very anxious to get the money as soon as he can. Write right away and let us know what to do in the matter, as Bazil will be in Holton next Saturday and wants to know about the money then if he can possibly.

Hoping to hear from your right away, we remain.

                                              Truly Yours.
                                              R J Orr

Refer in reply to the following:

Finance   **Department of the Interior.**
Cl. 106854   OFFICE OF INDIAN AFFAIRS
                    WASHINGTON,   March 25, 1899.

Lee Patrick,
    U.S. Indian Agent,
        Sac and Fox Agency, Oklahoma.
Sir:-

    Acknowledging receipt of your letter of September 24, 1898, inclosing the application of Theresa Big Ear for any money that may be due the estate of Hay-we-coo-lah, deceased member of the Sac and Fox Indians of Iowa, I have to inform you that the rolls of the tribe in this office show that the following amounts are still due and unpaid, viz: Voucher No. 8, 2nd quarter, 1891, and Voucher No. 10, 4th quarter, 1892, - 80--Hay-we-coo-lah, $15.40 payment of June 11, 1892.

    On Voucher 4, 2nd fractional 2nd quarter, 1894, the amount $19.35 is receipted by Lizzie Springer, - this being the 1st payment after death, Hay-we-coo-lah having died in May, 1893, - as only one payment is allowed after death, the estate is therefore not entitled to any payments after that date.

    Before action can be taken toward settlement of this claim, it is necessary that you furnish your certificate as to whether or not the two sums referred to above as unpaid, are still due and properly payable.

    In your reply, please refer to file mark at the head of this letter.

                                          Very respectfully,
                                          AC Tonner
C.A.H. (G)   Acting Commissioner.

Sac & Fox – Shawnee Estates
1885-1910 Volume I

Refer in reply to the following:

Land.
31034-1897

Department of the Interior.
OFFICE OF INDIAN AFFAIRS
WASHINGTON, August 30, 1899.

Lee Patrick,
   U.S. Indian Agent,
      Sac and Fox Agency,
         Oklahoma Territory.

Sir:-

    The attention of this office has at various times been called to the unsatisfactory manner in which the personal estates of deceased Indians and of minor Indian wards are managed, it being reported that in many cases the administrators and guardians are ir-responsible and their sureties worthless, so that the proper heirs and the Indian wards get very little or no benefit from what is rightfully due them. Section 6 of the General Allotment Act of February 8, 1887 (84 Stats., p. 388), provides that all Indians who have received allotments are entitled to the rights of citizenship and shall have the benefit of and be subject to the laws of the State or Territory in which they reside. By virtue of this law the personal estates of deceased Indians and Indian wards are under the control of the County or Probate Judges, who appoint the administrators and guardians and pass upon their acts as such.

    After considering various plans for the correction of the abuses referred to, it has been concluded that the co-operation of the Courts in which such citizen Indians reside, in the appointment of guardians and administrators and in the administration of estates, &c., should be secured. The Acting Secretary of the Interior has directed this office to give you proper instructions to that end.

    I have therefore to direct that you arrange for a conference with the County or Probate Judge at your earliest convenience, explain to him fully the situation and the wishes of this Department, and is possible effect an arrangement with him whereby in the future only such administrators and guardians as first meet with your approval, and whom you judge to be proper and fit persons for such trusts, shall be appointed. You will also endeavor to secure the concurrence of the Judge to a plan requiring you to first examine and approve all the accounts and other papers of administrators and guardians before they are filed with the court and approved by it.

    With such plans harmoniously arranged and faithfully carried out, and with the appointment in the future of proper and responsible persons only, with good sureties; the evil now complained of should be reduced to a minimum. As the arrangements suggested will materially aid the courts in securing the honest and impartial administration of estates - a thing to be desired alike by the Government and the local authorities - I am sure the County Judge will gladly cooperate with you in arranging and carrying out the plans suggested. You will make every proper endeavor to have the same effected.

I have also to direct that you examine the records of the County Court and ascertain the names of all persons who are now acting as administrators and guardians, whether Indian or white, who their sureties are, and then proceed to investigate the character and responsibility of all the parties. Should you find that any changes are desirable in these positions of trust you will present the matter fully to the Court and endeavor to have them effected.

All annuity moneys are under the absolute control of this Department. If irresponsible or improper persons be appointed by the local courts as guardians for Indian minors and a change in such guardianship cannot be effected, you will withhold the payment of annuities in such cases and the same should be returned to the Treasury and held, subject to future disposition for the benefit of the annuitant, under the direction of this office.

As affecting the good of the Indian service and the interests of individual Indians, this entire subject is one of the most important coming under your jurisdiction as an Agent. You will give the same your personal attention and put forth every effort in your power to secure an improvement in the administration of Indian estates and the suppression of the abuses now so frequently complained of.

You will acknowledge the receipt of this letter and in due time report the steps taken by you under the above instructions and the success, if any, attending your effort. Should you desire any further instructions in connection with this matter, you will promptly advise this office.

Very respectfully,
AC Tonner
Acting Commissioner.

J.R.W.

REFER IN REPLY TO THE FOLLOWING:

Department of the Interior.

Land.
46348-1899.

OFFICE OF INDIAN AFFAIRS

WASHINGTON,   October 12, 1899.

Lee Patrick, Esq.,
   U.S. Indian Agent,
      Sac and Fox Agency,
         Oklahoma.

Sir:

Sac & Fox – Shawnee Estates
1885-1910 Volume I

The office is in receipt of your letter dated September 26, 1899, stating that some years ago an Indian child was adopted by an Indian relative who has treated the child as his own and has drawn the annuity payments of the former ever since adoption. The father having died leaving no relatives, you inquire whether the adopted son is the heir of the deceased father.

You also seem to have another case in mind, as you inquire whether a child adopted as above set forth would share with the actual children in the estate of a deceased father. You say the desired information is needed in order to adjust some matters now under consideration at your Agency.

In reply, I have to say that the office is unable to give specific answers to your inquires, as you fail to give the names of the parties or data in detail that would enable the office to arrive at a conclusion. However, it may be stated in general that is the Indians you have in mind have received their allotments in severalty, they are citizens of the Territory of Oklahoma, entitled to the protection and benefits of the laws thereof. Any personal estate left by a deceased Indian would therefore have to be probated in the usual way by the local court having jurisdiction, especially if insisted upon by the heirs, if any, and there is a sufficient amount of property to render such a course advisable.

Attention is invited in this connection to office letter to you dated August 30, 1899, in relation to the appointment of administrators and guardians by probate courts.

In the case of lands allotted to Indians which are held in trust by the United States, this office holds that the probate court has no jurisdiction thereover. The same descends, however, as provided in the patents in accordance with the laws of the State or Territory in which the land is situated.

Should you desire some specific instructions, you should so advise the office, at the same time furnishing the names of the parties, the amount and kind of property left by the deceased Indian, together with such other data and information in detail as is required for a full understanding of the same.

Very respectfully,
AC Tonner
Acting Commissioner.

J.R.W. (L'e)

REFER IN REPLY TO THE FOLLOWING:

Land.
49300-99.

Department of the Interior.

OFFICE OF INDIAN AFFAIRS

Washington,   Oct. 26, 1899.

Sac & Fox – Shawnee Estates
1885-1910 Volume I

Lee Patrick, Esq.,
    U. S. Indian Agent,
        Sac and Fox Agency, Oklahoma.
Sir:

    This office is in receipt, by your reference through Special Agent Taggart, of a communication from Moses Keokuk, chairman, and Charles Keokuk, secretary, of the Sac and Fox council, dated October 13, 1899, in which they submit for decision the question as to the inheritance of a certain allotment. It appears that in 1891 allotment was made or the SE/4 of the SE/4, Sec. 10, the SW/4 of the SW/4 of Sec. 11, the NW/4 of the NW/4 of Sec. 14, and the NE/4 of the NE/4 of Sec. 15, all in T 12, R 4, to Jennie V. Powers, a white woman, the widow of George Powers, a halfbreed Sac and Fox Indian, who died in 1889, before the agreement was made with the Sac and Fox Nation; that said Jennie V. Powers died November 28, 1894; that diligent search and inquiry since that time has failed to develop any surviving blood relatives near or remote; but that the said Jennie V. Powers did several years before allotments were made adopt by Indian custom, two white children and two halfblood Sac and Fox children, to-wit: Frank W. Hamblin and his sister, Mrs. Johnson, nee Hamblin, (white), and Galbert White and Mary Barnes, nee Cluther, (halfbloods), and by will recognized them as her heirs, giving to the two males money, proceeds of her personal property, and to the females her allotment, as above described; that this land is not now under lease, but was at one time for two years, $117.50 being now on deposit in the sub-Treasury to the credit of George Powers' heirs; and that the land is not of great value, but can be leased for $50 or $60 per annum. The council request a decision as to the rights of these adopted children, particularly the two halfbloods, in and to said allotment, as in case they cannot inherit, it will, by the laws of Oklahoma, revert to the Territory.

    Section 3571 of the Statutes of Oklahoma, 1893, provides as follows:
"The person adopting a child, and the child adopted, and the other persons whose consent is necessary, must appear before the Probate Judge of the County where the person adopting resides, and the necessary consent must thereupon be signed, and an agreement be executed by the person adopting, to the effect that the child shall be adopted and treated in all respects ad his own lawful child should be treated."

    Section 3572 provides that the Probate Judge must examine all persons appearing before him pursuant to the above section, each separately, and if satisfied that the interests of the child will be promoted by the adoption he must make an order declaring that the child shall thenceforth be treated and regarded in all respects as a child of the person adopting. The child adopted in accordance with the above provisions inherits from its adopted parents the same as other children.

Sac & Fox – Shawnee Estates
1885-1910 Volume I

As the adoption of these children appears to have been had before the Sac and Fox Indians became citizens of the United States it is possible that said adoption took place before the passage of the statute above quoted, in which case it may be that adoption according to the Indian custom would be valid. But this is a question that can be determined by the proper courts alone. In case there are no legal heirs of Jennie V. Powers in existence, the land would escheat to the Territory, as suggested, but such fact would have to be determined by proper judicial proceedings to be instituted by the proper authorities of the Territory. In the meantime the land might be leased and the proceeds retained to be disposed of as the court may hereafter determine.

It is remarked that on the allotment schedule the name of Mrs. Powers appears as F. V. Powers.

Very respectfully,

AC Tonner
Assistant Commissioner.

J.F.A. (G)

Department of the Interior.
INDIAN SERVICE.

Ponca &c. Agency, Whiteagle, Oklahoma
November 2, 1899.

Hon. Lee Patrick,
  U. S. Indian Agent,
  Sac and Fox Agency, Okla.

Sir:-
  Silas Leclair, a Ponca Indian, states that he has been informed that you are paying to Pottawottomie[sic] Indians money appropriated to pay depredation claim held by them against the government. Leclair claims an interest in some of this money for reasons briefly stated as follows.

He married Ahk-nah Leclair, a Pottowottomie Indian, but who was afterwards dropped from the Pottowottomie rolls and enrolled with the Poncas[sic] and allotted with them. Ahk-nah Leclair was the daughter Martwas, who was a sister of Peter the Great. Leclair claims that Martwas had in a claim against the government for $500 and that Peter the Great had in a claim for $600. He claims that Martwas and Peter the Great are both dead; that his wife Ahk-nah, who is also dead would be her mother's only heir; and that she would also be heir to half the amount paid Peter the

Great, for the reason that he left neither wife nor children, and only two sisters - both of whom are dead.

Leclair claims to have gotten his information from one Eli Nadead, who lives at your Agency. I would thank you to advise me as to the facts in this matter, and whether or not Silas has any foundation for his claim.

Very respectfully,
[Name Illegible]
U. S. Indian Agent.

AFFIDAVIT

Oklahoma Territory
          ss
Pottawatomie County

Personally appeared Wah-ko-qua, who being first duly sworn deposes and ways: I am a Mexican Kickapoo woman, 53 years of age and the mother of Nep-peth-ske, who is now 21 years of age and lives with the Mexica Kickapoo Indians of Oklahoma. For a good many years he was sent away to school he elected to live with his aunt, Ken-no-qua, but I never gave my consent to him being adopted by her, except that he might live with her and help her take care of her ponies if he desired to do so. Nep-peth-ske's father was a Mexican Kickapoo indian[sic] named "Ken-wa-the" and he was an only brother of Ken-no-qua and died before the Kickapoo lands were allotted by Moses Neal. I make this statement with out prejudice for or against any one.

Signed   Wah-ko-qua   her X mark

Witness to mark.
  [Name Illegible]
  [Illegible] Goodner

Subscribed and sworn to before me this 13 day of Nov, 1899.

[Illegible] Goodner
U.S. Commissioner 3rd Judicial
District, Oklahoma.

I certify that I speak both the English and Kickapoo language[sic] and that I was present and interpreted for Wah-ko-qua in the above affidavit and that I explained the contents of the same to her and that I believe that she fully and perfectly understand it, when she signed her name by making her mark.

Sac & Fox – Shawnee Estates
1885-1910 Volume I

[Name Illegible]
[Illegible] Goodner

[Name Illegible]
INTERPRETER.
his x mark

Please state your name, age and residence. Frank A. Thackery, age 35, Residence, Shawnee, Oklahoma.
Q. What official position, if any, do you hold with the United States Government? A. Superintendent and Special Disbursing Agent in charge of the Shawnee Indian School and of the affairs of the Mexican Kickapoo Absentee Shawnee and Citizen Pottawatomie Indians.
Q. Have you a record in your office showing the names of the allotments owned by each member of the tribe of Kickapoo Indians? A. Yes, sir.
Q. Have you that record with you? A. Yes, sir.
Q. Please refer to your record and state what member of this tribe, if any, owns the north half of the southwest quarter of Sec. 18, township eleven, range three east, Indian Meridian, in Pottawatomie County, State of Oklahoma? A. It was allotted to Pen-ah-tho, Mexican Kickapoo allottee No. 172. The record shows it was allotted to her,--I don't say she owns it now,--she is dead.
Q. Is this Indian living or dead, do you know? A. She is dead.
Q. If dead, when did she die, as near as your[sic] are able to state? A. She died prior to October 1st, 1901,--that is as near as I am able to state. Q. Do you know whether or not she was dead on the 23rd day of July, 1906? A. Yes, she was.
Q. Was a quit claim deed signed by C. J. Beason, the plaintiff herein, made out to the heirs of Pen-ah-tho to this same piece of land ever delivered to you by the plaintiff herein? A. I received such a deed through the mail.
Q. State about when? A. It has been about a year, I guess, as near as I can remember.
Q. Did you have that deed recorded, and where? A. I had it recorded at the county recorder's office of this county, the office of the register of deeds at Tecumsch, and then I mailed it to the United States Attorney for his further action.
Q. Have you that deed yet in your possession? A. No, the United States Attorney has it.

Sac & Fox – Shawnee Estates
1885-1910 Volume I

Sett. No. 25113.

Treasury Department
Office of Auditor for the Interior Department
Washington, D.C.   November 21, 1899.

U. S. Indian Agent,
　　Sac and Fox Agency, Oklahoma.

Sir:

　　The claims of the following named Absentee Shawnee Indians were allowed by this office this date. When warrants issue the Treasurer will mail them to your address, viz:

Anna Bull Frog,			$103.00
Bin-mik Pecan,			$103.00
Wah-thah-pea-se,	(	joint heirs of	$ 51.50
Otha-ke-se,	(	Frank Hill, decd.	$ 51.50

　　　　　　　　　　Respectfully,
　　　　　　　　　　　[Name Illegible]
　　　　　　　　　　　　Auditor.

Refer in reply to the following:

Accounts
53872-99
1 Encl.

Department of the Interior.
OFFICE OF INDIAN AFFAIRS
Washington,　December 9, 1899.

Mr. Lee Patrick,
　　U. S. Indian Agent,
　　　Sac and Fox Agency, Okla.

Sir:-

　　The enclosed communication from Special Agent Taggart is referred to you for a full investigation and report relative to the complaint of Fannie Gibson, an Absentee Shawnee woman against Eliza Panther, whom it is alleged drew a greater proportion of the money due Betsy Gibson, the mother of Fannie, than she was lawfully entitled to and, further, that she is in possession of the patent to the allotment of Mrs. Gibson.

Sac & Fox – Shawnee Estates
1885-1910 Volume I

You are directed to personally investigate this complaint and to make a full report of your findings in the case, as outlined by the enclosed letter, and submit the same to this office at the earliest date practicable.

Very respectfully,
WA Jones
Commissioner.

Refer in reply to the following: **Department of the Interior.**
3366-1900   OFFICE OF INDIAN AFFAIRS
                          WASHINGTON,   January 23, 1900.

Lee Patrick, Esq.,
     U. S. Indian Agent,
         Sac and Fox Agency,
             Oklahoma Territory.

Sir:-

     The office is in receipt by Department reference of the 16th instant, for reply to the writer, of a letter from Eli Burkloo[sic], Esq., of date the 9th instant, in which he protests against the approval of a deed in favor of A. T. Jobe, covering the NW1/4 of SE1/4 and NE1/4 of SW1/4 of Sec. 32, T. 10 N., R. 3 E., in the County of Pottawatomie, Territory of Oklahoma.

     Enclosed with his communication is an incomplete farming and grazing lease (in triplicate) covering the land described, between Jim Lewis, sole heir of Debbic Lewis, deceased Absentee Shawnee allottee, and Eli Burkleo, for three years from January 1, 1898; consideration $20.50 per annum.

     Attached to the lease is a letter from yourself notifying the lessee that he must pay the rent, or you will be forced to put him off the land; a notice from the Agency Farmer to Mr. Burkleo that the Agent wants to see him at the Indian School; and a receipt for $20.50 on account of semi-annual payment of rent due July 1, 1898, on lease of 120 acres of land.

     He states that he has "broke" about 30 acres of the tract and fenced the same and if the land is to be sold, he would like to buy it himself, and would pay as much in cash as Mr. Jobe has offered; that he has made this offer to the Agent but he would not accept it.

     He further states that he has been to the Agency to have the lease completed but was told that when he was wanted he would be sent for as he had cleared himself of the law; and he asks the office to notify him what he shall do.

     No deed has been received in the office covering the tract of land as yet.

Sac & Fox – Shawnee Estates
1885-1910 Volume I

The papers in the case are transmitted to you, herewith, for report and recommendation.

Please return the enclosures.

         Very respectfully,
         [Name Illegible]
         Commissioner.

****

Jan. 23, 1900

Relative to protest made by Eli Burkleo to the approving of a deed given by Jim Lewis to A. T. Jobe.

****

Refer in reply to the following:

Land.   **Department of the Interior.**
61739-1899   OFFICE OF INDIAN AFFAIRS
        WASHINGTON, Jan. 8 1900

Lee Patrick, Esq.,
 U. S. Indian Agent,
  Sac and Fox Agency, Okla.

Sir:

 Replying to your communication of the 26th ultimo, relative to the disposition of rents from the allotment of Samuel Ely, deceased, you are advised that the office concurs in your decision that Albert Ely is the legal heir of his deceased son Samuel Ely, and is, therefore, the proper person to receive said rents, and not the mother.

         Very respectfully,
         WA Jones
         Commissioner.

J. L. D. (B)

****

Sac & Fox – Shawnee Estates
1885-1910 Volume I

Refer in reply to the following:

Land.   **Department of the Interior.**

OFFICE OF INDIAN AFFAIRS

Washington,   December 19, 1899.

Lee Patrick, Esq.,
   U. S. Indian Agent,
      Sac and Fox Agency,
         Oklahoma.

Sir:

    James Cleghorne, an Otoe Indian, who is at present in this city, has made a statement to the office for and on behalf of Jane Ely, an Iowa allottee, in regard to a farming and grazing lease executed by herself as sole heir of her deceased son, Samuel Ely, to the office that you have refused to pay her the rents due under said lease, and have informed her that Albert Ely, her former husband, is the proper person to receive said rents.

    He further states that Albert and Jane are separated, each having remarried; that Albert has denied that he is the father of Samuel, and Jane, the mother, admits that he is not; and that only recently Albert claimed that Samuel was his son in order to draw the rents from his allotment.

    The files of the office show that the S1/2 of the NE1/4 of Sec. 30, T. 16, R. 1 was leased by Jane Ely as the sole heir of Samuel Ely, deceased Iowa allottee No. 27, to William E. Briggs, for five years from January 1, 1897, at an annual consideration of $70; approved April 8, 1897.

    As this office is not in possession of sufficient evidence to determine who is the legal heir of Samuel Ely, you are requested to report to the office all facts pertaining to the case that are in your possession or that you may be able to obtain by investigation, in order that intelligent action may be taken.

                                  Very respectfully,
                                    AC Tonner
                                    Commissioner.

J.L.D.
C

Sac & Fox – Shawnee Estates
1885-1910 Volume I

GEO. L. ROSE,
ABSTRACTS
𝔣𝔞𝔯𝔪 𝔞𝔫𝔡 𝔠𝔥𝔞𝔱𝔱𝔢𝔩 𝔏𝔬𝔞𝔫𝔰

* * *

TECUMSEH, OKLA.   Mch 22, 19oo[sic].

Hon. Lee Patrick,
    Sac and Fox Agency [illegible]

Dear Sir:-

    I herewith hand copy of letters of Administration certified to by the Clerk of the Probate Court in the matter of the estate of Frank Pak-sh-kah deceased as per your suggestion in letter received some few days ago. I am very anxious to get this matter closed up in order that Mr. McGuire may get his deed.
    If we have complies with all the requirements will you please forward the deed to the Bank of Tecumseh and notify me of the fact. I judge from your letter that the certificate of deposit will be mailed to me, however, the deed is what I want to get now.

                  Yours very truly,
                  Geo L Rose

****

Tecumseh O.T.
Mch 22nd 900[sic]
George L Rose

Transmits letters of administration from the Probate Court in the matter of the estate of Frank Rah-sh-itah.

Refer in reply to the following:

Land.   𝔇𝔢𝔭𝔞𝔯𝔱𝔪𝔢𝔫𝔱 𝔬𝔣 𝔱𝔥𝔢 𝔍𝔫𝔱𝔢𝔯𝔦𝔬𝔯.
14964-1900   OFFICE OF INDIAN AFFAIRS
                WASHINGTON,   March 30, 1900.

Lee Patrick, Esq.,
    U. S. Indian Agent,
        Sac and Fox Agency, Oklahoma.

Sac & Fox – Shawnee Estates
1885-1910 Volume I

Sir:

Referring to your communication dated March 23, 1900, in which you return the letter from this office dated August 18, 1899, in regard to the allotment of an orphan boy named Willie Dole, deceased, and state that said letter was received during your severe illness last summer and fall, you are advised that this office desires the information asked for (which had not been furnished) as soon as practicable. Said letter is, therefore, returned.

        Very respectfully,
        AC Tonner
         Commissioner.

Refer in reply to the following:
Land.
19618-1900

Department of the Interior.

OFFICE OF INDIAN AFFAIRS
WASHINGTON, April 24, 1900.

Lee Patrick, Esq.,
 U. S. Indian Agent,
  Sac and Fox Agency, Okla.

Sir:

This office is in receipt of your letter of April 16, 1900, submitting for office confirmation, the decision as to the legal heirs of Doctor John, deceased. I agree with you if the facts be as presented in our letter, the Scott Foreman should not be considered as an heir of Doctor John, deceased, for the reason that there is nothing to show that Doctor John and Sallie Thompson married under Indian custom, nor that they ever lived together.

The question submitted is one for judicial determination. If you have any doubt as to the conclusion reached by you as to the legal heirs, the matter should be submitted to the courts for definite answer.

        Very respectfully,
        AC Tonner
         Acting Commissioner.

R. F. T. (B)

Sac & Fox – Shawnee Estates
1885-1910 Volume I

Sallie Spybuck saw John Spybuck yesterday evening. She tell him that he has to pay for the sixded[sic] dollars And John Spybuck said that he was not going [sic] do it pay her. this is all.

****

Hon Lee Patrick: Agent,

Dear Sir: The above in pencil was handed me by Mrs. Sallie Spybuck who has been appointed guardian of Frank Spybuck & has qualified. In July last, John Spybuck got $60^{00} belonging to the moma when Sallie ought to have had it as she is keeping the boy. Can't you devise some way to compel John to pay back this money?

Yours
W.S Pendleton, Probate Judge

Refer in reply to the following:
Finance.
Cl. 119386
2 Incls.

Department of the Interior.

OFFICE OF INDIAN AFFAIRS

WASHINGTON,   June 5, 1900.

The U. S. Indian Agent,
    Sac and Fox Agency, Oklahoma.

Sir:
    There is inclosed herewith the application of W. C. Boyer, Administrator for the estate of Ethel Higginbotham, with the request that you attach your certificate to the same that the amount claimed has not been paid, as shown by the records of your Agency, etc.

Very respectfully,
AC Tonner
McC. (G)   Acting Commissioner.

Sac & Fox – Shawnee Estates
1885-1910 Volume I

[Letter below typed as given]

                                        Reserve Ka
                                      June the 1900
                                                   30

                            Mr Major Patrick

Sir   I receved your leter of the 26 [illegible] Regard to Relative to the White Cloud Estate   Sir I can get all the ~~that~~ proof that may be nessery to proove that som of them down ther and som up here   I never staid with my father as my mother did when I was an infant and my uncle and aunt Raised me   I have one uncle up here James Chief White Cloud
            Eliza Morris

                                        Shawnee Oklahoma
                                              Aug 8, 1900

Lee Patrick Esq.
U.S. Ind^n Agent
    Sac and Fox Agency

Sir:

    The allotment of my sister, Ellen Deleware[sic], who died Jan. 1890 has been for the last 3 years illegally leased by Jane Smith nee Deleware who is also one of the heirs of said allottee and rent has been at devers[sic] times collected by her without our knowledge

    I respectfully request that steps be taken at once to stop this illegal renting of said land and that it be leased legally by all ~~them~~ heirs so as to get benefit equally from proceeds of said rent. I enclose you herewith a diagram of[sic] showing the relationship of the heirs for your information.

                                        Yours respectfully,
                                        Boletha Hood

per T.W. Alford

Sac & Fox – Shawnee Estates
1885-1910 Volume I

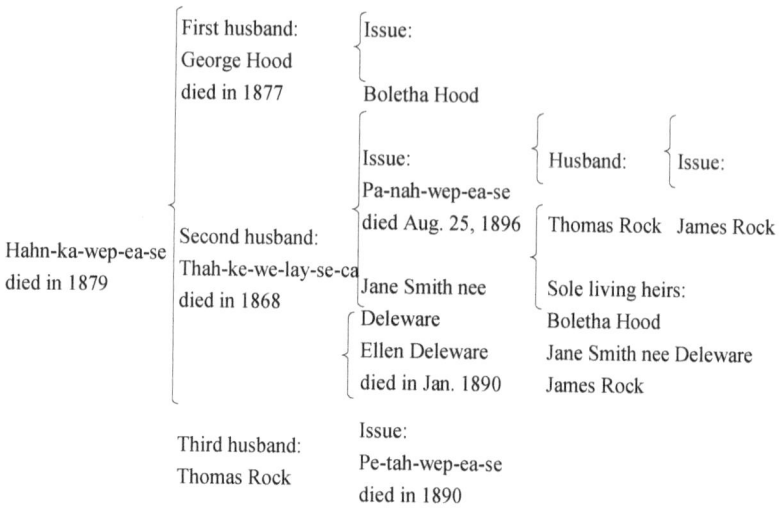

Refer in reply to the following:
Finance.
Cl. 119335

Department of the Interior.

OFFICE OF INDIAN AFFAIRS

WASHINGTON, August 31" 1900

U. S. Indian Agent,
    Sac and Fox Agency, Okla.

Sir:

    This office addressed a communication to you under date of July 7" relative to the claim of John Longman for the amount of $103.00 due his deceased wife, Jennie McCoy and inclosed therewith a list of questions to be answered by him, under oath, showing that he was the sole surviving heir of decedent.

    To this communication no attention was paid by you and under date of August 7" another communication was sent you on the same subject asking you to inform this office when the papers would be returned. No reply has been made thereto and you are now called upon to explain your continued delay in replying to the above letters. An immediate reply will be expected to this communication.

Sac & Fox – Shawnee Estates
1885-1910 Volume I

>Very respectfully,
>AC Tonner
>Acting Commissioner.

McC.

>Holton,
>Jackson Co. Kansas
>Sept. 18, 1900.

To Lee Patrick,
    Indian Agent Sac & Fox, O.T.
Dear Sir:

    There are four of us children here that are nearest heirs of the Mary Bennett or Kewa che wah no qua estate. I am the only one that is of age and the rest are not their ages are eight, fourteen and nineteen and I am twenty one and will be twenty two in December.

    Our father was a sister[sic] to Mary Bennett and therefore was our aunt. I have a letter here that I got from her after our father died.

    It might show that she was our aunt and we have proofs here if there is any doubts about our heirship.

    I would like to get my share of the property and the rest will have to have a guardian and I suppose I would have to wait for my share until the guardian sells the property.

    Tell me what can be done and will be looking for a reply from you soon.

>I remain yours truly,
>Dennis Numott Spear
>Holton,
>   Kansas

Sac and Fox Agency, Oklahoma Territory,
September 25, 1900.

IN THE MATTER OF THE SETTLEMENT OF THE ESTATE OF POLLY LITTLEAX OR SIME-HA-THLE, DECEASED.

    The personal property of the deceased consisting of 5 ponies, 4 head of cattle, and $1000 in cash.

Sac & Fox – Shawnee Estates
1885-1910 Volume I

We, The undersigned heirs to the estate hereby consent and gree[sic] to the following division of said estate:

In consideration of the care of the deceased during her late sickness, her daughter, Nah-wah-lah-pea-se, shall receive the 4 head of cattle.

The 5 horses shall be divided as follows: William Littleax to have the first choice, Stella Bluecoat, Gertrude Alford, Claude Tyner, Charley Tyner, and James Washington second choice, Switch Littleax third choice, Peter Washington and John Ax and Jesse Washington fourth choice, and Nah-wah-lah-pea-se fifth choice.

The $1000 in cash is to be divided as follows: William Littleax $200, Switch Littleax $200, Nah-wah-lah-pea-se $200, Peter Washington $66.66, John Ax $66.66, Jesse Washington $66.68, Stella Bluecoat $40, Gertrude Alford $40, Claude Tyner $40, Charley Tyner $40. and James Washington $40.

Witness our hands this 25th day of September, 1900.

William Little Ax   his x mark   Charlie Tyner
Switch Little Ax   his x mark   Stella Bluecoat
Nah-wah-lah-pea-se   her x mark   Gertrude Alford
James Axe
Jesse Washington
Claude Tyner

Acknowledged before me this 25th day of September 1900.

U. S. Indian Agent.

I, William Hurr, U. S Interpreter, hereby certify on honor that the foregoing agreement was explained to and fully understood by the heirs before they signed the same and that I have no interest whatever in this claim.

U. S. Interpreter.

Refer in reply to the following:
Accounts
47317-1900
1 Inclosure   W.O.O.

Department of the Interior.
OFFICE OF INDIAN AFFAIRS
Washington,   Oct. 1, 1900.

The U. S. Indian Agent,
   Sac and Fox Agency, Oklahoma.

Sac & Fox – Shawnee Estates
1885-1910 Volume I

Sir:

Referring to your communication of the 21st ultimo, relative to the disposition of the $500 on deposit with the Shawnee National Bank in favor of Joe Charley, deceased, and suggesting that this Office establish Susan Bob as the sole heir of the said Joe Charley, so that the money may be paid to her direct instead of to white men who appear to be so solicitous in her behalf, you are advised that you should take the necessary steps to have Susan Bob appointed administratrix of the estate of her father, thus avoiding the complications which may arise if any other course is pursued. The certificate of the Shawnee National Bank is herewith returned.

        Very respectfully,
        AC Tonner
(L.)   Asst. Commissioner.

Territory of Oklahoma,) and Pottawotamie[sic] County.)	In the Probate Court in and for said county Territory.
In the matter fo[sic] the estate of Joe Charley-deceased.))))	Order and decree of distribution.

And now on this 1st. day of December 1900, the same being a regular judicial day of the regular November term came on for hearing on the petition of Susan Bob Administratrix of the estate of Joe Charley –deceased, and the Court finds from said verified petition that the petitioner, Susan Bob, is the sole heir of said Joe Charley-deceased, and that there are no other heirs or legatees of said estate; and the the[sic] personal property of said estate consists of money, in the sum of $500.00 now in the hands of Lee Patrick, U.S. Indian Agent, and $300.00 in the hands of Nancy Charley; that there are no debts against said estate of any kind, and that tere[sic] are no taxes due and unpaid and that said sum of $500.00 is ordered paid by said Lee Patric[sic] 7.[sic]S. Indian agent to said Susan Bob, Administratrix of said estate in her representative capacity as said Administratrix; and it is further ordered that Nancy Charley pay to said to Susan Bob, Administratrix the sum of $300.00 as Such Administratrix apon[sic] the service of a certified copy of the Ordered and decree; It is therefore by the Court ordered and decreed that Lee Patrick, U.S. Indian Agent pay Susan Bob Administratrix the sum $500.00 apon[sic] the service of a certified copy of this order apon[sic] said Lee Patrick, U.S. Indian Agent, aforesaid, and it further ordered that

Sac & Fox – Shawnee Estates
1885-1910 Volume I

Nancy Charley pay to said Susan Bob, administratrix of the estate of Joe Charley-deceased the sum of $300.00 apon[sic] the service of a certified copy of the order and decree. It is further ordered and decreed that said sum of money and each of them above stated and decreed be and the same hereby is set apart and distributed to said Susan Bob sole heir of said Joe Charley-deceased as sole heir thereof. All of which is, by the court, so ordered and decreed.

J.D.F. Jennings
Probate Judge.

Oklahoma Territory, Pottawotamie[sic] County.
I, J.D.F. Jennings, duly elected and acting Probate Judge in and for the county aforesaid, do hereby certify that on this day, Dec. 1st 1900 Susan Bob was duly appointed Administratrix of the estate of Joe Charley-deceased; and that the above is a true and complete copy of the findings and decrees of this Court as appears of record in my office. Witness my hand and official seal Dec. 1st, 1900.

J.D.F. Jennings
Probate Judge.

Refer in reply to the following:

Land.   **Department of the Interior.**
57296-1900   OFFICE OF INDIAN AFFAIRS
                       WASHINGTON,   Dec. 15, 1900.

Lee Patrick, Esq.,
    U. S. Indian Agent,
       Sac & Fox Agency,
          Oklahoma.
Sir:

    There is transmitted, herewith, for investigation, report and recommendation, a complaint of Lawrence Horton, a Pottawatomie Indian dated at Choctaw City, Oklahoma, the 17th ultimo, in regard to the disposition of the land allotted to his mother. He states that one Charles Hawkins is in possession of 80 acres of the land, claiming that it was willed to him by the allottee. He also complains of the non-payment of the rents due the estate.

    You will please return Mr. Horton's communication with your report.

Very respectfully,
WA Jones
Commissioner.

J.D.D.
   L.

Sac & Fox – Shawnee Estates
1885-1910 Volume I

Refer in reply to the following:
Land.
60168-1900

Department of the Interior.

OFFICE OF INDIAN AFFAIRS
WASHINGTON, Dec. 18, 1900.

Lee Patrick, Esq.,
    U. S. Indian Agent,
        Sac & Fox Agency,
            Oklahoma.

Sir:

    There is transmitted herewith for investigation, report and recommendation, a letter from Tena Foreman White Turkey, complaining as to the disposition of the rent money due from the estate of White Turkey deceased Absentee Shawnee allottee.

    You will please return said communication with your report.

                      Very respectfully,
                      AC Tonner
                        Commissioner.

J.L.D.
L.

Refer in reply to the following:
Land.
56629-1900

Department of the Interior.

OFFICE OF INDIAN AFFAIRS
WASHINGTON, Dec. 21, 1900.

Lee Patrick, Esq.,
    U. S. Indian Agent,
        Sac and Fox Agency, Okla.

Sir:

    Referring to your letter of October 27, 1900, forwarding for approval a deed dated October 12, 1900, from the heirs of Isabella Clardy conveying to William H. Bates for $1200, the SW/4 of the NE/4, the NW/4 of the SE/4, the SW/4 of the SE/4 and SE/4 of NW/4, Sec. 21, - 6 N., R 5 E., containing 160 acres. I now return said deed that you may have a ten-cent war revenue stamp attached to the certificate of C. M. Campbell, clerk of the southern district of Indian Territory, that J. W. Hooker, before whom said deed was acknowledged, was a notary public at the time of the acknowledgment.

59

Sac & Fox – Shawnee Estates
1885-1910 Volume I

>   Very respectfully,
>   WA Jones
>   Commissioner.

R.F.S. (B)

DEPARTMENT OF THE INTERIOR
UNITED STATES INDIAN SERVICE.

Sac and Fox Agency, Oklahoma Territory,
December 26, 1900.

C. J. Benson, President,
    Shawnee, Oklahoma.

Sir:

Please make a new certificate of deposit in lieu of your No. 123 to read as follows: " This certifies that J. B. Deen has deposited with the Oklahoma State Bank $1400 payable to the order of B. J. Clardy and others as per indorsement on the back on return of this certificate properly indorsed, etc" On the back make an indorsement, " Pay to the order of B. J. Clardy, A. H. Clardy, William Clardy, Annie Boyer, Joshua Clardy, Carrie B. Clardy and Lucy I. Clardy when a deed to the N/2 of SW/4 etc. is approved by the Secretary of the Interior." and indorse the certificate yourself and forward same to me at your earliest convenience.

>   Very respectfully,
>   Lee Patrick

M.   U. S. Indian Agent

12/28-1900
    Herewith certificate as requested

>   CJ Benson
>   Pres

>   Belvue, Kansas
>   Jan 8th 1901

Mr Lee Patrick...
            Dear Sir as I have land there I would like to know what it would cost to get a deed for it or will it cost anything as I am one of the minor[sic] of

Sac & Fox – Shawnee Estates
1885-1910 Volume I

~~Mrs~~ Mary E Hurd as she had three hundred and twenty acres and there is four sirs I want to know how much it will cost to have it divided or if it will cost any thing that will make me 160 acres all together with the eighty I have alloted[sic] to me.

Yours Truly

Mrs. Piercie Rimer,
Belvue Kan.

Perkins O.T. Jan 14/01

Hon Lee Patrick
   Sac & Fox Agency

Mr Dear Sir:-   My [sic] at Washington has informed me that the case of "Wallace vs The heirs of Willie" contesting the defendants right to the N² N.W.⁴ of Sec. 15-17 3 had been referred to you on Nov. 27 1900 He says your report had not reached the Sec. yet. If the hearing has not been had kindly inform me when you will order the case to be called so that I may be present. I think I can show without a doubt that Willie Dole was dead at the time allotment was made.
I am most truly

Chas. A. Wallace

[Letter below typed as given]

Neadean[sic] Kansas
Jan 17ᵗʰ 1901

   Sac and Fox Agency
   Agent of the Sac and Fox Agency.
Sir. will you please send me the numbers of my Granpa[sic] land. his name was Mo-cho-win and please let me know what you done with his pay-ment. you are the only one that knows I think because your father and you payed the Pottawattomies[sic] off. he is dead now so write and if you sent it back let me know and this Agent will send for it. Yours Trully[sic]

Marry Wes-ken-no or
Little Bird

Sac & Fox – Shawnee Estates
1885-1910 Volume I

Refer in reply to the following:
Land
2309-1901

Department of the Interior.

OFFICE OF INDIAN AFFAIRS

Washington, Jan. 24, 1901.

Lee Patrick, Esq.,
    U. S. Indian Agent,
        Sac and Fox Agency, Oklahoma.

Sir:

    There is transmitted herewith an affidavit executed by Joseph Tenwas, January 8, 1901, in which he states that Mnes-no-que Pak-sh-kah, allottee No. 200, died January 4, 1900, leaving some personal property. And also the following lands: the E/2 of the SW/4 and the NW/4 of the SW/4 of Sec. 18, T. 7, R 4 E. The deponent further states that he is one of the heirs, and asks the Department for an order for possession of the above property, he being a first cousin of the deceased.

    You will investigate and report as to who are the heirs of the said deceased allottee.

                              Very respectfully,
                                  AC Tonner
                                      Commissioner.

J.F.A. (G)

Refer in reply to the following:
Land
7020-1901

Department of the Interior.

OFFICE OF INDIAN AFFAIRS

Washington, March 16, 1901.

Lee Patrick, Esq.,
    U. S. Indian Agent,
        Sac and Fox Agency, Okla.

Sir:

    There is transmitted herewith a communication from Joseph Moose, Secretary National Business Committe[sic], dated January 31, 1901, writing at the request of Joseph Tenwas in regard to the rights of Tenwas in the allotment of Frank Pah-sh-rah, who died July 16, 1899.

    You will investigate the statements of Mr. Moose and return his letter with your report and recommendation in the premises.

                              Very respectfully,
                                AC Tonner

J.F.A. (B)   Commissioner.

Sac & Fox – Shawnee Estates
1885-1910 Volume I

Shawnee, O.T. 1/26, 1901

Hon. Lee Patrick, U.S. Ind. Agt.
   Sac & Fox Agency, OF

Dear Sir:

   I just rec'd a letter from Mr. H.D. Price, calling on me for a certificate from County Clerk of Pottawatomie County that I was a Notary Public at the time I took the acknowledgement to deed from the heirs of Pep-ka-wa or Mary Peanna deceased for N^2NW^4 - 34 - 6 - 4 E.

   My certificate of official character is attached to lease of Ben Bullfrog to Jefferson P. Fullen - SW^4SE^4 - 22 10 - 2 E

   Hereafter will a reference to this case be sufficient in that regard or should I file such certificate with each acknowledgment?

                    Very respectfully
                    Frank W Boggs

Shawnee O.T. 1/26-1901

Hon. Lee Patrick, U.S. Ind. Agt.
   Sac & Fox Agency, OF

Dear Sir:

   Enclosed please find two affidavits as to residence of John Axe, one to be attached to the deed from John Axe to William B. Fowlers for $N^2 SW^4$ - 30 11 -5 E, the other to the deed from John Axe to C. J. Benson for the $S^2 SW^4$ - 30 - 11 - 5 E

   I wish you would please let me know if a certificate of official character of the Notary will be required to accompany these two affidavits or is it only required in acknowledgements?

                    Yours truly,
                    Frank W. Boggs

Sac & Fox – Shawnee Estates
1885-1910 Volume I

Shawnee, Oklahoma Territory.
Jan. 26, 1901.

Hon. Lee Patrick
   Sac and Fox Agency Okla.

Dear Sir,-

   I hereby apply for the payment for my share of the per capita shares due Rhoda White and Mabel White, now both dead, Absentee Shawnees, on the roll paid by Litchfield in 1872, amounting to 103\underline{^{00}}$ each.

   I claim the estate by reason [paper torn] Rhoda White and Mabel being sisters.

   I further state that I h[paper torn] father and mother living [paper torn] they both refused to j[paper torn] in the application for [paper torn] due the deceased.

   This money has never b[paper torn] and is now held in the[paper torn]

   Enclose find affia[paper torn] members of the tribe wh[paper torn] acquainted with the [paper torn]

                 Very respect[paper torn]
                 Toneley [paper torn]

            ****

Territory of Oklahoma }
Pottawatomie County } ss

We <u>Jacob Buckheart and Chas Switch</u> being duly sworn each for himself deposes and says; He was well acquainted with Roda White and Mabel White during their life time; that Roda White died April 1st, 1900 and that Mabel White died March 25th, 1899, At the ages of about 28 and 11 years respect~~ably~~ ively, and left as their sole and only surviving heirs Tonley Worther, and Hiram White who bear the relation to the~~m~~ of[sic] brothers; that also Mrs Bob White is an heir of said estate by reason of Roda and Mabel being her daughters.

   We further swear that we have no interest in the attached application of Tonley Worther for the money due the deceased.

                              Jacob Buckheart
                              Chas Switch

Sac & Fox – Shawnee Estates
1885-1910 Volume I

Subscribed and sworn to before me this the __26th__ day of __January__ 1901.
My commission expires __Oct 26, 1903__.

            H A Basham
            Notary Public

| HOFFMAN & EMBRY | ROY HOFFMAN |
| ATTORNEYS at LAW | JOHN EMBRY |

         Chandler, Okla.,   1/30/1901.

Hon. Lee Patrick,
   U.S. Indian Agent,
     Sac and Fox Agency, O.T.

Sir:--

   Will you kindly furnish us copy of your report in the matter of your investigation of the allotment made to the Indian, Lucinda?. We understood from your ~~appearance~~ former notice that the case was set for hearing on the 28th inst. and all the witnesses and heirs summoned to appear before you at that time. We desire this information, since we are going on the theory that this land is subject to homestead entry, and a client of ours has a homestead application therefor.

   Thanking you in advance for the courtesy, we are

          Very truly,

            Hoffman and Embry
             Per K

G. A. OUTCELT
    ATTORNEY AT LAW

         TECUMSEH, O. T.   2/15"   1900

Friend Patrick –

   Whats[sic] the matter with the Morton estate matter? Sc^r Rains signed af[sic] receipts all ok and [illegible] now ready for adjustment. Please see to ok bro Patrick

          Your friend John [Illegible]

Sac & Fox – Shawnee Estates
1885-1910 Volume I

A. E. HAMMONDS,
ATTORNEY AT LAW.

SHAWNEE, OKLA., March 23rd, 1901

Hon. Lee Patrick,
Sac & Fox Agency, Okla.,
Dear Sir:-

I am informed that the S.E. one forth[sic] of sec. 8, township 9, range 4 East, was allotted to Sampson Day, that the Shawnee Committee have recently filed their opinion with you that Katie Ellis the wife and Sam Day, minor child, are the only heirs of of[sic] Sampson Day deceased; am I correct? if so, what will a certified copy of the finding [illegible] opinion of the commitee[sic] and your finding thereon cost me?

Thanking you for past favors,
I am to remain,
Very truly yours,
A. E. Hammonds

DEPARTMENT OF THE INTERIOR.
UNITED STATES INDIAN SERVICE.

Shawnee, Oklahoma Feb. 3rd 1901

Mr. Lee Patrick,
U.S. Indian Agent
Sac and Fox Agency, Oklahoma.

Dear Sir:

I herewith enclose you triplicate copy of testimony taken to day in the matter of the estate of William Cherokee, deceased. It appears that the real heirs in this case are the two children who survive Cherokee, and the wife with whom he was living at the time of his death. Lucy Pecan, wants the land divided equally between the two children and she desires to retain that portion belonging to her child for her own occupancy.

Sac & Fox – Shawnee Estates
1885-1910 Volume I

>Very respectfully,
>M J Bentley
>A/S Indian Agt

HORACE A. SMITH, JUDGE GEO. W. FOSTER, SHERIFF ERNEST W. ADAMS, CLERK

Probate Court Noble County.

Perry, Oklahoma, Feb. 28" 1901.

Indian Agent Sac and Fox Agency

Dear Sir:--------

One White horse wishes me to write you and state that Elwood Oldman Grant's son is dead, and that sometime before his death he parted from his wife. That they [illegible] the money coming due him & his mother Mrs Grant, and that it is his desire that the money be paid to her.

>H. A. Smith

Territory of Oklahoma,
County of Lincoln,

Personally appeared before me, Lee Patrick, Notary Public, in and for the above County and Territory Dick Ellis and Jeptha Wilson of lawful age, who being duly sworn upon oath, say that they are members of the Absentee Shawnee Band of Indians in Oklahoma; that they knew Size-ha-thle during her lifetime; that they were present at her death which occurred in the Creek Nation, Indian Territory on the 17th day of May, 1900, caused by burning of body by fire started in bedding accidentally by match in hands of deceased. That the deceased leaves as her surviving heirs: Nah-wah-lah-pea-se, daughter William Littleax, son, Switch Littleax, son and Peter Washington, John Ax, Claude Tyner, James Alford, Stella Bluecoat, Jesse Washington, James Washington and Charlie Tyner, grandchildren, all of which are living at the Sauk and Fox Agency, Oklahoma.

Witnesses
Mary Antoine
R.E.L. Daniel

Jeptha Wilson his
Dick Ellis   x mark

Sac & Fox – Shawnee Estates
1885-1910 Volume I

Subscribed and sworn to before me this 18th day of March, 1901.

My Com Ex 2-25-1902   Lee Patrick
                                   Notary Public.

    Also personally appeared at the same time and place Thomas Washington and Jim Spoon of Bank [illegible] Agency two reputable disinterested parties who being duly sworn upon oath say that they have heard the contents of the foregoing affidavit of Jeptha Wilson and Dick Ellis and believe the same to be true as stated and that they knew Nah-wah-lah-pea-se, daughter William Littleax, son, Switch Littleax, son, Peter Washington, John Ax, Claude Tyner, James Alford, Stella Bluecoat, Jesse Washington, James Washington and Charlie Tyner, children of deceased and children of decedant[sic], to be the only surviving legal heirs of Size-ha-thle, deceased, and that they have no interest in this claim.

    Witnesses   Thomas Washington   his
    Mary Antoine   John Spoon   X
    R.E.L. Daniel   mark

Subscribed and sworn to before me this 18th day of March, 1901.

My Com Ex 2-25-1902   Lee Patrick
                                   Notary Public.
    Sauk and Fox Agency, Oklahoma Territory,

    I certify on honor that the foregoing affidavit is correct as shown by the records of this office and that the heirs therein mentioned are the sole beneficiaries of the estate of Size-ha-thle, deceased.

                Lee Patrick
                U. S. Indian Agent.

Refer in reply to the following:
Land
4884-1901

Department of the Interior.
OFFICE OF INDIAN AFFAIRS
WASHINGTON,   March 20, 1901.

Lee Patrick, Esq.,
    U. S. Indian Agent,
        Sac and Fox Agency, Okla.

Sac & Fox – Shawnee Estates
1885-1910 Volume I

Sir:

This office is in receipt of a letter dated January 21, 1901, from Caleb Deshane of Catale, Indian Territory, forwarding a copy of Probate Court proceedings respecting the estate of Joe Charley, and respecting a deed of a portion of Joe Charley's land in Oklahoma Territory, by Susan Bob and her husband.

These papers are transmitted for your investigation and report thereon.

Very respectfully,
W A Jones
Commissioner.

R.F.T. (B)

JACOBS HARDWARE COMPANY.
HOLDENVILLE, INDIAN TERRITORY

Holdenville, I. T. 3/27 *190*1

Hon. Lee Patrick
    Sac & Fox Agency, O.T.

Dear friend   Simply writing for information as to Shawningo's children viz. Stella Shawningo & John Shawningo. I want to know if they share in Old Bob Deer's estate or any of his land. I was appointed their Admistrator[sic] by the U.S. Court last May 1890 which I [illegible] little of administration to explain its[sic] self. Some parties are trying to buy Bob Deer's land if they share in said proceeds. I expect I would have to sign deeds to. And there is one 40 acre belonging to their sister deceased. I want to know whether I can sell same or not. proceeds of the sale they can [illegible...]   I don't know what kind of land these are but if I am interested I would want to know & look after same. Please write me & return letter of admistration[sic] & explain to me these questions.

Your frd,
John A Jacobs

P.S. Under my administrating the Estate, I think I ought to receive rent money & report same to U.S. Court.

Yours truly
JAJ

****

Sac & Fox – Shawnee Estates
1885-1910 Volume I

JACOBS HARDWARE COMPANY.
HOLDENVILLE, INDIAN TERRITORY

Holdenville, I. T.   Apr 1   1901

Hon. Lee Patrick
    Sauk & Fox Agency, O.T.

Dear Sir: In reply to yours of the 29th I will say that Stella & John Shawningo is children of Bob Deerr's daughter "Tilda" I have been told that they would ~~have a~~ share in the Estate.

    You will also advise me who would be the right party to receive Stella & John Shawningo's rent money when comes due.

                            Yours Truly,
                            John A. Jacobs

Refer in reply to the following:
Land.
15774-1901

Department of the Interior.
OFFICE OF INDIAN AFFAIRS
WASHINGTON,   March 29, 1901.

Lee Patrick, Esq.,
    U. S. Indian Agent,
        Sac & Fox Agency,
            Okla.

Sir:

    The office is in receipt of your letter of the 19th instant, submitting for cancellation one farming and grazing lease, executed by Jennie Segar, sole heir of Anna King, deceased Absentee Shawnee allottee, in favor of William W. Collins for the SE/4 of SE/4 of 25-10-3, 40 acres, for one year from January 1, 1900; consideration $130. This lease expires by limitation on January 1, 1901.

    You also submit for approval a lease covering the same land for the same time in favor of Pierre B. McClanahan for the same consideration.

    You state that the lessee Collins is a minor and could not make a legal contract and has since left the country; that McClanahan has occupied the land and paid the rent up to <u>January 1, 1901</u>, but is delinquent on that payment; and you request that the last named lease be approved at once, in order that you may bring suit against Mr. McClanahan to recover the last semi-annual payment, should it become necessary.

Sac & Fox – Shawnee Estates
1885-1910 Volume I

The McClanahan lease was submitted to the office for approval with your letter of March 17th 1900. It was returned for further consideration on June 28th last, because of the existence of the prior lease in favor of Collins.

The office records show that this land has been sold to James M. Toney. The deed is dated September 6, and was approved October 29, 1900.

Before submitting these leases to the Secretary for action, the office would like further information as to why they were not submitted for action before the expiration of the term and also as to what understanding was had with the purchaser Toney in regard to the McClanahan lease, when Toney was given possession, &c. There is nothing in the deed to indicate that it was subject to the lease.

If McClanahan paid up to January 1, 1901, he is not delinquent. It is supposed that he paid to July 1, 1900.

All papers submitted with your letter are returned for further consideration, as above indicated.

Very respectfully,
W A Jones
Commissioner.

J.L.D.

  L.

Oklahoma City O. T. April 22nd, 1901
Lee Patrick Esq.
Sac & Fox Agency
I.T.

    Friend Patrick:-

Will you kindly inform me if there is any good prospect of our geting[sic] our claim against the Estate of Wm Shawnee who died in Norman Okla, and was taken to Shawnee to day by Mr Shaffer who is my pardner[sic] in our store at Norman O.T. Mrs Shawnee was over to Norman some time ago, and told Dr Threadgill Supt of the Insane Asylum, in case of the death of Mr Shawnee to fix him up nicely and send his remains to Shawnee. We went to a good deal of expense to embalm him gave him a nice Broadcloth Casket, and paid all expenses over there, accompanying his remains. His wife had no collateral to offer, and all we could do was to take her receipt for the remains, and O K the bill, and trust to the future to get our money from the Estate. Please write me any information as how to proceed to secure the amount. Will take it as a personal favor for any or all information you can furnish.

Sac & Fox – Shawnee Estates
1885-1910 Volume I

Thanking you in advance for the favor.
I am Very truly
J H Reid

Office of
GEO. M. SOUTHGATE,
County Clerk,
Pottawatomie County.

Tecumseh, Oklahoma. May 13   *190* 1.

Lee Patrick,
    U.S. Indian Agt.
        Sac Fox Agcy

Dear Sir

    Has there been a deed sent to your office from Susan Bob & George Bob her husband as heir to Joe Charley for the N $^{1/2}$ SE $^{1/4}$ Sec 23 Twp 20 Range 4 E.[sic] Mr. Gilbert my father in law wants to purchase the land if it has not been sold and will give 6\underline{00}$ per acre for it.

    Please let me hear from you soon.

Yours truly
Geo M Southgate

WM. C. BAYLIS,
ATTORNEY AT LAW,
ROSSVILLE, KANS.
May 29 1901

Hon Lee Patrick,
  U-S Indian Agent,
    Sac & Fox Agency,
      Oklahoma

      Sir, Your attention is called to the following matter: Grace Doud an allottee of Pottawatomie Indian land died sometime in the Summer of A.D. 1900 was about 9 years old at the time of selecting land. under the law as known and called the Daws Bill and Law.

Her Father Leroy Palmer Doud and Mother Zora Doud nee Zora Acton are bothe[sic] alive – by the death of Grace Doud, a single person the Father is the sole heir and

Sac & Fox – Shawnee Estates
1885-1910 Volume I

entitled to the rents issues and profits of said allotment. he reports to me that their[sic] is 31 acres in Cultivatin[sic] renting for 2^{00} per acre or 62^{00} rest being pasture land it's subdivision – S^2 of NE^4 Sect 1 or 2 township 6 range 1
You are respectfully requested to hold any monies or renewells[sic] of lease subject to his (the Father of said Grace Doud, Leroy Palmer Doud) Order – and further will you please let him know if last year's rent is payed or been collected, an interchange of correspondence is respectfully requested in relation to said matter.

       Yours with due respect

Post Office address,   Leroy P Doud
Rossville,   by Wm C Baylis
Shawnee Co, Kans.

        Buck Head O T
        5/22/1901

Mr Lee Patrick

 Dear Sir
   in regard to the Charley Rodd land I have not got to see the heirs and dont[sic] believe that I can do anything with them so as far as I am conserned[sic] I shall drop the matter and thanking you for past favors I remain
       Yours truly
       H.A. Myers
       Buck Head O T

J. H. Harry, President *C. H. Cade, Vice Pres.* *Willard Johnston, Cashier*
      No. 5095
    First National Bank

       May 31, 1901.

Lee Patrick, U. S. Indian Agent,
  Sac & Fox Agency.
Dear Sir:-
  Yours of the 29" inst with Certificate of Deposit for $1150.00 payable to the heirs of Spanish Wilson, (deceased) and a deed from said heirs to W. H. Brown, received, and as requested, I herewith inclose our draft on St. Louis for $380.33

payable to your order: also enclose the two receipts which you requested me to sign as guardian, and have notified Mr. Brown that the deed was here, and to call for same, and we will send you the receipts for it as soon as he comes in.

    I have gone according to your directions, Mr. Patrick, but it seems to me like there is a mistake, as the Certificate of Deposit is for $1150.00, one third, Nancy Wilsons[sic] share, would be #383.33, and you say you only paid her $380.33, and I only remitted you the draft for that amount. The other $3.00 I will pay to her. The other receipts that I signed as guardian, you have made out for $616.67, and I have received $766.67 so if you want these receipts changed, return them to me and I will receipt you as stated, and if this $3.00 should come to you instead of her, advise me at once.

                        Respectfully yours,
                         Willard Johnston
                              Cashier.

Refer in reply to the following:
Land
28999-1901

Department of the Interior.
OFFICE OF INDIAN AFFAIRS
        WASHINGTON,   June 5, 1901.

Lee Patrick, Esq.,
    U. S. Indian Agent,
        Sac and Fox Agency, Okla.

Sir:

    This office is in receipt of your letter of May 25, 1901, forwarding for approval a deed dated April 20, 1901, from the heirs of Etienne Kahdot, conveying to C. W. Miller, for $400, the W/2 of the SW/4 of Sec. 13, T 7 N, R 4 E, I. M.

    I now return said deed as the records of this office show that the above described land was allotted and patented to Peter Tesson, Citizen Potawatomi reservee No. 919.

                        Very respectfully,
                            W A Jones
                              Commissioner.

R.F.T. (G)

Sac & Fox – Shawnee Estates
1885-1910 Volume I

C. W. MILLER, Pres.   I. H. WALKER, Vice Pres.   W. A. REGGLES, Cashier

Tecumseh State Bank.

PAID UP CAPITAL STOCK $10,000.00

Tecumseh, Okla.   June 6th 190 1

Lee Patrick, U.S. Ind. Agt.
    Sac & Fox Agency

Dear Sir I have been trying to find the allotment Patent to E^2 25 [illegible] of Wezo Curly

    Wezo said her brother Andy had the Patent and Andy says it is at the agency If you have it we would like to have it to record

                  Yours
                    E.W. Miller

Refer in reply to the following:
Land
23644-1901

Department of the Interior.

OFFICE OF INDIAN AFFAIRS

Washington,   June 10, 1901.

Lee Patrick, Esq.,
    U. S. Indian Agent,
        Sac and Fox Agency, Oklahoma.

Sir:

    This office is in receipt of your letter of April 29, 1901, forwarding for approval a deed dated March 7, 1901, from the heirs of Ellen Delaware, Absentee Shawnee reserve No. 237, conveying to Estelle Wilson, for $800 the W/2 of the NE/4 of Sec. 13, T 9 N., R 4 E., I. M., containing 80 acres of agricultural land, with accompanying papers.

    I now return said deed that you may furnish a certified copy of the proceedings of the proper probate court that Mary C. Williams has been appointed legal guardian of James Rock, a minor and one of the heirs of Ellen Delaware; also authority from said court to said guardian to sell the rights and interests of said minor, James Rock, in and to the aforesaid land.

Sac & Fox – Shawnee Estates
1885-1910 Volume I

Very respectfully,
W.A. Jones
Commissioner.

R.F.T. (B)

Refer in reply to the following:
Land
28870-1901

Department of the Interior.
OFFICE OF INDIAN AFFAIRS
WASHINGTON, June 10, 1901.

Wm. H. Mallicoat, Esq.,
    Tecumseh, Oklahoma.

Sir:

    This office is in receipt, by Department reference through the Commissioner of the General Land Office, of your letter of May 11, making inquiry respecting a deed from the heirs of Ellen Delaware, Absentee Shawnee reservee No. 227, conveying to you the SE/4 of the NE/4 and the SE/4 of the NW/4 of the NW/4 of Sec. 10, T 9 N., R 4 E., I. M., containing 80 acres of grazing land, you are informed that said deed was this day returned to Agent Patrick unapproved for the reason that it was not accompanied by any evidence showing the appointment of Mary C. Williams as guardian of James Rock, one of the minor heirs, nor of any authority granted her to sell the interest of said minor in said land. As soon as this evidence shall have been furnished in legal form, this office will be prepared to take action on said deed.

Very respectfully,
W.A. Jones
Commissioner.

R.F.T. (B)

****

Mr J W. Rigas
I inclose within note which explaines[sic] it's[sic] self please let me know what to do immediately and oblige

W.H. Mallicoat

Sac & Fox – Shawnee Estates
1885-1910 Volume I

Shawnee O.T.
June 11th 1901

Mr Lee Patrick
　　Dear Sir
　　　　I enclose deed from Mary Ross heirs for W^2 SW 1/4 Sec 25 Tp 10 R 8 E and W^2 NW 1/4 Sec 36 Tp 10 R 8 E. Please give me what assistance you can in getting it through. Any thing you do will be highly appreciated. I would be glad to get it through as soon as possible.

　　　　　　　　　Yours Truly
　　　　　　　　　J W Hand

CERTIFICATE

Territory of Oklahoma, Lincoln County, ss.

　　I, 　S. A. Cordell 　　　Probate Judge of said County and ex-officio Clerk of the Probate Court of said County, do hereby certify that the records of said court show that 　P. S. Hoffman 　　　　　　　is the duly appointed qualified and acting Administrator 　　of the Estate of William Thrift, deceased, and that his Letters as such are within full power and effect

　　　　　　Witness my hand and official seal affixed at my office in Chandler, Lincoln County, Territory of Oklahoma this 　5th 　　day of July 　　　　190 1

　　　　　　　　　S. A. Cordell
　　　　Probate Judge and ex-officio Clerk of the Probate Court.

****

Sac & Fox – Shawnee Estates
1885-1910 Volume I

The United States,

To P.S. Hoffman Admitted. William Thrift   Dr.

DATE			DOLLARS	CTS
1901				
July	3	To Balance of Individual Indian Money due Estate of William Thrift	104	31

Received, at Sauk & Fox Agency O.T.   , 190 1,
of Lee Patrick US Ind. Agent, One hundred four ($104.31) & 31/100 *dollars,*
in full of the above account.

* *Witness:*   WR Gulick   P.S. Hoffman Adm

I certify, on honor, that the above account is correct and just, and that I have actually, this 3rd *day of* July   *, 190* 1 *paid the amount thereof.*

                                        Lee Patrick

NOTES.— All vouchers must show a sufficient explanation of the objects and necessity of the expenditure, and be made in triplicate. The dates, rates, and places at which services were rendered must, in all cases, be stated.
  * Signatures of Indians and all signatures by mark must be witnessed.

Sac & Fox – Shawnee Estates
1885-1910 Volume I

Geo. L. Rose,
Farm and Chattel Loans
TECUMSEH, OKLA.

July 13, 1901.

Mr. Lee Patrick,
    Sac & Fox Agency, O.T.

Dear Sir:-

Can you give me any information as to the deed made by the heirs of Zah-jah-no, deceased to Joseph N. Villines, conveying the E/2 of SE/4 of 19-7-5 E. This matter went to your office some time in Jan. or Feb.

Yours very truly,
Geo. L. Rose

GEO. D. LATHAM   C. W. COOMBS

The Cleveland County Leader,

Latham & Coombs, Proprietors.

ESTABLISHED 1891.   CIRCULATION 1000.

Lexington, O. T.   July 17   1901

Lee Patrick
    U.S. Ind Agt.
    Dear Sir

Inclosed find affidavit by Indians by blood to the Eason[sic] heirs also Natay[sic] Certificate will forward the other Certificate and business committe[sic] certificate soon.

By request of Howard Friend who is buying the Easton heirs[sic] land.

Geo. D. Latham

Sac & Fox – Shawnee Estates
1885-1910 Volume I

DEPARTMENT OF THE INTERIOR.
UNITED STATES INDIAN SERVICE.

Sac and Fox Agency, Iowa.
Toledo, July 22, 1901.

Hon. Lee Patrick,
    U. S. Indian Agent,
        Sac And Fox Agency, Okla.
Sir:

    Relative to the claim of Maggie Picket being the only heir of Wa-Ta-To-Wah, I personally know nothing, but will make inquiries into the matter. He had no claim on any land of which I have been informed, and I think there is a small amount of unpaid annuity still due to him.

    This unpaid annuity matter is being investigated at the Indian office in Washington, and when results are reached, if there is anything due to the said Wa-Ta-To-Wah, deceased, I will ascertain who the rightful heirs are, and settlement will be made accordingly. When I hear from the Department, I will apprise you of the fact, so that Maggie Picket can file her claim.

                      Very respectfully,
                        W.G. Malin
                        U. S. Indian Agent.

U. S. POST OFFICE

SACRED HEART, OKLA.

Mr. A.B. Jones.
    Dear Sir:

                Please find out the status of a deed from Joseph Na-kna-chkuk, and other heirs, conveying a piece of land down on the Canadian river, to a person, the name of whom they do not know. They say that you know all about the deal. They are here now and want you to trace the deed up, and hurry it through for them, as they need the money, and the deed has been gone about six months.

I believe the name of the Granter is Robinson.

I spoke to the Brickmaker and he say[sic] that he will sell good bricks for $7.00 per M. in smaller quantities $1.00 per C.

Sac & Fox – Shawnee Estates
1885-1910 Volume I

Very truly yours
Bro John Laracy

Lee. Do you know any thing of the above deed. Will order brick for vault as above.

A.B.J.

Traders INSURANCE CO. CHICAGO

Dowagiac Michigan
July 26, 1901

Hon Lee Patrick
    Sac and Fox Agency

Dr Sir

Will you kindly inform as to the disposition of the estate of Frank Pa ksh kah, a Pottawatomie who died in Oklahoma a year ago last winter. This may be a larger task than you care to assume, if so, kindly give me the name of someone who can help me. This man has two nieces here and they keep getting letters from parties at Avoca asking for a power of attorney to sell the property, a farm - and they think best to go to you. He may have died before the time I state, but the letters commenced there. You may write to Mrs Lawrence   (Mix)
A M Moon   Justice Joh[sic] Pearce   Dowagiac Mich

J. H. Harry, President   *C. H. Cade, Vice Pres.*   *Willard Johnston, Cashier*

No. 5095

First National Bank

Shawnee, O.T.   August 8, 1901

Lee Patrick, U. S. Indian Agent,
    Sac and Fox, O.T.
Dear Sir:-
    I have your letter in regard to Certificates of Deposit for $400.00 and $450.00 payable to the order of the heirs of James Little Bear (deceased) and I note what you say about our refusing to pay these certificates, and that would place same in

Sac & Fox – Shawnee Estates
1885-1910 Volume I

the habds[sic] of an United States attorney. You say you know of no steps having been taken to stop payment. In this you are mistaken, as I notified the Stroud State Bank at the time we returned them, because of an order from the Probate Judge, who has the jurisdiction in these cases, and I would rather obey his orders than take my chances in paying out against his orders and instructions, because if I paid this out against the orders of the court, and it had been squandered, we would probably have had to pay it again, and I can't help but believe that if you had been placed in my position, you would have done as I have done.

I did not know, Mr. Patrick, that you had paid this money back. I suppose of course it was being paid to Shawnee Little Bear. The Probate Judge has now authorized us to pay this money to you. He said you should have notified him that you held it, and in that case he would have released us from the order no to pay the money out, or if you had advised us yourself that you held it, I would have been willing to pay it out.

Enclosed find our draft for $850.00.

Yours truly,
Willard Johnston
Cashier.

Department of the Interior.

U.S. INDIAN SERVICE.

Sac & Fox Agency O.T.
Nov 3rd *190*2

Frank A. Thackery, Supt.
Shawnee, Okla
Dear Sir:-

In settling the estate of Mattie Shantey a deceased Sac & Fox, we find that she is a sister of the Littlebears, the amount in our hands is 62\underline{50}$ and there are eight of the heirs. There is an [illegible] of 39\underline{60}$ and balance which would be $286 each for the heirs. All of the adults have signed and received their share. More are two minors viz: Janie and Lillie Littlebear girls two children of Lucy Littlebear, deceased, who are minors who would receive their mother's share.

Can you give me the names of the guardians of these minors and would you get their signatures and the necessary court certificates if I send the money to you.[sic]

Respectfully
W N Galick
Clerk in charge.

Sac & Fox – Shawnee Estates
1885-1910 Volume I

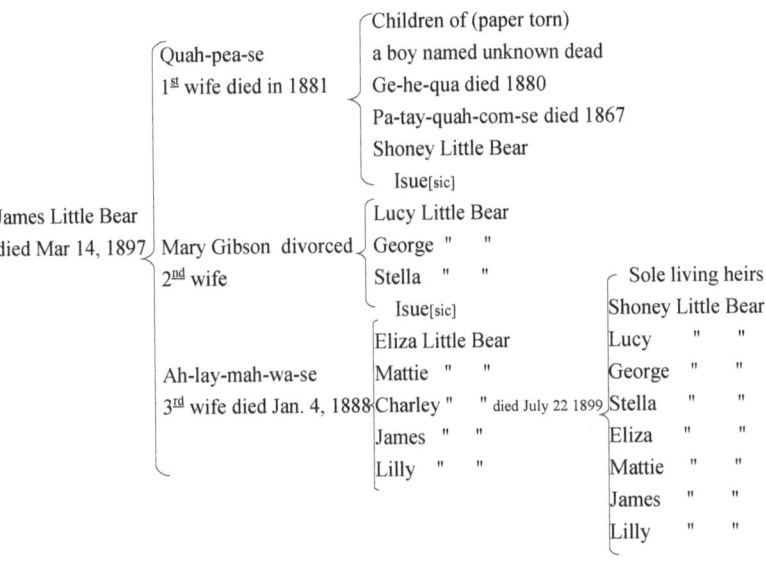

We the undersigned members of the Absentee Shawnee Business Committee do hereby certify on honor that the above shown heirs of James Little Bear, deceased, and Charley Little Bear, deceased, are the identical persons they represent themselves to be and that their relationship shown therein is correct.

                                        Thomas W. Alford
                                        John C. King

Department of the Interior.

U. S. INDIAN SERVICE.

if I send the money to you?
                    Respectfully
                    W.R. Gulick   , *190*__
                    Clerk [illegible]

    The above letter got covered up & was lost sight of. Am not sure of these children having a legal Gdn at present time, but Shoney Little Bear is their nearest relative & also their natural guardian & I would suggest paying the amt direct to him & taking his receipt as such. If this meets with your approval you can send amt to this office & Shoney LB. can sign receipts, and money either given to him or to the children, who are in this school.

Sac & Fox – Shawnee Estates
1885-1910 Volume I

Yours respectfully
Frank A. Thackery
Supt. & S.D.A.
Cox Clk.

Hico, Okla. Ter.
Aug. 10th 1901

U.S. Indian Agent
    Sac & Fox Agency
        Okla.

I would like to know whether the Department has decided about the Douglas Deere estate of 160 acres, that I and Sam sold for $1000.^{00} and would like to know when we will get the money and would like to know how long it will take to be decided. The land we sold I and Sam sold lies just adjoins where Thomas Pierce leased from us, it joins on the west side from Thomas Pierce's lease. I dont[sic] know the No's of the land that I and Sam sold to a man in Shawnee. I wish you would write and let me know when the Department would decide the ownership of the Douglas Deere land case, when the deed would be approved by the Secretary. Wish you would answer me soon about the matter, to Hico. Okla.

        Very Respectfully
        Amos Deere

Shawnee. Oklahoma. Territory.

        Aug. 15th. 1901

Hon Lee Patrick.
    Sac and Fox Agency.
Dear Sir, will you please tell me if the Heirs of Emma Johnson Decd have ever signed the Deeds that was fowered[sic] to your Office for them to sign. the[sic] parties are anxious to know. please[sic] let me know at your earlest[sic] conveance[sic]

        Respectfully. Yours.
        Florien B [Illegible]

Sac & Fox – Shawnee Estates
1885-1910 Volume I

Sacred Heart O.T. 8/16/1901

Major Lee Patrick,

Dear Sir, Yours notifying me of the approval of the deed of the heirs of the heirs of Adelaide Bertrand, was [illegible] while I was in Lawton. You ask about the death of B. B. Bertrand one of the grantors. He is not dead, but it was the grantee Lawrence J. Bertrand who died, and his widow Mary, under my advice took out letters of administration on his estate last June. The deed can be sent to the bank at Parcell. My brother Lawrence transacted all his banking business there.

Now I wish you would if convenient send my certificate of deposit directly to me here, you can endorese[sic] on the back of the certificate that the deed mentioned has been duly approved, and I can cash it in Shawnee. I[sic] will be very inconvenient for me to go to Parcell, as I would have no other business there. You can sent my brother Benards[sic] certificate to the First National Bank at St. Marys, Kansas. With any certificate of deposit you can send such receipt as you wish for me to sign. If it suits you better you can send my certificate and receipt to Brother [blacked out] our Postmaster

Yours truly R. R. Bertrand

If you have the necessary influence I will you would get me the job of surveying the [illegible] of Ashor. I believe that I have surveyed more times than any other engineer in the Territory.

I have the very best instruments costing over $200. [Illegible] latest railroad transit and 100 foot steel chain, also leveling instruments, And forty years practice

---

Bear[sic]

RECEIVED
AUG 29 1911
SAC & FOX AGENCY,
OKLAHOMA.

Shawnee, Okla.
August 28, 1911.

Mr. W. C. Kohlenberg,
Dear Sir:-

Will write for grand ma (Sarah Bear) as she has asked me to do so. I would like for you to notify me when you a (Court) folks are going to discuss over Bertha's Pattequa's land or property. You said for me to tell you about this matter in September [end of letter]

85

Sac & Fox – Shawnee Estates
1885-1910 Volume I

O. B. CLEVENGER
   Lawyer and Notary Public.

Bartlesville I. T. September 20, 1901.

Lee Patrick Esq.,
   Sac & Fox Agency.
Dear Sir:-
   On June 19th. last one Edd Rhodd of this place made a deed before me to some land in Oklahoma, to his brothers[sic] land, with the understanding that he was to receive his share of this land, when the deed was made, and he has never heard from it since.
   Now what he wants to know is what was done by the rest of the heirs, did the rest of them sign it and was the sale consummated or did some of them fail or refuse to sign the deed And the sale fall through, if the sale was made why was Edd not sent his share as agreed?
   Please let him know as soon as possible in regard to this, I was the Notary before whom his quit claim deed was acknowledged and sent the deed to you when he signed it.

Yours Resp,
O. B. Clevenger

Purcell Ind. Terr
Sept 17, 1901

Agent Patrick
   Sac & Fox, O.T.

Dear Sir
as I understand the law of Okla – where a wife is left with no children the land goes one half to her and the other half to the heirs of her husband – now what I want you to tell me is there any law or can I compel the heirs to pay me for my improvements, this is in regard to allotted land I wrote the Secy of Indian Affairs and he referred me to you so would be glad if you would let me hear from [sic] at once-

Respectfully
Mattie J Clardy

Sac & Fox – Shawnee Estates
1885-1910 Volume I

Refer in reply to the following:
Land
70653-1901

Department of the Interior.
OFFICE OF INDIAN AFFAIRS
Washington,   Dec. 13, 1901.

Lee Patrick, Esq.,
    U. S. Indian Agent,
        Sac and Fox Agency, Oklahoma.

Sir:

    Referring to your letter of December 2, 1901, forwarding receipts for deed and money from the heirs of Caesar Beaver, Absentee Shawnee reservee No. 83, who conveyed to William H. Dill the SE/4 of the NE/4 of Sec. 16, T 10 N, R 3 E, I now return said receipts, stating that the land sold was the SE/4 of the NW/4 of said Sec. 16.
    Please obtain receipts for the correct description of land.

                Very respectfully,
                W A Jones
                    Commissioner.

R.F.T. (G)

Refer in reply to the following:
Land
69392-1901

Department of the Interior.
OFFICE OF INDIAN AFFAIRS
Washington,   Dec. 13, 1901.

Lee Patrick, Esq.,
    U. S. Indian Agent,
        Sac & Fox Agency,
        Oklahoma.

Sir:

    The office is in receipt, by reference of the Hon. D.T. Flynn, of a letter from A.T. Ross, dated Shawnee, Oklahoma, November 20th last, stating that one G.A. Hawkins was administrator of the estate of Rose Horton, a deceased Potawatomi Indian who was allotted the S/2 of Sec. 24, T 8 N., R 1 E., in Cleveland Co., Oklahoma; that the estate was administered in the Probate Court of Crowley County, Kansas; that Hawkins made final settlement and was discharged as such administrator December 8, 1898; that at the time he made final settlement there was due him, as administrator's fees, the sum of $48., which sum is still due him; and he asks for an investigation, and

Sac & Fox – Shawnee Estates
1885-1910 Volume I

if the claim is found to be correct, that an order be issued providing for the payment of said sum out of the lease money.

The letter is transmitted, herewith, and you are instructed to make a full investigation of this matter and report your findings to this office with such recommendation as you think proper.

Please return said enclosure with your report.

Very respectfully,
AC Tonner
Acting Commissioner.

J.L.D.
L.

DEPARTMENT OF THE INTERIOR.
UNITED STATES INDIAN SERVICE.

SAC AND FOX AGENCY, IOWA.
Toledo, June 30", 1902.

Hon. Ross Guffin,
    U.S. Indian Agent,
        Sac and Fox Agency, Okla.

Dear Sir:

Your favor of the 27th, instant, relative to the estate of Wa-To-Ta-Wa, is at hand, and replying will say, that there is but the meager sum of $43.83, due to the said Wa-To-Ta-Wa, and he owes over $50.00 to one man in Montour, Iowa, and a smaller sum to another person in the same town. It has been decided by the friends of the said Wa-To-Ta-Wa, that this sum which is due him, shall be paid Pro- rata, to his creditors, which decision I know you will approve.

Very respectfully,

U.S. Indian Agent.

****

DEPARTMENT OF THE INTERIOR.
UNITED STATES INDIAN SERVICE.

SAC AND FOX AGENCY, IOWA.
Toledo, Nov. 14, 1901.

W. R. Gulick,
    Sac and Fox Agency, Okla.

Sac & Fox – Shawnee Estates
1885-1910 Volume I

Sir:

Your favor of the 11th, instant at hand. Relative to the claim of Maggie Pickett as being the only heir of Wa-To-Ta-Wah[sic], Deceased, I will say, that I have made inquiries concerning this matter, and find, That there are two heirs of the said Indian living here who have equal claims with Maggie Pickett, whose claim is acknowledged by the Chief, and she will be accorded her share of the back annuity due him, when settlement is made. One of these heirs is dead, but he, or she, left two children, who I think, justly claim the share due to their parent, and the Chief and the head men of the tribe have so adjudged.

This matter will be settled, as soon as the small-pox subsides, so that the quarantine can safely be raised.

Very respectfully,

U. S. Indian Agent.

Wrote April 10th 1902
Wrote June 27th 1902

Department of the Interior.
INDIAN SCHOOL SERVICE.
OFFICE OF SUPERINTENDENT

Sauk & Fox Agency 1901
Toledo, Aug. 19, ~~190~~

Hon Lee Patrick
   Indian Agent
      Sac & Fox Agency O.T.

Sir

I have the honor to hereby acknowledge the receipt of your favor of the 14th instant relative to the claim made by Maggie Pickett. I can find no record of the name of Pah Te Ko Ta on any of the Pay Rolls in this office, which only date back to the year 188[?]. I find his name on some old records in 1857 but nothing later. Wau-ma-kee, is 62 years of age and [illegible...]. that there are no moneys due the said Pah-Te Ko Ta and I have no knowledge of any land ever belonging to him. I will make inquiry into this matter of the Head Man of the tribe, and if Maggie proves her claim she shall have justice done here if any estate be found

Very respectfully
WG Malin
US Indian Agent

Sac & Fox – Shawnee Estates
1885-1910 Volume I

Refer in reply to the following:
Land.
49686-1902.

Department of the Interior.
OFFICE OF INDIAN AFFAIRS
WASHINGTON,
September 12, 1902.

Ross Guffin, Esq.,
    U. S. Indian Agent,
        Sac and Fox Agency, Oklahoma.
Sir:-

    Referring to your letter of August 2, 1902, recommending the appointment of -

        1. McKosito,
        2. Moses Keokuk,
        3. Alexander Connolly,
        4. Kaw-tope,
        5. William Pattequa,

as a business committee for the Sac and Fox tribe of Indians in Oklahoma, in passing upon the question of heirship of deceased allottees, you are informed that the Department on the 19th instant confirmed said nominations as such business committee.

    I transmit herewith a copy of Department letter for the files of your office.

                Very respectfully,
                      W.A. Jones
                            Commissioner.

R.F.T. (G)

                ****

                (COPY)
        DEPARTMENT OF THE INTERIOR,
            Washington, August 19, 1902.
The Commissioner of Indian Affairs -
    Sir:-

        In accordance with your recommendation of the 6th instant, the nomination by the Sac and Fox tribe of Indians in Oklahoma of the following members of said tribe as a Business Committee, are hereby confirmed: -

        1. McKosito;

Sac & Fox – Shawnee Estates
1885-1910 Volume I

2. Moses Keokuk;
3. Alexander Connolly;
4. Kaw-tope;
5. William Pattequa.

The inclosure to your letter is herewith returned.

Very respectfully,
Thos. Ryan
Acting Secretary.

7441, Ind. Div. 1902.
1 inclosure.
M.E.W.

LETTERS OF GUARDIANSHIP.

The State of Kansas,
Shawnee County, } ss.

In Probate Court.

To all to Whom these Presents Shall Come - Greeting:

Know Ye, *That whereas,* Ernest Ray Green, Minor child and Heir at law of John Green, deceased.

ha*S.*. *property, rights and credits, in said county and elsewhere, that may be lost, destroyed, or diminished in value, if speedy and proper care be not taken of the same : to the end, therefore, that the estate, rights and property, and the person of the said minor..... be properly care for and protected, I,* W. E. Fagan

Probate Judge in and for the aforesaid county,

do hereby constitute and appoint J. N. Dolley

of said county, Guardian of the person......, estate and property of whatsoever kind that may appertain or belong to said minor........, with full power and authority to collect and dispose of any or all his *estate, property, rights and credits, according to law; and in general, to do and to perform all other acts and things which are, or hereafter may be, required of* him *by law, or the decree of any court having jurisdiction.*

IN TESTIMONY WHEREOF, I, W. E. Fagan
Judge of the Probate Court in and for said county, do hereto set my hand and affix the seal of said court, this 13th day of September 190 2

(seal)

W. E. Fagan   Probate Judge.

LETTERS OF GUARDIANSHIP.

The State of Kansas,
Shawnee *County,* } *ss.* In Probate Court.

To all to Whom these Presents Shall Come - Greeting:

Know Ye, *That whereas,* Herbert Reinhart Green, minor child and heir at law of Christina Eliza Green, deceased.

ha s.. *property, rights and credits, in said county and elsewhere, that may be lost, destroyed, or diminished in value, if speedy and proper care be not taken of the same : to the end, therefore, that the estate, rights and property, and the person of the said minor...... be properly care for and protected, I,* W. E. Fagan

Probate Judge in and for the aforesaid county, do hereby constitute and appoint J. N. Dolley vice John Green, deceased, *of said county, Guardian of the person........, estate and property of whatsoever kind that may appertain or belong to said minor.........., with full power and authority to collect and dispose of any or all* his *estate, property, rights and credits, according to law; and in general, to do and to perform all other acts and things which are, or hereafter may be, required of* him *by law, or the decree of any court having jurisdiction.*

IN TESTIMONY WHEREOF, I, W. E. Fagan
Judge of the Probate Court in and for said county, do hereto set my hand and affix the seal of said court, this 13th day of September 190 2

(seal) W. E. Fagan Probate Judge.

****

W. F. SCHOCH
I, ~~R. F. HAYDEN~~ *Judge and ex-officio Clerk of the Probate Court within and for the County of Shawnee and State of Kansas, do hereby certify that the above and foregoing is a full, true and correct copy of* Letters of Guardianship in the estate of Herbert Reinhart Green, minor child and heir at law of Christena Green, deceased and Ernest Ray Green, minor child and heir at law of John Green, deceased.
as the same appears *of record* *in my office.*

IN WITNESS WHEREOF, I have hereunto set my hand and affixed the seal of said County at my office in the City of Topeka, this *11th* day of *February* 190 2

W. F. Schoch *Probate Judge.*

Sac & Fox – Shawnee Estates
1885-1910 Volume I

Territory of Oklahoma.)
: ss
Pottawatomie County,)

In Probate Court in and for said County and Territory,

in the matter of the estate of) Decree
Ralph Dunn (Mahaw-taw-waw-pah-wah) deceased.)

Be it remembered that on the 23d day of September A.D. 1902 the same being a regular day of the September term of said Court the above matter came on to be heard upon the application for final settlement and distribution, of F. W. Christher[sic] the duly appointed, qualified and acting administrator of said estate, and after hearing the proofs offered and testimony introduced in said matter the court finds as follows:-- That due notice of the filing of the application for final hearing was given according to law. That there are no debts, claims or demands outstanding and unpaid against said estate. That the said Ralph Dunn (Mahaw-taw-waw-pah-wah) deceased, died in Pottawatomie County Oklahoma Territory in the year 1898, and was a resident of said County and Territory at the time of his death, leaving no father or mother. That he left no personal property, and that he left real estate situated in Pottawatomie County, Oklahoma Territory described as follows to-wit:-- The South West Quarter of Section 1.2[sic] Township 11 N of R 5 E of the I.M, the same being an allotment from the United States Government and containing 160 acres more or less according to the Government survey. That he left surviving him his widow Caroline Dunn, Albert Dunn, his son now deceased and Ada Duncan his daughter age 22 years who died leaving Richard Duncan her husband as her sole and only heir, as the only heirs at law of the said Ralph Dunn, deceased.

Wherefore it is ordered, adjudged and decreed that the said estate be partitioned and distributed among the said heirs hereinbefore set forth as follows to-wit:-- The said Caroline Dunn one-third and the said Richard Duncan two-thirds. That the said heirs pay the cost of administration of said estate taxed at   dollars and that the said F.W. Christner, administrator be and is hereby discharged.

In testimony whereof I have hereunto set my hand and caused the great seal of said court to be attached hereto this 23d day of September A.D. 1902.

W. S. Pendleton
Probate Judge.

Sac & Fox – Shawnee Estates
1885-1910 Volume I

Territory of Oklahoma.)
: ss
Pottawatomie County,)

I, W. S. Pendleton, Probate Judge in and for said County and Territory hereby certify that the above and foregoing is a true and certified copy of the final order and decree in the matter of said estate of Ralph Dunn (Mah-taw-was-pah-wah) deceased, now a matter of record in the office of said court in the city of Tecumseh, Territory of Oklahoma.

Given under my hand and the seal of said court this 23d day of September A.D. 1902.

W. S. Pendleton
Probate Judge.

****

Territory of Oklahoma.)
: ss
Pottawatomie County,)

In Probate Court in and for said County and Territory,

in the matter of the estate of)
Albert Dunn (Maw-maw-kaw-she) deceased) Decree

Be it remembered that on the 23d day of September A.D. 1902 the same being a regular day of the September term of said Court the above matter came on to be heard upon the application for final settlement and distribution, of F. W. Christner the duly appointed, qualified and acting administrator of said estate, and after hearing the proofs offered and testimony introduced in said matter the court finds as follows:-- That due notice of the filing of the application for final hearing herein was given according to law. That there are no debts, claims or demands outstanding and unpaid against said estate. That the said Albert Dunn (Maw-Maw-kaw-she) deceased, died in Pottawatomie County Oklahoma Territory in the year 1900 and was a resident of said County and Territory at the time of his death, leaving no father, no mother, no wife, or children. That he left no personal property, and that he left real estate situated in Pottawatomie County, Oklahoma Territory described as follows towit:-- The North West Quarter of Section 12 Township 11 N of R 5 E of the I.M, the same being his allotment from the United States Government and containing 160 acres more or less according to the Government Survey. That he left surviving him his sister Ada Duncan aged 22 years who died April 2d 1901 leaving her husband Richard Duncan

Sac & Fox – Shawnee Estates
1885-1910 Volume I

and McKinley Duncan her son as her only heir at law. Who died leaving Richard Duncan his father as his sole heir

Wherefore it is ordered, adjudged and decreed that the said estate be partitioned and distributed among the said heirs herein before set forth share and share alike, that the said heirs pay the cost of administration of said estate taxed at dollars and that the said F.W. Christner, administrator be and is hereby discharged.

In testimony whereof I have hereunto set my hand and caused the great seal of said court to be attached hereto this 23d day of September A.D. 1902.

W. S. Pendleton
Probate Judge.

Territory of Oklahoma.)
: ss
Pottawatomie County,)

I, W. S. Pendleton, Probate Judge in and for said County and Territory hereby certify that the above and foregoing is a true and certified copy of the final order and decree in the matter of said estate of Albert Dunn (Mah-Maw-kaw-she) deceased, now a matter of record in the office of said court in the city of Tecumseh, Territory of Oklahoma.

Given under my hand and the seal of said court this 22d day of September A.D. 1902.

W. S. Pendleton
Probate Judge.

AMENDED RULES

(Dated October 2, 1902)

FOR

CONVEYANCE OF INHERITED INDIAN LANDS,

To be observed in lieu of the rules heretofore approved in the conveyance of inherited land allotted to members of any tribe of Indians, for which trust or other patents have been issued with restriction upon alienation, under the provisions of the act of Congress approved February 8, 1887 (24 Stats., 388), or other act of Congress, or any treaty stipulation, as authorized by section 7 of the act of May 27, 1902 (32 Stats., 245, 275), viz:

That the adult heirs of any deceased Indian to whom a trust or other patent containing restrictions upon alienation has been or shall be issued for lands allotted to him may sell and convey the lands inherited from such decedent, but in case of minor heirs their interests shall be sold only by a guardian duly appointed by the proper court upon the order of such court, made upon petition filed by the guardian, but all such conveyances shall be subject to the approval of the Secretary of the Interior, and when so approved shall convey a full title to the purchaser, the same as if a final patent without restriction upon the alienation had been issued to the allottee. All allotted land so alienated by the heirs of an Indian allottee and all lands so patented to a white allottee shall thereupon be subject to taxation under the laws of the State or Territory where the same is situate: *Provided*, That the sale herein provided for shall not apply to the homestead during the life of the father, mother, or the minority of any child or children.

I. (1) Owners of such inherited lands desiring to sell the same may petition the Indian agent, or other officer having charge, within whose territorial jurisdiction the land is located, praying that the land therein described may be sold under said act in accordance with the regulations. The petition shall be signed by all the lawful heirs, and, in case of minors by their legal representatives, and shall set forth every material fact necessary to show full title under the laws applicable.

(2) When the land is not located within such jurisdiction the owners may petition the most convenient Indian agent, or other officer in charge of an Indian agency or Indian tribe, who shall take like action thereon as if the same were within the territorial limits of such agency or tribe.

(3) When such Indian agent, or other officer in charge, shall be satisfied that the facts alleged in the petition are sufficient, he shall cause a memorandum record of the same to be made in a book to be kept for that purpose and shall file the petition in his office. A

6—111

copy of such petition shall be immediately forwarded to the Commissioner of Indian Affairs by such agent or other officer in charge, who shall indorse thereon the date the same was received by him and the date the land described therein will be listed for sale. He shall, on each Monday morning, post in a conspicuous place in his office in such large letters and figures as will be clearly legible, for a period of ninety days, a list of the lands described in the petitions received by him during the week preceding each such Monday, showing in separate columns the names of the owners, the descriptions of the lands, the dates when listed and the date when bids will be opened, and such list shall be accessible to the public at all times in business hours of the office. On each Monday the Indian agent or other officer in charge will forward to the Commissioner of Indian Affairs a complete list of all lands posted in his office for sale.

(4) When any tract of land has been so listed, the Indian agent, or other officer in charge, when competent from his general personal knowledge of the value of the land, shall visit, view, and appraise the same at its true value, according to his best judgment. If such agent or officer is not so competent, he shall require the appraisement to be made in like manner by the most competent officer or employee under his charge. A certificate of said appraisement, signed by the person making it, shall be sealed and not opened until the sealed bids are opened. The appraisement shall not be made public, but no bid less than the appraised value shall be considered. If the appraisement is made by other than the agent or officer in charge, such agent or officer shall add his certification of the qualifications and integrity of the appraiser, and that he believes the appraisement to be the true value of the land.

(5) Bids will be received by such agent, or other officer in charge, at his office for any land so listed at any time before the day on which the bids are opened. No bidder will be permitted to include more than one allotment in any bid. If a prospective purchaser desires to bid on more than one allotment, he must submit a separate bid for each allotment which he desires to purchase, and if he wishes to purchase less than an entire allotment, he may submit a bid for one or more legal subdivisions of such allotment.

(6) All such bids shall be inclosed in a sealed envelope which must be marked by the bidder "Bid for inherited land," and the legal description of the land must also be written thereon by him. Each bid must be accompanied by a duly certified check on some solvent bank payable to the Commissioner of Indian Affairs for the use of the grantors, for 25 per cent of the amount offered, as a guaranty for the faithful performance, by the bidder, of his proposition. If the bid shall be accepted, and the successful bidder

shall, within a reasonable time, after due notice, fail to comply with the terms of his bid, such check shall be forfeited to the use of the owner of the land.

(7) The right to reject any or all bids is reserved, and bids will only be accepted by such agent, or other officer, subject to the approval of the owner of the land.

(8) Purchasers shall pay all costs of conveyancing, and, in addition thereto, the following sum, to wit: If the purchase price is $1,000, or less, seventy-five cents; if it is more than $1,000 and less than $2,000, one dollar; and where the purchase price is more than $2,000, one dollar and twenty-five cents; to be used by the Commissioner of Indian Affairs for giving due public notice, as hereinafter provided, that the lands will be sold.

(9) Bidders and other interested persons may be present when bids are opened. When opened, the bids shall be so recorded in a book to be kept for that purpose as to show name of bidder, description of land, amount offered, and action taken thereon.

(10) Listed land not disposed of at the appointed time may, if the owner so desires, be relisted under the same rules as governed its original listing.

(11) The Commissioner of Indian Affairs shall cause an advertisement to be published in some local paper of general circulation in the section of the country in which lands authorized to be listed are located, and such other newspapers as he may deem advisable, by which the public will be informed that inherited Indian lands within the limits of the agency, offered for sale under the act of May 27, 1902, will be publicly listed at the agency, where sealed proposals for any tract on the list will be received during the ninety days following the date when the same was listed, in accordance with regulations which may be had on application, in person or by letter, to the agent or officer in charge.

II. The deed or other instrument of conveyance must be executed in the presence of two subscribing witnesses and acknowledged before the Indian agent or superintendent of an Indian training school in charge of the Indian agency or Indian tribe if the grantors reside within the limits of an Indian agency; but the purchaser may, if he so desires, at his own expense, have an additional acknowledgment taken before some officer authorized by the laws of the State or Territory to take acknowledgments, but such acknowledgment must not be of a date prior to the date of the Indian agent's acknowledgment.

In case the grantors do not reside within the limits of an Indian agency, the deed of conveyance may be acknowledged before a notary public, a justice of the peace, or other person duly authorized to take acknowledgment of deeds, whose official character must be certified by the clerk of a court of record under the seal of such court.

III. Such deed or instrument of conveyance, when submitted for the Secretary's approval, must be accompanied by the original petition, the appraisement, all bids and checks relating to the lands covered by such deed, and a full report by the agent or other officer in charge of all proceedings previous to the execution of the deed; also—

(1) By a certificate signed by two members of a business committee, if there be such, or by at least two recognized chiefs, or by two or more reliable members of the tribe, setting forth that the allottee to whom the land was originally allotted is dead, giving as nearly as possible the date of death. Such certificate shall also show the names and ages of the heirs, adults and minors, of such deceased allottee, but the Department reserves the right to require, if in its judgment it shall be considered necessary, such further and additional evidence relative to heirship as may be deemed proper. If the persons who certify to the death of the allottee are, from their own knowledge, unable to certify as to who are the heirs (with their names and ages) of such deceased allottee, an additional certificate made by persons of one of the three classes herein specified, showing who are the heirs and giving their names and ages (adults and minors), must be furnished.

(2) By a certificate from the Indian agent, superintendent of school, or other officer having charge of the Indian tribe, that the contents, purport, and effect of the deed of conveyance were explained to and fully understood by the grantors; that the consideration specified in the deed is a fair price for the land; that the same has been secured to be paid to the grantors in lawful money of the United States; and that the conveyance is in every respect free from fraud or deception; and that said allottee did not reside upon his homestead or allotment, nor cultivate the land sold during his lifetime and immediately preceding his death. If the allottee did reside upon such land, then it must be shown of whom the family of the deceased allottee consisted, their ages, and relation to said deceased allottee, in order to determine whether it is a case in which a sale is authorized under the said act of May 27, 1902.

(3) The consideration money must in no case be paid to the grantors; but a certificate from the cashier, or other officer, of some reputable bank, or, in case there is no bank convenient, from a United States Indian agent, showing that the stipulated price named in the deed for the land has been deposited in such bank, or with such agent, as the case may be, to be paid to the grantors or their order, upon the presentation of the deed duly approved

by the Secretary of the Interior, or by the President, must accompany such deed.

(4) When the deed is acknowledged before an officer other than an Indian agent or superintendent, it must be accompanied (in lieu of the certificate of the Indian agent in other cases required) by a certificate of the officer taking the acknowledgment as to the facts required to be certified by the Indian agent; or, if such facts shall not be known to such officer, they must be verified by the affidavits of at least two credible disinterested persons who are cognizant of these facts, whose veracity must be certified by such officer.

(5) Where these rules specify two or more officers or other persons to perform certain duties, preference must, in all cases, be given to such officers or persons in the order named.

(6) The affidavits of the grantors and the grantees must accompany such deed, showing that there is no contract, agreement, nor understanding (written or verbal) whereby the consideration money or price paid for the land, or any portion thereof, is to be refunded to the purchaser after the approval of the deed; nor any live stock, implements, other article or thing, are to be exchanged or taken in lieu of said consideration money or purchase price, or any portion thereof, for such land. Each deed must be accompanied by an affidavit of the grantee, stating that he is not a party to any association or combination of persons to acquire lands under said law at less than their fair value or to prevent open and fair competition in the purchase and sale of lands; that he is not directly or indirectly connected with or interested in any device, scheme, or plan to prevent or interfere with fair competition in the purchase of such lands or to secure them at less than their fair market value, and that the contract under which the deed presented for approval was executed was not procured through or by means of any such plan or scheme; that such contract was not secured through false representations to the grantor, or suppression of facts as to the value of the land or as to any other feature of the transaction, and that neither the grantor nor anyone acting for him or in his place has been given or promised any money or other thing by the grantee, or by anyone with his advice, consent, or knowledge, except the consideration named in the deed, to induce him to agree to such sale of his land.

(7) The testimony and all papers pertaining to the conveyance must be properly authenticated under seal, and in all other respects the conveyance must conform to these rules.

IV. When the land conveyed, or any part thereof, is less than a legal subdivision, or does not conform to the public survey, a diagram prepared by a competent surveyor, or an authenticated copy of the official plat of survey indicating all the land intended to be conveyed, and all former sales by the grantors, or allottees, must be furnished for the use of the Indian Office.

V. No deed of conveyance for an undivided interest in any tract of land will receive approval. All the heirs of a deceased allottee must unite in one deed conveying their entire interest in the land. If the land of a deceased allottee has been partitioned among his or her heirs, any such heir may sell the portion set off to him in and by such partition. Where there have been court proceedings, a certified copy thereof must accompany the deed.

VI. If in the case of any deceased allottee there shall have been or shall hereafter be probate or other court proceedings establishing who are the heirs of such deceased allottee, a certified copy of the final order, judgment, or decree of the court showing and determining such heirship must be furnished; but where such court proceedings have not been had a compliance with the requirements of the provisions of paragraph 1 of section III of the rules as amended will be deemed sufficient to establish the heirship. In the case of sales by guardians, the deed must be accompanied by certified copies of the orders of the proper court appointing the guardian and authorizing him to make the sale.

In all cases the probate judge, or officer having probate jurisdiction, is respectfully requested and urged, in taking the bond of guardian, to require such guardian to give a trust and guarantee company, wherever practicable, as surety.

VII. A form of deed of conveyance has been prepared and printed for gratuitous distribution by the Indian agent, superintendent, or other officer in charge of the Indian tribe, which must be used or conformed to in all cases of transfer of inherited Indian lands.

No proceeding or action under these regulations shall affect in any respect the right of the Secretary of the Interior to exercise the discretion given him by law relative to approval of deeds for these lands.

A. C. TONNER,
Acting Commissioner Indian Affairs.

Approved October 4, 1902.
THOS. RYAN,
Acting Secretary.

Sac & Fox – Shawnee Estates
1885-1910 Volume I

DEPARTMENT OF THE INTERIOR.
UNITED STATES INDIAN SERVICE.

Nov 18" 1902

Maj
Ross Guffin
 U.S. Ind Agent

   Sac and Fox Agency Okla
Sir:

 Herewith inclosed find my official CA No.# 261940 Mrs Kashenay $415.00 semiannual lease payment due Oct 10 1902 with receipts in triplicate for her signature. Since making up the [illegible] for their payment I have learned that Mrs Kashenay has no claim to the allotment of Ida Kashenay dec'd which is [illegible] in this lease.

 I was informed through James Cleghorn that Ida Kashenay was married to William Hillis and she died leaving Wm Hillis her husband an heir to her estate and that through subsequent marriages and deaths Lidda Anderson and Jim Cleghorn are the legal heirs to this estate. Will you kindly investigate this claim and you find them to be the legal heirs to this estate they will be entitled to $118.12 out of this check

      Respectfully
      H R Donnell
      U S Ind Agt

OFFICE OF
COUNTY ATTORNEY,
TAMA COUNTY.

TOLEDO, IOWA.

U. S. Indian Agent,
 Sac & Fox Agency,
  Oklahoma.
Dear Sir:-

 Will you kindly inform me whether under the laws of your territory a half brother would inherit from a half sister?

 Thanking you in advance for this information, I am,

      Yours truly,
      SC Huber

Sac & Fox – Shawnee Estates
1885-1910 Volume I

SAC AND FOX AGENCY, IOWA.
Toledo, March 10, 1903.

Hon. Ross Guffin,
    U.S. Indian Agent,
        Sauk and Fox Agency, Okla.
Sir:

    Your favor of the 6th. instant, in which you inform us of the action and decision of the Sac and Fox Council as your Agency, relative to the claim of On-A-Wot, a Sac and Fox Indian residing at this Agency to an allotment, originally made to Ah-Squa-Sup-Pit, deceased, and which the said On-A-Wot claims, being the nearest of kin by blood, is before me.

    I have just received authority from the Indian Office, to have the Indian Council appoint a Committee, to whom shall be referred all claims of this character for adjudication and I very respectfully request that final action be deferred by your Council, until the official report of the Council at this Agency is received by you, which will be in a very few days. Please present by compliments to your Council, and report that the matter be not closed, until this report is received, as this will give the whole matter more of a judicial aspect, and as having been properly adjudicated, and settled.

                Very respectfully,

                      W. G. Malin
                      U. S. Indian Agent.

Refer in reply to the following:
Land
19628-1903

Department of the Interior.
OFFICE OF INDIAN AFFAIRS
WASHINGTON,
March 31, 1903.

Ross Guffin, Esq.,
    U. S. Indian Agent,
        Sac and Fox Agency, Oklahoma.
Sir:

    Acknowledging the receipt of a petition forwarded by you March 23, 1903, of the heirs of Jane Moore, allottee No. 498, your attention is invited to said petition where it is stated that the above named heirs (petitioners) "are the sole and only heirs left surviving the said Mary Neal, deceased," - which is not understood by this office, and hence a request is made that you explain the same inasmuch as the petitioners claim to be the heirs of Jane Moore.

Sac & Fox – Shawnee Estates
1885-1910 Volume I

Another defect of the petition sent in is the lack of designating the tribe to which the allottee belongs. The tribe of the heirs is usually given but it frequently happens that the heirs are of a different tribe from the allottee.

Please examine these petitions closely as to these facts before forwarding the same to this office and thereby save the office the time required to examine the tract books and schedules to find out the facts in the case.

Very respectfully,

R.F.T.(G)   Acting Commissioner.

Refer in reply to the following:
Land
20519-1903

Department of the Interior.
OFFICE OF INDIAN AFFAIRS
WASHINGTON,
April 9, 1903.

Ross Guffin, Esq.,
    U. S. Indian Agent,
        Sac and Fox Agency, Oklahoma.
Sir:

At the solicitation of William Jones, a member of the Sac and Fox tribe of Indians in Iowa, that a business committee be appointed from said Indians, for the purpose of determining the heirs of deceased Sac and Fox Indians to whom lands were patented in Oklahoma whenever any of such heirs are residents of Iowa, this office reported favorably on the 27th of March to the Department upon the proposition, and submitted the names of five Sac and Fox Indians in Iowa nominated as a business committee and reported by Agent Malin, of the Sac and Fox Agency, consisting of:

                Wa-pelluka,
                Na-saq-pa-phia, - John Allen,
                Push-E-to-neke-qua, - Chief,
                Sha-wa-na-qua-huk, - James Morgan,
                On-A-wa-ta, - James Onawat.

If in the sale of inherited Indian lands you should find that it is probable some of the heirs are residents of Iowa, you should correspond with Agent Malin and have him call his business committee together to determine the question so far as his Indians are concerned.

A copy of Department letter of March 31st, confirming said nominations, is herewith enclosed for your information.

Sac & Fox – Shawnee Estates
1885-1910 Volume I

Very respectfully,
AC Tonner
Acting Commissioner.

R.F.T.(G)

DEPARTMENT OF THE INTERIOR
UNITED STATES INDIAN SERVICE.

SAC AND FOX AGENCY, IOWA.
Toledo, May 1st. 1903.

Hon. Ross Guffin,
    U.S. Indian Agent,
        Sac and fox Agency, Okla.
Sir.

I have the honor to herewith present the claim of On-A-wot, a Sac and Fox Indian enrolled as an annuitant at this Agency, to the estate of Ah-squa-sa-pi-ta, deceased, together with the findings in the case, as arrived at by the Official Committee as this Agency, to whom it was referred for their decision, as to the relationship existing between the said On-A-wot, and Ah-squa-sa-pe-ta[sic], or Ah-squa-sup-pit. The statement of the committee is as follows, viz:

    Ah-na-ka-wa, and We-sho-wa, were father and mother, respectively, of On-A-wot.

    Ma-ma-wah, and Na-ha-pa-no-qua, were father and mother, respectively of Ah-squa-sa-pe-ta.

    Ah-ne-ka-wa, and Na-ha-pa-no-qua, were full brother and sister, making On-A-wot, and Ah-squa-sa pe-ta full first cousins.

    The following named persons who constitute the Official Committee at the Sac and Fox Agency, Iowa, whose nomination is confirmed by the Honorable Secretary of the Interior, will back up the above statements of facts with their affidavits, if necessary. The above is signed by

    Na-sa-pe-phia   (John Allen)
    Wa-pellu-ka,
    Push-E-to-neke-qua,   (Chief)
    Sha-wa-na-qua-huk,   (James Morgan)

Sac & Fox – Shawnee Estates
1885-1910 Volume I

DEPARTMENT OF THE INTERIOR
UNITED STATES INDIAN SERVICE.

SAC AND FOX AGENCY, IOWA.
Toledo, May 2nd. 1903.

Hon. Ross Guffin,
    U.S. Indian Agent,
        Sac and fox Agency, Okla.
Sir:

    I herewith present the claim of On-A-wot, or On-A-wa-ta, to the estate of Ah-squa-sa-pe-ta, or Ah-squa-sup-pit, as stated by him, and verified by the official Committee, whose names are attached to their findings.

    I believe the findings of this Committee is entitled to credit, and I believe they are as honest and reliable as any Indians in their convictions of right, and I think they are in a condition to know more of their tribal relations than any other tribe of Indians can know, and that they also base their conclusions upon blood relationship, and not upon their clan, as stated in your letter of March 4th, 1903.

    Relative to the testimony of the Committee at your Agency, with refference[sic] to the relationship of On-A-wot and Ah-squa-sup-pit, they have entered no denial of the relationship claimed by On-A-wot to Ah-squa-sup-pit, because this relationship does not descend through the father of the latter, but through his mother, who they admit to have been Na-ha-pa-no-qua, who was the sister of On-A-wot's father.

    It is a preposterous assumption, that On-A-wot did not know his own fathers[sic] name, and that he would not know his father's brothers and sisters, and the further statement by this Committee, "They say that they were well acquainted with On-A-wot, and that they had always understood that his father was a white man", while he can abundantly substantiate the fact, that he is a full blood Fox Indian, and can prove his genealogy by a number of men who have been intimately associated with him from his infancy. This statement alone, is sufficient to discredit the testimony of the Committee, regarding this whole matter.

    If I am correctly informed, the decisions of the Committee, appointed to inquire into these matters, at this Agency, are of equal force with those of the Committee at other Agencies, and if the Committee at your Agency ignores the evidence herewith transmitted, On-A-Wot's only recourse will be to carry the matter into the Courts.

    2nd. The case of Wa-wa-to-sa, which was clearly set forth in my letter of Dec. 24, 1902, needs not to be reiterated. The statement that Waw-waw-ko had a sister who was living at the time of the death of the former, and that this sister died, leaving a husband and son, would seem to dispose of Wa-wa-to-see's claim, and now, that the Committed at this Agency have affirmed the claim of the said Wa-wa-to-see without

Sac & Fox – Shawnee Estates
1885-1910 Volume I

material change, if your committee can prove the statements made, relative to the sister who survived the said Waw-waw-ko, then the claim of Wa-wa-to-see is clearly outclassed.

Believing that you will refer these cases to your committee in the spirit if[sic] fairness to which they are entitled, to the end that justice may be meted out to these contestants, I am,

Very respectfully,
Wm G. Malin
U. S. Indian Agent.

****

DEPARTMENT OF THE INTERIOR
UNITED STATES INDIAN SERVICE.

SAC AND FOX AGENCY, IOWA.
Toledo, Dec. 26, 1902.

The U.S. Indian Agent,
    Sac and fox Agency, Ok.

Sir:

Some of the Indians, at this Agency, notably On-a-wot[sic], and Wa-wa-To-sah have been in my office, interviewing me in regard to some claims they think they have to some land in Oklahoma. As for On-a-wot, or An-a-wa-ta, who claims to be the only living heir to one Es-qua-sa-pi-ta, deceased, ~~and~~ states that he and the said Es-qua-sa-pi-ta are, or were first cousins, being the children of brother and sister.

On-a-wot[sic] statement is to this effect; That the said On-a-wot's father, and Es-qua-sa-pi-ta's mother were full brother and sister, and that the said Es-qua-sa-pi-ta had and[sic] an allotment, in Oklahoma, that he is dead, and that he left no children, and had neither brother or sister, and that he, (On-a-wot) being his nearest relative, is legal heir to said land, and other belongings of the said Es-qua-sa-pi-ta, deceased.

The other case is like this: Wa-co-se-ne-ne and Na-na-ah-pa-ma-qua, (both deceased), were brother and sister, Wa-co-se-na-ne, had one son, Wa-wa-to-sah, who is enrolled, and is living at this Agency.

Na-na-ah-pa-ma-qua, had one son, Ma-ma-na-wa, who in turn, had one daughter named Wa-wa-co. The said Wa-wa-co, had an allotment in Oklahoma, and is dead,

Sac & Fox – Shawnee Estates
1885-1910 Volume I

leaving no children, and having neither brother or sister, that the said Wa-wa-to-sah is full first cousin to the father of the said Wa-wa-co, and is her nearest blood relative, and therefore the legal heir to the said allotment, left by the decedett[sic] Wa-wa-co.

I am informed, that there is a committee of the Sauk Indians at our Agency, to whom is assigned the duty of determining to whom property descends, where there are no direct heirs, as appears in the cases cited above. If my information is correct, will you please place this letter in the possession of the said committee, or in the hands of the proper tribunal, whose duty it is to determine such questions.

When these Indians are in my office, I will elicit any further information relative to these claims, and forward the same to you. Will you please inform me as to the modus operandi of proceedings in such cases with your people.

Very respectfully,
Wm G. Malin
U. S. Indian Agent.

****

SAC AND FOX AGENCY, IOWA.
Toledo, February 10, 1903.

Hon. Ross Guffin,
    U. S. Indian Agent,
        Sac and Fox Agency, Okla.
Sir:

In receipt of your favor of the 29th, ultimo, relative to certain claims made by On-A-wot and Wa-wa-to-see, Fox Indians enrolled at this Agency to certain lands in Oklahoma, because of being the nearest relatives of deceased Indians, formerly resident in said Oklahoma, is hereby acknowledged.

At a meeting of the Chief and head men of the Sac and Fox tribe of Indians living in Iowa to-day, at my office, the following facts were elicited, which can be substantiated by the affidavits of the Chief, and at least two members of his council, and other of the older members of the tribe living in Iowa.

Ma-ma-wa was a Fox Indian, and was father to Es-qua-sa-pi-ta, or Ah-squah-sup-pit and Na-ha-pa-no-qua was his mother.

Ha-ne-ka-wa, another Fox Indian was father to On-A-wot, or Ah-no-wa-ta, and his mothers[sic] name was We-sho-wa.

Ha-ne-ka-wa, On-A-wot's father, and Na-ha-pa-no-qua, Es-qua-sa-pi-ta's mother were full brother and sister and were full blood Fox Indians.

Push-E-to-Neke-Qua, chief, and Wa-pellu-ka and Na-sa-pa-phia, old men and members of the council, say they personally know this relationship to exist, because they personally knew these parties, and will make affidavit to the facts above stated.

Sac & Fox – Shawnee Estates
1885-1910 Volume I

There are also other old people in the camp, who will do likewise, if it be necessary. William Jones, an educated Fox Indian, who holds a position in the Historical Department of the Anthropological Society in New York City, and who spent some weeks among the Indians at your Agency during the latter part of the year 1902, informs me that he could find no evidence of relationship existing between Es-qua-sa-pi-ta, and any of the Indians in Oklahoma, but that he did find evidence of the relationship claimed, between On-A-wot and Es-qua-sa-pi-ta.

The Indians here make the claim, and it is not without merit, that Es-qua-sa-pi-ta being a Fox Indian, and the Committee to whom this matter was referred were Sauks, they did not know, and could not reasonably be expected to know of the relationship existing between the Fox Indians.

It would seem from the above cited evidence, that On-A-wot has a clear claim to relationship to the decedent in question, and that if no nearer relationship that[sic] first cousin can be shown, his claim is good to the land in question.

In the second case, these Indians reiterate the statement sent forward to your office, namely: That Wa-wa-to-see and the father of Wa-wa-co, were full first cousins, that the said Wa-wa-co had neither brother nor sister, nor any other relatives by blood connection, which leaves the said Wa-wa-to-see her legal heir. I again repeat their statement, viz: Ta-co-se-ne-ne and Na-na-ah-pa-ma-qua, were brother and sister, and are both deceased. Wa-co-se-ne-ne had one son, Wa-wa-to-see, who is living and is enrolled at this Agency. Na-na-ah-pa-ma-qua had one son, Ma-ma-na-wa, and in turn had one daughter, Wa-wa-co. This Wa-wa-co had neither brother or sister, and is dead. she[sic] had an allotment, and left no blood relatives but the said Wa-wa-to-see, and that these people were all Fox Indians.

They are willing to substantiate these statement by affidavits from the best men of this tribe, who speak from personal knowledge of the facts stated above. A copy of this letter has been forwarded to the Indian office.

Very respectfully, Wm G. Malin U.S. Indian Agent.

Refer in reply to the following:
Land
27,508-1903.

Department of the Interior.
OFFICE OF INDIAN AFFAIRS
WASHINGTON,   May 5, 1903.

Ross Guffin, Esq.,
U. S. Indian Agent,
Sac and Fox Agency, Oklahoma.

Sac & Fox – Shawnee Estates
1885-1910 Volume I

Sir:

This office is in receipt, by your reference, of a petition of the heirs of Eva Brown, allottee No. 24, for the sale of certain tracts of land. This petition is returned to you that there may be stated in said petition to what tribe of Indians the said Eva Brown belongs.

Very respectfully,

A.C. Tonner
Acting Commissioner.

(B.F.T.)
P.

DEPARTMENT OF THE INTERIOR
UNITED STATES INDIAN SERVICE.

Nadean Kans
May 5th 1903

Mr Ross Guffin
U S Ind Agent

Sauk and Fox Agency Okl

Sir

Inclosed herein find Certif of Deposit No 3188 on the Bank of Horton Kans for One hundred and fifty dollars with receipt in triplicate covering the share due Po-Ko-hom-a-way one of the three heirs of the Wah-se[?]-se-quah Estate on the Sauk & Fox of the reservation in Kansas. I have paid as follows from the rental receipts –

For 1901-	Mrs Margaret Margrave	150.00
" 1902-	Wap-pe-ko-[?]-ah	150.00
" 1903-	Po-Ko-hom-a-way [illegible]	150.00
	Total paid	$450.00

The amounts reported paid on the collections for the 3 years 1901- 2- &3- the place is leased for 1904 for $100.00 with a contract to enclose the allotment with a good [illegible] in fence. If you will kindly deliver this certif and take her receipt therefore I will be under renewed obligations.

Respectfully
W.R. Donnell
U S Ind. Agent

****

Sac & Fox – Shawnee Estates
1885-1910 Volume I

DEPARTMENT OF THE INTERIOR
UNITED STATES INDIAN SERVICE.

Nadean Kans
May 12th 1903

Ross Guffin
U S Ind Agent

Sauk and Fox Agency Okl

Sir

I think the [Illegible] of Po Ko hom-a-way can sign for herself and as Nat guard for the minor child, and the adult heir sign the receipt will be sufficient.

Respectfully
W. R. Donnell
U. S. Ind Agent

DEPARTMENT OF THE INTERIOR
UNITED STATES INDIAN SERVICE.

SAC AND FOX AGENCY, IOWA.
Toledo, May 19. 1903.

The U. S. Indian Agent,
Sac and Fox Agency, Okla.

Sir:

I write for information relative to some property from which an Indian enrolled at this Agency drew some lease money, as one of the heirs to said property, after the death of the person ^ to whom an allotment had been made. [I do not know his name] The name of the Indian referred to was On-na-ka-wa-na or John Canoe. After the death of said John Canoe, one payment of the ren[sic] money due him was sent to his mother, (if I am correctly informed), whose name was Pau-au-che-qua, and who died with small pox during the prevalence of that scourge at this agency in 1901. The said Pau-au-che-qua, left one son, whose name is Wa-ne-ce-wa-ha, who claims to be the heir of the said On-na-ka-wa-na, deceased. Any information you may impart will be gladly received.

Very respectfully,
Wm G. Malin
U. S. Indian Agent.

Sac & Fox – Shawnee Estates
1885-1910 Volume I

S. C. HUBER
ATTORNEY AT LAW

OFFICE OF
COUNTY ATTORNEY,
of TAMA COUNTY, IOWA.

OFFICES:
COURT HOUSE, TOLEDO, IOWA.
SOLEMAN BLOCK, TAMA, IOWA.

Tama, Iowa, June 12th, 1903.

Mr. Ross Guffin,
    U. S. Indian Agent,
        Sac & Fox Agency, Oklahoma.

Dear Sir:-

    Your favor of May 19th in reference to the lease money of the allotment of Abby Redrock was duly received. Yesterday I took up the matter of the heirship to the land in question with the Sac & Fox Council which was then in session.

    Mah-Mah-Ke-Ah, the brother of Abby Redrock, died a number of years before she did. The exact date of his death I cannot give but should it be found necessary to have it at any time, it can be found from the records in the agent's office. This determines one question in the case.

    As to the claims of Ko-Naw-Paw-Kah, our council does not agree with his claim. Our council stated that the father of Abby Redrock was Pe-To-Ke-Mo and that her mother was No-To-Kah and that Ko-Naw-Paw-Kah- is not a brother of either of the two Indians last names, who were the father and mother of Abby Redrock, and hence Ko-Naw-Paw-Kah could now be the uncle by blood of Abby Redrock. Ko-Naw-Paw-Kah has two brothers, Pa-Me-Ka-Wo and We-Pe-Lu-Ka, and a sister, the wife of John Allen, all living here, and Wa-Pe-Lu-Ka is a member of the council and was present at the meeting yesterday and is very positive in his statement that Ko-Naw-Paw-Kah is not a relative of Abby Redrock.

    It seems from the above that there is a direct conflict as to these several claims and the facts of the case should, if possible, be ascertained at this time. I would suggest that you ascertain from Ko-Naw-Paw-Kah just how he claims his relationship to Abby Redrock, and that you send such statement to me or to Agent Malin, that we may submit it to the council here and see if we cannot obtain any further light on the subject.

    From my experience in determining the relationship of these indians[sic], I have had more or less difficulty on account of the fact that they use terms designating relationship with a different meaning from what we do, but in this instance I took considerable time and a great deal of pains with the council and believe I have their meaning correctly.

                Yours truly,
                    S C Huber

Sac & Fox – Shawnee Estates
1885-1910 Volume I

DEPARTMENT OF THE INTERIOR
UNITED STATES INDIAN SERVICE.

Potawatomi &c Agency,
Nadeau, Kansas. June 30, 1903.

Hon. Ross Guffin,
    Sac & Fox Agency, Okla.

Sir:

    I enclose you herewith a letter of E. L. Conklin's which is self-explanatory. I also hand you herewith my official check on the Bank of Horton for $150.00 payable to your order for the heirs of Po ko hom a way, deceased. I presume these heirs have already received the money as Mr. Conklin cashed the certificate of deposit that was payable to the order of Po ko hom a way and the bank declined to honor the same for the reason that they did not deem the evidence sufficient that the heirs of Po ko hom a way had endorsed said certificate and received the money.

                Very respectfully,
                W.R. Donnell
                U. S. Indian Agent.

Refer in reply to the following:
Accounts,
38198-1903.
2 enclosures.

Department of the Interior.
OFFICE OF INDIAN AFFAIRS
WASHINGTON, July 9, 1903.

Mr. Ross Guffin,
    Superintendent, &c.,
        Sac and Fox Agency, Okla.

Sir:

    Referring to your letter of April 25, 1903, to Superintendent Thackery, of Shawnee School, Oklahoma, in regard to the sum ($7.55) shown by your records to be die the estate of O-gih-mah-quah, deceased, you are instructed to obtain from the chiefs and headmen a certificate as to who is the proper person to receive and receipt for the money, and, if Ne-bah-quah, the surviving husband of the deceased, is designated as the beneficiary, to prepare a claim for him on the enclosed blanks and submit it, in duplicate, with the certificate of the chiefs and headmen, to this office for settlement.

> Very respectfully,
> WA Jones
> Commissioner.

Refer in reply to the following:
Land
41648-1903

Department of the Interior.
OFFICE OF INDIAN AFFAIRS
WASHINGTON,   July 10, 1903.

Ross Guffin, Esq.,
    Superintendent Sac and Fox Agency,
        Oklahoma Ter.

Sir:

    Replying to your letter of July 2, 1903, concerning the allotment of Henry Davis, or Henry Shaquine, in which Moses Keokuk claims heirship, being, as shown by the records of this office, Lots 3 and 4 in SW/4 Sec. 10, T. 1, R. 17, Sac and Fox reservation in Kansas, you are informed that the said land appears unsold.

    Should petition for the sale of the land be made, you will be notified in order that Moses Keokuk may have opportunity to present his claims therefor before action is taken by the Department.

    In the meantime the necessary steps should be taken by Keokuk to establish his rights in the premises by the filing of the affidavits and other papers, in support of his contention, with this office.

> Very respectfully,
> WA Jones
> Commissioner.

<u>CFH</u>
C

Sac & Fox – Shawnee Estates
1885-1910 Volume I

DISTRICT COURT OF BROWN COUNTY	**COURT CONVENES**
	FIRST MONDAY IN Paper torn
R. W. HICKS, CLERK	FIRST MONDAY IN
	FIRST MONDAY IN NOV
	HON. W^m. I. STUART, JUDGE.

HIAWATHA, KANSAS   JUNE 19-1903.

ROSS GRIFFIN[sic], ESQ.,
    U.S. India,[sic] Agent,
        Oklahoma Territory.

DEAR SIR:-

    Yours of 16th, inst. just received. The suit you have refference[sic] to was brought by Wa-tho-tha as plaintiff against Moses Keokeuk and the unknown heirs of Henry Sha-qui-nee, Deceased, and came on for trial and was heard on the 18th. day of last May. It was a partion[sic] or to quiet title.

    A certified copy of the petition and the court decree will cost you $2.30

        Very Resp'y,
            R W Hicks
            Dist Clerk

SAC AND FOX INDIAN AGENCY, OKLAHOMA.

APRIL 7, 1904

Honorable Commissioner of Indian Affairs,
    Department of the Interior,
        Washington, D. C.

Sir:-

    I find among the unfinished business of this office some matters relating to the allotment of Henry Davis or Henry Shaquin (Indian name We-sko-sah) being a tract of land in the Sac and Fox Reservation in Kansa[sic] described as Lots 3 and 4 in the S.W. 1/4, Section 10, Township 1, Range 17, in which Moses Keokuk claims heirship.

    It seems that my predecessor, Maj. Ross Guffin, had had some correspondence with the Nebraska agent of these Indians and also with the Clerk of the Court of Brown County Kansas relating to certain legal proceedings instituted there in this matter.

    It appears from this correspondence that a purported decree of the District Court had been obtained in Brown County, Kansas, quieting the title to this tract of

Sac & Fox – Shawnee Estates
1885-1910 Volume I

land in one Wa-tho-tha. It further seems from investigation of this correspondence this decree was had without notice or service of summons of any kind upon Moses Keokuk. From conversation with various members of the tribe here it seems to me it can be abundantly established that Moses Keokuk was the lawful heir.

I also find among the correspondence two affidavits, one by Edgar Mack and the other of Jack Bear, members of the Sac ad[sic] Fox of the Mississippi Tribe of Indians, subscribed and sworn to before Ross Guffin relative to this matter. I also find your letter of July 10th to Mr. Guffin, copy of which is herewith enclosed, Land 41648-1903, Initials C.F.H.C. From all of which it appears that Mr. Guffin was attempting to talk steps to protect the interests of Moses Keokuk in accordance with your letter referred to in which he was doubtless interrupted by his serious illness and death. Accordingly I enclose herewith the affidavit of Edgar Mack and Jack Bear relating to this matter. I have supplemented the same with the affidavit of Charles Keokuk, son of Moses Keokuk. This in accordance with letter from you referred to and directions therein contained. This relationship can be established by various members of the Sa[sic] and Fox Tribe of Indians here as I am reliably informed and should any more evidence be desired upon the subject it can be supplied.

All of which is herewith respectfully submitted with a view to aid the service in establishing the right heir.

Respectfully,

L. W. CLAPP,
FARM MORTGAGE LOANS,
OLD COURT HOUSE.

WICHITA, KANSAS.   July 16, 1903.

U. S. Indian Agent,
Sac & Fox Agency, O. T.

Dear Sir:--

You will find enclosed a letter written by Mr. Lee Patrick and a statement of facts as to the family of Abraham Lincoln. From this statement it would appear that Abraham Lincoln left surviving a widow, Maggie Lincoln, and two children, Thomas Lincoln and Fullwood Lincoln, these three thus constituting the heirs of said Abraham Lincoln.

You will note that Mr. Patrick says that the deed to Mr. Razey for this land is ready to be forwarded to the Secretary. I am making a loan to Mr. Razey to supply the funds necessary to go with the deed; and hence, am desirous of being sure that the deed is signed by all the heirs.

Sac & Fox – Shawnee Estates
1885-1910 Volume I

Will you kindly, therefore, return me Mr. Patrick's letter, and statement of facts, advising me as to who has signed the deed; and I would thank you to sign the enclosed certificate, if the facts therein stated are correct as shown by your records; or by any information at your command.

If they are not correct, will you kindly either alter the certificate, or write it, so as to state the exact facts?

Yours truly,
L W Clapp

Toledo Iowa
Sept. 8, 1903

US Indian Agent
    Sac & Fox Agency Oklahoma,
Sir:-

My brother Ba O se dead was killed in Oklahoma about [sic] month ago. What are we going to do about our land that my dead brother and I have there? I have to get that land.

                          Yours respectfully,
Write to Agent. Toledo, Iowa   ta ta la ko

Kansas City Mo. 9-9- 1903

Hon Ross Guffin,
    Sac and Fox Agency.
Dear Sir:-

    Mr Bryan will again compleet[sic] the deed from the heirs of Fred Sanachez as soon as C. M. Carde returns from the west.

Sac & Fox – Shawnee Estates
1885-1910 Volume I

It may be some time befor[sic] I'll compleet my work with the citizan[sic] Pottawatomies[sic] up here. I will go to the Reservation tomorrow. Old K @ so as much as can be today Rain Rain haven't been out of room today.

Yours Respect-

F.B. Lusk

DEPARTMENT OF THE INTERIOR

UNITED STATES INDIAN SERVICE.

SAC AND FOX AGENCY, IOWA.

Toledo, Sept. 15, 1903.

Hon. Ross Guffin,
    Supt. & Spcl. Disb. Agent,
        Sac and Fox Agency, Okla.

Sir:-

William Davenport was in my office to-day, and expressed some anxiety because of a report that had reached him through some Indian correspondent at your Agency, with reference to his interest in some land in Oklahoma, as one of the heirs of John Mc.Kuck, deceased.

The report was to the effect, that some one had either sold his land or was attempting to sell it, and thus dispossess him of his rightful property. I told him that I would write you and ascertain the truthfulness, or falsity of the report. If there is any such scheme on foot to deprive these Davenports of their share of this allottment[sic], I respectfully request that you inform me of it at once. Will you please give me the status of this land, its value &c.

On-A-wot still maintaines[sic] that he is the rightful heir to the allot-[sic] of Ah-squa-sup-pit, and will never be satisfied, until the courts decide the matter, either one way or the other. Please inform me when your Court having jurisdiction over probate matters, can be applied to for a settlement of this claim.

Very respectfully,

Wm G. Malin

U. S. Indian Agent.

Sac & Fox – Shawnee Estates
1885-1910 Volume I

Refer in reply to the following:
Land
53512-1903.

Department of the Interior.

OFFICE OF INDIAN AFFAIRS

WASHINGTON, Sept. 15, 1903.

Ross Guffin,
    Superintendent Indian School,
        Sac and Fox Agency, Oklahoma.

Sir:

    Referring to your letter dated July 28, 1903, you are advised that in accordance with the recommendation of this office of August 12, 1903, the Secretary of the Interior, on August 15, 1903, approved a deed dated June 22, 1903, from Charlie Crane and Mary E. Crane, his wife, as heirs of May Conger (Mesh-shaw-che), deceased Sac and Fox allottee No. 389, conveying to R. P. Carpenter, for $1920, the NE/4 Section 22, Township 16 N., Range 6 E., Oklahoma, containing 160 acres. The conveyance is made subject to the legal lease on the premises, the vendee to receive the benefits therefrom.

    A certificate of deposit No. 5286 dated July 3, 1903, for $1920, issued by the Deming Investment Company, of Oswego, Kansas, to the order of Charles Crane, the grantor, is attached to the deed.

    The deed has been recorded in Deed Book Inherited Indian Lands, volume 2, page 110.

    You are instructed to make proper delivery of the deed to the grantee, and of the consideration money to the grantors, taking receipts for the same in duplicate and transmitting one copy of each receipt to this office.

                                       Very respectfully,
                                           A. C. Tonner
                                           Commissioner.

EBF/LKS.

****

Sac & Fox – Shawnee Estates
1885-1910 Volume I

Land 53512 – 1903 – Sept 15-1902 App Aug 18

Nov. 23 , *190* 3.

Received of W.C. Kohlenberg Supt &C. ~~U. S. Indian Agent,~~

a warranty deed dated June 22 , *190* 3 , *given by*
Heirs of May Conger Mesh shawche *to* R. P. Carpenter

for the NE/4 Sec 22 twp 16 Range 6 E

Consideration, $ 1920⁰⁰ RP Carpenter

****

Sac and Fox Agency, O.T.
Nov. 18th, 1903.

Received from W.C. Kohlenberg Certificate of Deposit for Nineteen hundred twenty ($1920.00) and 00/100 dollars, No. 5286 drawn on the Deming Investment Co Oswego Kansas made payable to the order of Charlie Crane in consideration for warranty deed made by him to R.P. Carpenter conveying the NE/4 22-16-6

A. D. Wright
Administrator estate
Charlie Crane, deceased.

See certified copy Letters of Administration attached

****

Sac & Fox – Shawnee Estates
1885-1910 Volume I

Letters of Administration [paper torn]

Territory of Oklahoma, County of Lincoln,

    A. D. Wright is hereby appointed administrator of the estate of Charles Crane deceased.

Witness S. A. Cordell Judge of the Probate Court of the County of Lincoln, with the seal thereof affixed, the 14th day of November 1903

    Judge of the Probate Court.

Territory of Oklahoma, County of Lincoln, ss.

    A. D. Wright do solemnly swear that I will perform according to law the duties of administrator of the estate of Charles Crane deceased. So help me God.

    A. D. Wright

Subscribed and sworn to before me, the 14th day of November 1903

    Lucy Clark
    Notary Public

(Seal) My Com Expr 7-22" 1907

****

Letters of Administration
CERTIFICATE.

Territory of Oklahoma, Lincoln County, ss.

    I, S. A. Cordell Probate Judge of the County of Lincoln, in the Territory of Oklahoma, and ex-officio Clerk of the Probate Court of said County of Lincoln do hereby certify.... that A. D. Wright is the duly appointed, qualified and acting Administrator of the estate of Charles Crane, deceased and the attached and foregoing to be a true, full and correct copy of his letters as such Administrator

with the endorsements thereon as the same appears on file and of record in my office.

    IN WITNESS whereof I have hereunto set my hand and affixed my official seal at Chandler, Lincoln County, Oklahoma Territory this 25th day of November A.D. 1903

    S.A. Cordell
    Probate Judge and ex-officio Clerk of Probate Court.

Sac & Fox – Shawnee Estates
1885-1910 Volume I

DEPARTMENT OF THE INTERIOR
UNITED STATES INDIAN SERVICE.

SAC AND FOX AGENCY, IOWA.

Toledo, September 23, 1903.

Hon. Ross Guffin,
Supt. & Spcl. dis. Agt.
Sac and Fox Agency, Okla.

Sir:-

Pa-phia-na, We-pau-sa-qua and Ma-ke-so-pe-at, children of Pa-nau-see, who was a brother of Na-she-ta, deceased, who died at your Agency some time ago (they cannot give me the date), and they claim that the the[sic] said Na-she-ta, (their aunt), died without direct heirs, and they request information concerning this matter. These people have had some correspondence with friends at your Agency, who claim that there are no direct heirs to the allottment[sic] left by the said decedent, and that these above named children of the brother of the said Na-she-ta, are the rightful heirs to the said estate. Any information relative to this matter will place me under obligations.

Ta-ta-pau-go, an Indian enrolled at this Agency, I am informed left his home here on Monday, to visit your Agency on business relative to the death of his brother who was killed a short thie[sic] ago in Oklahoma, or Indian Territory, and whose name was Pa-sa-sha-she-ha, and who had an allottment[sic] in Oklahoma. Any assistance that you can give this man in his investigation will be duly appreciated.

Very respectfully,
W^m G Malin
Naw-hah-she-law   U. S. Indian Agent.

PETITION FOR THE SALE OF INDIAN LANDS.

To Frank A. Thackery

Supt. and Spec. Dist. Agt.
Shawnee, Oklahoma.

Sir:

In compliance with the amended rules dated October 2, 1902, for the conveyance of Inherited and other Indian lands   we   the undersigned   Arthur Ketch-Kum-ee (M Spitto)   and   Francis Ketch-Kum-ee (Wabahaw)   heirs of   Louise Ms-cop-go   allottee No. 1406   to whom the South half of south east quarter of section

Sac & Fox — Shawnee Estates
1885-1910 Volume I

18 Township 6 North Range 3 of the Indian Meridian, Oklahoma Territory was allotted under the Act of February 8, 1887 do respectfully petition that you take such action as will cause the sale of the said land in accordance with the amended rules referred to above and we further agree to sign a deed of said tract of land to the highest bidder for the same provided the said highest bid is not less than the valuation placed upon the said land by the Government appraiser and is in our opinion a fair price for the said land. We further represent that we are the sole heirs or owners of said land as shown below. If this represents an heirship case the matter must be fully set forth showing relationship and ages of all heirs.

Louise Ms cop go died thirteen years ago or in 1895. She was the legal wife of Arthur Ketch Kum ee (M. Spitto) and the issue was and is Francis Fetch-Kum-ee[sic] (Wab shaw) a son. If further reference required correspond with L.A. Scott (clerk) Nadeau, Kansas, Pottawatomi Agency.

Witnesses to signature
Wm Covney
R L Miller
Mayetta Kan

William Rileh Kumee
M Spitto

Refer in reply to the following:
Land
64328-1903.

Department of the Interior.

OFFICE OF INDIAN AFFAIRS
WASHINGTON, Oct. 12. 1903.

E. L. Chalcraft, Est.,
    Supervisor in Charge, Sac and Fox Agency, Okla.

Sir:
    Referring to Agency letter dated August 22, 1903, you are advised that in accordance with the recommendation of this office of September 30th, the Acting Secretary of the Interior on October 5, 1903, approved a deed dated June 1, 1903, from Leo Gokey and Lizzie, as heirs of Amelia Mitchell (Pah-she-ko-kaw), deceased Sac and Fox allottee No. 56, conveying to F. M. Rice for $2604 the NE/4 of Section 25, Township 17 North, Range 5 East, Oklahoma, containing 160 acres. The conveyance is made subject to the lease on the land, the benefits of the same to succeed to the vendee. A certificate of deposit dated August 5, 1903, for $2604, issued by the Sac and Fox Bank, of Stroud, Oklahoma, to the order of Leo Gokey is

Sac & Fox – Shawnee Estates
1885-1910 Volume I

attached to the deed. The bank issuing this certificate is understood to be now known as the Stroud State Bank.

Said deed has been recorded in Deed Book Inherited Indian Lands, volume 2, page 189.

You are instructed to make proper delivery of the deed to the grantee and of the consideration money to the grantor, taking receipts for the same in duplicate and transmitting one copy of each receipt to this office.

Very respectfully,
WA Jones
Commissioner.

EBF/LKS.

****

Sac & Fox Agency Okla, Dec 5, *190*3.

Received of W C Kohlenberg Supt & SDA ~~U. S. Indian Agent,~~

a warranty deed dated June 1 , *190* 3 , *given by*

Heirs of Amelia Mitchell *to* F. M. Rice

for the NE/4 25 - 17 - 5E 160 acres

Consideration, $ 2604 $\underline{00}$

F. M. Rice

****

(Land 64328 1903- Oct 12)

Certf of Deposit Aug 5 - 1903
Stroud State Bank

$ 2604^{00} Sac & Fox Agency Okla, Nov 3, *190* 3.

Received of Edwin Chalcraft, Supervisor in Charge ~~U.S. Indian Agent,~~

Twenty six hundred and four ———————————— *Dollars,*

consideration in deed, dated June 1st *190* , *to*

F M Rice *for* NE/4 of Sec 25 Tp 17 north of range 5E IM - 160 acres

WITNESS

William [Illegible] Leo Gokey

Horace Guffin Lizzie Gokey

Sac & Fox – Shawnee Estates
1885-1910 Volume I

Refer in reply to the following:
Land.
64327-1903.

Department of the Interior.

OFFICE OF INDIAN AFFAIRS
WASHINGTON,   Oct. 12, 1903.

E. L. Chalcraft, Esq.,
    Supervisor in Charge,
        Sac and Fox Agency, Oklahoma.

Sir:

    Referring to agency letter dated September 1, 1903, you are advised that in accordance with the recommendation of this office of September 30, 1903, the Acting Secretary of the Interior on October 5, 1903, approved a deed dated August 24, 1903, from Hiram Thorpe and Julia, his wife, as heirs of Charles Thorpe, deceased Sac and Fox allottee No. 245, conveying to Hunter Montgomery, for $2200, lots 1 and 5 of the NW/4 of Section 13, and lots 1, 2, 3, and 4 of the NE/4 of Section 14, Township 10 North, Range 4 East, Oklahoma, containing 157.88 acres. The conveyance is made subject to the lease on the premises.

    Certificate of deposit No. 267 dated August 26, 1903, for $2200 issued by the State National Bank of Shawnee, Oklahoma, to the order of Hiram Thorp is attached to the deed. Said deed has been recorded in Deed Book Inherited Indian Lands, volume 2, page 188.

    You are instructed to make proper delivery of the deed to the grantee and of the consideration money to the grantor, taking receipts for the same in duplicate and transmitting one cop of each receipt to this office.

                      Very respectfully,
                            W.A. Jones
                              Commissioner.

EBF/LKS.

                    ****

(Land 64327 1903 Oct 14)

Sac & Fox Agency Okla, ~~Dec~~ Nov 12, *190* 3.

Received of Edwin L Chalcraft Supervisor in Charge ~~U. S. Indian Agent,~~

a warranty deed dated   August 24   , *190* 3 *, given by*

Hiram Thorpe & Julia Thorpe   *to*   Hunter Montgomery

for the Lot 1&5 of NW/4 of Sec 13 and Lot 1,2,3&4 of NE/4 Sec 14 10 - 4E IM

Consideration, $ 2200$\underline{00}$ Hunter Montgomery

Sac & Fox – Shawnee Estates
1885-1910 Volume I

****

Land 64327 - 1903

$2200⁰⁰   Sac and Fox Agency Nov 10th, 1903.
Received of Edwin L Chalcraft, Supervisor in Charge ~~U.S. Indian Agent,~~
Twenty two hundred (2200⁰⁰)and ⁰⁰/₁₀₀   Dollars,
consideration in deed, dated   August 24th   190 3 , *to*
Hunter Montgomery   *for* Lots 1&5 NW/4 Sec 13
                Lots 1&2&3 and 4 NE/4 Sec 14 Twp 10N R4 E IM
WITNESS   157.88
Horace Guffin   Hiram Thorpe his x mark
Mary Antoine   Julia Thorpe her x mark

Cert of Deposit Aug 26th 03 State Nat'l Bank

Refer in reply to the following:
Land
64330-1903.

Department of the Interior.
OFFICE OF INDIAN AFFAIRS
WASHINGTON,   Oct. 17, 1903.

E. L. Chalcraft, Esq.,
  Supervisor in charge Sac and Fox Agency, Oklahoma.

Sir:

Referring to agency letter dated September 1, 1903, you are advised that in accordance with the recommendation of this office of September 30th the Acting Secretary of the Interior, on October 5, 1903, approved a deed dated August 24, 1903, from Isaac McCoy and Mary, his wife, as heirs of Jacob McCoy, deceased Sac and Fox allottee No. 77, conveying to David N. Meek, for $1600, the NE/4 of Section 12, Township 12 North, Range 5 East, Oklahoma, containing 160 acres. The conveyance is made subject to the lease on the land, the vendee to receive the benefits therefrom.

Certificate of deposit No. 269 dated August 28, 1903, for $1600, issued by the State National Bank of Shawnee, Oklahoma, to the order of Isaac McCoy, is attached to the deed.

The deed has been recorded in Deed Book Inherited Indian Lands, volume 2, page 191.

You are instructed to make proper delivery of the deed to the grantee and of the consideration money to the principal grantor, taking receipts for the same in duplicate and transmitting one copy of each receipt to this office.

Sac & Fox – Shawnee Estates
1885-1910 Volume I

Very respectfully,
AC Tonner
Acting Commissioner.

EBF/LKS.

****

(Land 64330 1903 Oct 17)
Sac & Fox Agency Okla, Nov 22, *190* 3.
Received of Edwin L Chalcraft Supervisor in Charge ~~U. S. Indian Agent~~,
a warranty deed dated August 24 , *190* 3 , *given by*
Heirs of Jacob Puckett *to* David N Meek
for the NE/4 Sec 12 P 12 North range 6 E IM 160 acres
Consideration, $ 1600$\underline{^{00}}$ David N Meek

****

(Land 64330 1903 Oct 17)
$ 2200^{00} Sac & Fox Agency Okla Nov 2 , *190* 3.
Received of Edwin L Chalcraft, Supervisor in Charge ~~U.S. Indian Agent~~,
Sixteen hundred ─────────────── Dollars,
consideration in deed, dated August 24   *190* 3 , *to*
David N Meek   *for* NE/4 Sec 12 Tp 12 north
      range 5 E I M   160 acres
WITNESS
Horace Guffin   Isaac McCoy
                      her
Mary Antoine   Mary x McCoy
                       mark

Certificate of Deposit
State National Bank

Refer in reply to the following:
Land
68441-1903.

Department of the Interior.
OFFICE OF INDIAN AFFAIRS
WASHINGTON,
October 26, 1903.

E. L. Chalcraft, Esq.,
 Supervisor in charge,
  Sac and Fox Agency, Okla.

Sac & Fox – Shawnee Estates
1885-1910 Volume I

Sir:

Referring to Agency letters dated August 20, September 18 and September 19, 1903, you are advised that in accordance with the recommendation of this office of October 1st, the Acting Secretary of the Interior on October 23, 1903, <u>disapproved</u> a deed dated August 18, 1903, from Wilson McKinney, as father and heir of Jefferson McKinney, a deceased Sac and Fox allottee, conveying to John B. Howard, for $3500.00, the NE/4 of Sec. 35, T. 13 N., R. 4 E., Oklahoma, containing 160 acres, it having been shown by Agency letter of September 18, 1903, that the grantor does not wish to complete the transaction, and that the grantee has no objection to the cancellation of the sale.

A certified check dated August 15, 1903, for $875.00 drawn by J. B. Howard on the Union National Bank of Chandler, Oklahoma, to the order of the Commissioner of Indian Affairs, and made payable by endorsement to the order of John B. Howard, the grantee, is herewith returned for delivery to Mr. Howard. It appears that Mr. Howard did not deposit the balance of the consideration money. The disapproved deed will be retained in the files of this office.

Very respectfully,
WA Jones
Commissioner.

EBF-CGC

Refer in reply to the following:
Land
64329-1903.

Department of the Interior.
OFFICE OF INDIAN AFFAIRS
Washington,   Oct. 17, 1903.

E. L. Chalcraft, Esq.,
    Supervisor in charge Sac and Fox Agency, Oklahoma.
Sir:

Referring to agency letter dated August 22, 1903, you are advised that in accordance with the recommendation of this office of September 30th the Acting Secretary of the Interior on October 5, 1903, approved a deed dated June 15, 1903, from Josie Springer and Joe Springer, her husband, and Lydia Dupuis and John Dupuis, her husband, as heirs of Way-ho-nee-mie, deceased Iowa allottee No. 100, conveying to Roy Hoffman, for $1204, the S/2 of the NW/4 Section 30, Township 16 North, Range 1 East, Oklahoma, containing 76.53 acres.

A certificate of deposit dated July 30, 1903, for $1204, issued by the Stroud State Bank of Stroud, Oklahoma, to the order of Josie Springer and Lydia Dupuis, is attached to the deed.

Sac & Fox – Shawnee Estates
1885-1910 Volume I

The deed has been recorded in Deed Book Inherited Indian Lands, volume 2, page 190.

You are instructed to make proper delivery of the deed to the grantee and of the consideration money to the principal grantor, taking receipts for the same in duplicate and transmitting one copy of each receipt to this office.

Very respectfully,
AC Tonner
Acting Commissioner.

EBF/LKS.

****

Certf of Deposit July 29 1903 Stroud State Bank

$1204⁰⁰   Sac & Fox Agency Okla Nov 11 , 1903.
Received of Edwin L Chalcraft, Supervisor in Charge ~~U.S. Indian Agent,~~
Twelve hundred and four ———————————— Dollars,
consideration in deed, dated   June 15   190 3 , *to*
Roy Hoffman   *for* S/2 of NW/4 Sec 30 Tp 16 north
    of range 1 E I M 86[sic] acres
WITNESS
[Name Illegible]   Lydia x Dupuis
William [Illegible]   Josie x Springer

****

(Land 64329 1903 Oct 17)

Certif of Deposit Stroud State Bank July 303, 1903 - $1204.⁰⁰/₁₀₀

            Sac & Fox Agency Okla, Oct 30 , 1903.
Received of Edwin L Chalcraft Supervisor in Charge ~~U. S. Indian Agent,~~
a warranty deed dated   June 15   , 190 3 , *given by*
Heirs of Way-ho-nee-mie   *to*   Roy Hoffman
for the S. 1/2 of NW qr. Sec 30 Tp 16 N. R. 1 E I.M.

Consideration, $ 1204 ⁰⁰/₁₀₀   Roy Hoffman

Sac & Fox – Shawnee Estates
1885-1910 Volume I

Refer in reply to the following:
LAND
67576-1903

Department of the Interior.
OFFICE OF INDIAN AFFAIRS
WASHINGTON,   November 4, 1903.

E. L. Chalcraft, Esq.,
 Supvr. in Charge Sac and Fox Agency,
  Sac and Fox Agency, Oklahoma.

Sir:

 Referring to agency letter dated August 22, 1903, you are advised that in accordance with the recommendation of this office of September 30th the Acting Secretary of the Interior, on October 19, 1903, approved a deed dated July 27, 1903, from Samuel L. Brown, Amos Black and Mary, his wife, Edith Mason, and Gracie Mason, as heirs of Eva Brown (Mook-kut-tah-o-so-que), deceased Sac and Fox allottee No. 24, conveying to John Foster for $1650, the S./2 of the N.W./4 and the N./2 of the S.W./4 of S. 10, T. 11-N., R. 4-E., Oklahoma, containing 160 acres.

 A certificate of deposit dated July 30, 1903, for $1650., issued by the Stroud State Bank of Stroud, Oklahoma, to the order of said grantors is attached to the deed.

 The deed has been recorded in Deed Book Inherited Indian Lands, Vol. 2, Page 240.

 You are instructed to make proper delivery of the deed to the grantee and of the consideration to the grantors as their interest may appear, taking receipts for the same in duplicate and transmitting one copy of each for this office.

       Very respectfully,
       WA Jones
E.B.F. - E.S.R.   Commissioner

     ****

Sac & Fox – Shawnee Estates
1885-1910 Volume I

$ 412⁵⁰   Sac & Fox Agency Okla Nov 17 , *190* 3.

  Received of W.C. Kohlenberg, Supt & SDA   ~~U.S. Indian Agent,~~

 Four hundred and twelve and ⁵⁰/₁₀₀ ─────────── *Dollars,*

consideration in deed, dated   July 27th   *190* 3 , *to*

 John Foster   *for* S/2 of NW/4, N/2 of SW/4 of S 10

  Twp 11 N of range 4 E I.M.   160 acres
WITNESS

 William [Illegible]

 Horace Guffin   Edith Mason

****

$ 412⁵⁰   Sac & Fox Agency Okla Nov 17 , *190* 3.

  Received of W.C. Kohlenberg, Supt SDA   ~~U.S. Indian Agent,~~

 Four hundred and twelve and ⁵⁰/₁₀₀ ─────────── *Dollars,*

consideration in deed, dated   July 27th   *190* 3 , *to*

 John Foster   *for* S/2 of NW/4 , N/2 of SW/4 of Sec 10

  Twp 11 N of range 4 E I.M.   160 acres
WITNESS

 William [Illegible]

 Mary Antoine   Gracie Mason

****

      Sac & Fox Agency Okla, Oct 30 ,   *190* 3.

  Received of W.C. Kohlenberg Supt SDA   ~~U.S. Indian Agent,~~

a warranty deed dated   July 27   , *190* 3 , *given by*

 Heirs of Eva Brown   *to*   John Foster

for the S² of NW⁴ and N² of SW⁴ 10-11-4 E I.M.

Consideration, $ 1650⁰⁰   John Foster

****

Sac & Fox – Shawnee Estates
1885-1910 Volume I

$412⁵⁰   Sac & Fox Agency Okla Nov 30 , *190*3.

Received of W.C. Kohlenberg, Supt & SDA   ~~U.S. Indian Agent~~,

Four hundred and twelve and ⁵⁰/₁₀₀ ———————— *Dollars,*

consideration in deed, dated   July 27th   *190* 3 , *to*

John Foster   *for* S/2 of NW/4 , N/2 of SW/4 of Sec 10

WITNESS Twp 11 N of range 4 E I.M.   160 acres

Horace Guffin   his

William [Illegible]   Samuel L Brown   X

                                                          mark

****

$412⁵⁰   Sac & Fox Agency Okla Nov 30 , *190*3.

Received of W.C. Kohlenberg, Supt & SDA   ~~U.S. Indian Agent~~,

Four hundred and twelve and ⁵⁰/₁₀₀ ———————— *Dollars,*

consideration in deed, dated   July 27th   *190* 3 , *to*

John Foster   *for* S/2 of NW/4 , N/2 of SW/4 of Sec 10

WITNESS Twp 11 N of range 4 E I.M.   160 acres

Mary Antoine

Horace Guffin   Amos Black

Refer in reply to the following:
Land
67828-1903

Department of the Interior.
OFFICE OF INDIAN AFFAIRS
               WASHINGTON,   November 5, 1903.

E. L. Chalcraft, Esq.,
    Supvr. in Charge Sac and Fox Agency,
       Sac and Fox Agency, Nebraska.

Sir:

     Referring to agency letter dated September 16, 1903, you are advised that in accordance with the recommendation of this office of October 9, 1903, the Acting Secretary of the Interior, on October 20, 1903, approved a deed dated September 7, 1903, from Webster Smith, as heir of Alexander Smith, deceased Sac and Fox allottee No. 38, conveying to Geo. T. Shoffner for $3004.00 lot 3 of the N.W./4 and lots 4 and

Sac & Fox – Shawnee Estates
1885-1910 Volume I

5 and the E./2 of the S.W./4 of S.30, T. 17-N., R.5-E., Oklahoma, containing 157.76 acres. The conveyance is made subject to the lease on the land; the vendee to receive the benefits therefrom.

A certificate of deposit dated September 14, 1903, for $3004. issued by the Stroud State Bank, of Stroud, Oklahoma, to the order of Webster Smith, the grantor is attached to the deed.

The deed has been recorded in Deed Book, Inherited Indian Lands, Volume 3, Page 1.

You are instructed to make proper delivery of the deed to the grantee and of the consideration money to the grantor, taking receipts therefor in duplicate and forward one copy of each receipt for the files of this office.

Very respectfully,
WA Jones
Commissioner.

E.B.F.
R.S.R.

****

Nov 19 , *190*3.

Received of W.C. Kohlenberg   Supt SDA   U.S. Indian Agent,

a warranty deed dated   September 7   , *190* 3 , *given by*

Heirs of Alexander Smith   *to*   Geo. T. Shoffner

for the Lot 3 of NW4 & Lots 4&5 &E/2 SW/4 Sec 30 - T17 5-E.

Consideration, $ 3004$\underline{00}$ George T Shoffner

****

$ 3004^{00} Nov 18th   , *190* 3.

Received of   W.C. Kohlenberg   Supt etc   U.S. Indian Agent,

Thirty hundred four   (3004$\underline{00}$) and $^{00}/_{100}$ *Dollars,*

consideration in deed, dated   September 8th   *190* 3 , *to*

Geo T Shoffner   *for*   Lot 3 of NW/4 and lots

WITNESS   4 & 5 and E/2 SW/4 Sec 30 - 18 - 5

Horace Guffin

William [Illegible]   Webster Smith   his x

Sac & Fox – Shawnee Estates
1885-1910 Volume I

Refer in reply to the following:
Land
69572-1903.

Department of the Interior.

OFFICE OF INDIAN AFFAIRS

WASHINGTON, November 18, 1903.

William C. Kohlenberg, Esq.,
    Supt., Sac & Fox Indian School,
        Sac & Fox Agency, Oklahoma.

Sir:

    Referring to Agency letter dated September 15, 1903, you are advised that in accordance with the recommendation of this office of October 9, 1903, the Acting Secretary of the Interior on October 26, 1903, approved a deed dated May 11, 1903, from Tecumseh Sherman, Jessie Lee, Philip Lee and Ida Roubideaux, as heirs of Bessie Lee, deceased Sac and Fox allottee No. 71, conveying to J. H. Maxey, for $1304.00, the SE/4 of Section 4, Township 11 North, Range 4 East, Oklahoma, containing 160 acres, more or less.

    For certificates of deposit, numbered 1060 - 1061 - 1062 and 1063, dated August 25, 1903, for $326.00 each, payable to the grantors above named, as the interest of each appears, are attached to the deed.

    The deed has been recorded in Deed Book Inherited Indian Lands, Vol. 3, Page 29.

    You are instructed to make proper delivery of the deed to the grantee, and of the consideration money to the grantors, taking a receipt for the same, in duplicate, and forwarding one copy of each for the files of this office.

                             Very respectfully,
                                 WA Jones
                                 Commissioner.

EBF-O.

****

$326.00   November 25, 1903   , *190* .

Received of W.C. Kohlenberg Supt & Sp. Disbg. Agent. ~~Indian Agent,~~

Three hundred twenty six ($326.00) and 00/100   *Dollars*,

consideration in deed, dated   May 11, 1903   *190* , *to*

J. H. Maxey   *for*   SE/4 of Section 4-11-4 E.

WITNESS

Horace Guffin

William [Illegible]   Jessie Lee

Sac & Fox – Shawnee Estates
1885-1910 Volume I

****

$ 326.00   November 25, 1903   , *190* .

Received of W.C. Kohlenberg Supt & Sp. Disbg. ~~r. Agent~~ ~~Indian Agent,~~

Three hundred Twenty six ($326.00) and 00/100   *Dollars,*

consideration in deed, dated   May 11, 1903   *190* , *to*

J. H. Maxey   *for*   SE/4 of Section 4-11-4 E.

WITNESS

Horace Guffin   My

William [Illegible]   Tecumseh Sherman   X mark

****

$ 326.00   November 25, 1903   , *190* .

Received of W.C. Kohlenberg Supt & Sp. Disbg. ~~r. Agent~~ ~~Indian Agent,~~

Three hundred Twenty six ($326.00) and 00/100   *Dollars,*

consideration in deed, dated   May 11, 1903   *190* , *to*

J. H. Maxey   *for*   SE/4 of Section 4-11-4 E.

WITNESS

Mary Antoine   His

Edw Leech   Philip Lee   X mark

****

$ 326.00   November 23, 1903   , *190* .

Received of W.C. Kohlenberg Supt & Sp. Disbg. ~~r. Agent~~ ~~Indian Agent,~~

Three hundred Twenty six ($326.00) and 00/100   *Dollars,*

consideration in deed, dated   May 11, 1903   *190* , *to*

J. H. Maxey   *for*   SE/4 of Section 4-11-4 E.

WITNESS

[Name Illegible]   her

Horace Guffin   Ida Roubideaux   X mark

****

Sac & Fox – Shawnee Estates
1885-1910 Volume I

Dec. 2, *190*3.

Received of W. C. Kohlenberg, Supt. & ~~U. S. Indian Agent~~ Sp. Disbg. Agent

a warranty deed dated May 11, 1903 , 190 , *given by*

The heirs of Bessie Lee *to* J. H. Maxey

for the SE/4 of section 4-11-4 E.

Consideration, $ 1304.00   JH Maxey

Refer in reply to the following:
Land. 70064-1903.

Department of the Interior.
OFFICE OF INDIAN AFFAIRS
WASHINGTON,   Nov. 24, 1903.

William C. Kohlenberg, Esq.,
   Superintendent Indian School,
      Sac and Fox Agency, Oklahoma.

Sir:

   Referring to agency letter dated September 1, 1903, you are advised that in accordance with the recommendation of this office of October 19th, the Acting Secretary of the Interior, on October 29, 1903, approved a deed dated August 17, 1903, from Edward Matthews and Ann Matthews, his wife, as heirs of Jesse Ridge (O-sha-ke), deceased Sac and Fox allottee No. 379, conveying to C. W. Carpenter, for $900.00, the NW/4 of Section 33, Township 17 North, Range 6 East, Oklahoma, containing 160 acres. The conveyance is made subject to the lease on the land, the benefits of the same to succeed to the grantee.

   The deed has been recorded in Deed Book Inherited Indian Lands, volume 3, page 44.

   You are instructed to make proper delivery of the deed to the grantee and of the consideration money to the principal grantor, taking receipts for the same in duplicate and transmitting one copy of each receipt to this office.

   There is also inclosed herewith a certificate of deposit dated September 1, 1903, for $900.00, issued by the Stroud State Bank of Stroud, Oklahoma, to the order of Edward Matthews, the principal grantor, for delivery to him.

Sac & Fox – Shawnee Estates
1885-1910 Volume I

Very respectfully,
WA Jones
Commissioner.

EBF/LKS.

****

$ 900.00	Nov 30, , 190 3.
Received of W. C. KOHLENBERG Supt. & Spl. Disb Agent ~~U.S. Indian Agent~~	
Nine hundred and 00/100	Dollars,
consideration in deed, dated Aug 17th	190 3 , to
C.W. Carpenter for NW/4 33-17-6	
WITNESS	
Horace Guffin	his
William [Illegible] Edward Matthews	X mark

****

	Nov 30th , 190 3.
W. C. KOHLENBERG Received of Supt. & Spl. Disb Agent	~~U.S. Indian Agent~~
a warranty deed dated August 17th	, 190 3 , given by
Heirs of Jesse Ridge to C. W. Carpenter	
for the NW/4 33 - 17 - 6	
Consideration, $ 900.00	CW Carpenter

Refer in reply to the following:
Land.
69821-1903.

Department of the Interior.
OFFICE OF INDIAN AFFAIRS
WASHINGTON,   Nov. 24, 1903.

William C. Kohlenberg, Esq.,
    Superintendent Indian School,
        Sac and Fox Agency, Oklahoma.

Sac & Fox – Shawnee Estates
1885-1910 Volume I

Sir:

Referring to agency letters dated September 1st and October 8, 1903, you are advised that in accordance with the recommendation of this office of October 19th the Acting Secretary of the Interior, on October 28, 1903, approved a deed dated August 10, 1903, from Frank Carter and Laura Carter, his wife, as heirs of Martha Carter, deceased Sac and Fox allottee No. 324, conveying to W. K. Nickel, for $3,600.00 lots 3 and 4 and the E/2 of the SW/4 of Section 19, Township 17 North, Range 6 East, Oklahoma, containing 160.17 acres. The conveyance is made subject to the lease on the land the benefits of the same to succeed to the grantee.

The deed has been recorded in Deed Book Inherited Indian Lands, volume 3, page 43.

You are instructed to make proper delivery of the deed to the grantee and of the consideration money to the principal grantor, taking receipts for the same in duplicate, and transmitting one copy of each receipt to this office.

There is also inclosed herewith a certificate of deposit dated September 1, 1903, for $3,600.00, issued by the Stroud State Bank of Stroud, Oklahoma, to the order of Frank Carter, the principal grantor, for delivery to him.

           Very respectfully,
            WA Jones
             Commissioner.

EBF/LKS.

****

	Nov 30th , *190*3.
Received of [Illegible]	~~U. S. Indian Agent,~~
a warranty deed dated August 10	, *190* 3 , *given by*
Heirs of Martha Carter *to* W. K. Nickel	
for the Lots 3 & 4 and E/2 SW/4 19 - 17 - 6	
Consideration, $ 3600^{00}	WK Nickel

****

Sac & Fox – Shawnee Estates
1885-1910 Volume I

$3600⁰⁰   November 30,   , 190 3.
         W. C. KOHLENBERG
  Received of Supt. & Spl. Disb Agent   ~~U.S. Indian Agent,~~
  Thirty six hundred and 00/100   Dollars,

consideration in deed, dated   Aug 10ᵗʰ   190 3 , *to*

  W.K. Nickel   *for*   Lots 3 & 4 and E/2 SW/4
            Sec 19 - 17 - 6
  WITNESS

  Horace Guffin

  Mary Antoine   Frank Carter

Sac and Fox Agency, Oklahoma,
December 28, 1903

Received from W. C. Kohlenberg, Supt. & Sp. Disb. Agent, certificate of deposit No. 127 dated July 20, 1903, for $900.00, received by the Stroud State Bank, Stroud, Oklahoma to the order of the heirs of Rebecca McClellan. The certificate of deposit was issued to purchase the NE/4 of Section 27- 8-6 E. The deed disapproved by the Department. Office letter dated December 23, 1903, "Land 79986-1903."

                                        CM Carpenter

****

Sac and Fox Agency, Oklahoma,
December 28, 1903

Received from W. C. Kohlenberg, Supt. & Sp. Disb. Agent, Certificate of deposit dated July 28, 1903, for $1500.00, received by the Stroud State Bank, Stroud, Oklahoma, to the order of Thomas J. Ruffalohorn. The certificate was issued to purchase the NE/4 of section 17-16-6 E. The deed disapproved by the Department. Office letter dated December 23, 1903, "Land 79986-1903."

                                        CM Carpenter

Sac & Fox – Shawnee Estates
1885-1910 Volume I

Department of the Interior.

Refer in reply to the following:
Land.
77566-1903.

OFFICE OF INDIAN AFFAIRS

Washington, December 11, 1903.

Wm. C. Kohlenberg, Esq.,
    Supt. in Charge Sac & Fox Agency,
        Sac & Fox Agency, Oklahoma.

Sir:

    Enclosed herewith is a letter dated November 20, 1903, from Horace K. Guffin, Esq., Financial Clerk at your agency, an administrator of the estate of Ross Guffin, deceased, enclosing the receipt of Martin Thorpe for an approved deed from Andrew Barker to Thorpe, dated July 6, 1903, conveying lots 1 and 2 of the S.E./4 of S.25, T.19-N., R.5-E., and lots 1, 2 and 3 of the S.W./4 of S.30, and lot 1 of the N.W./4 of the N.W.4 of S.31, T.19-N, R.6-E., Oklahoma, for $1304.00.

    Mr. Guffin states that the receipt from Andrew Barker, the grantor, for the $1304 consideration money in the above-mentioned conveyance, has been refused by Barker on the ground that he labored under a false impression as to the land conveyed, thinking it another quarter section of land, the ownership of which was obtained by him through inheritance. Mr. Guffin adds that by reason of Barker's refusal to receive the consideration money he has turned the money over to you.

    You are requested to investigate this transaction with the view of ascertaining whether or not there was any irregularity connected with it. Mr. Guffin's letter should be returned with your reply.

                  Very respectfully,
                        WA Jones
                        Commissioner.

E.B.F.
H.S.R.

****

Sac & Fox – Shawnee Estates
1885-1910 Volume I

Sept 21st. 1903.
Received of Ross Guffin Supt & Spl Disb Agent a warranty deed dated July 6th. 1903 with Andrew Barker to Martin Thrope[sic] for the Lots 1&2 SE/4 25-19-5 Lots 1&2 &3 of the SW/4 30 and Lot 1 and the NW/4 of the NW/4 31 -19-6 Consideration $1304.00

Martin Thorpe

****

Supt & Spl Disb Agent.
Received of Ross Guffin ^ a warranty deed described as follows:-
From Andrew Barker to Martin Thrope conveying the Lots 1&2 SE/4 25-19-5 Lots 1,2 & 3 of the SW/4 Sec. 30 and Lo 1 and the NW/4 of the NW/4 Sec. 31-19-6

Farmers and Merchants Bank

****

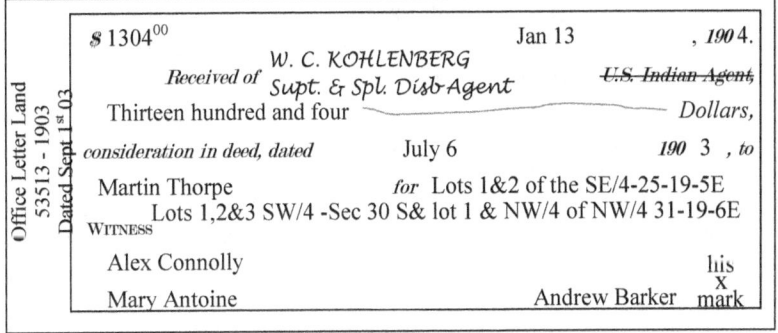

****

Sac and Fox Agency, Okla
November 28th, 1903.

Received of Horace K. Guffin, Administrator estate of Ross Guffin deceased, Late Supt & Spl Disb Agent, and Financial Clerk at this Agency. Certificate of Deposit drawn by Martin Thorpe on the Farmers & Merchants Bank of Cushing, Oklahoma for Thirteen hundred four ($1304.00) and 00/100 dollars, payable to the order of Andrew Barker in consideration for deed to Lots 1&2 SE/4 Sec. 25-19-5 E & Lots 1,2 &3 of SE/4 Sec. 30 and Lots 1 and NW/4 Sec 31-19-6, in which Andrew Barker and Martin Thrope[sic] both as aforesaid, appear as grantor and granted respectively.

Sac & Fox – Shawnee Estates
1885-1910 Volume I

[Illegible...] to Andrew Barker

WC Kohlenberg
Supt & Spl Disb Agent

****

Refer in reply to the following:
Land
53513-1903.

Department of the Interior.

OFFICE OF INDIAN AFFAIRS

Washington, Sept. 15, 1903.

Ross Guffin, Esq.,
    Superintendent Indian School,
        Sac and Fox Agency, Oklahoma.

Sir:

    Referring to your letter dated July 28, 1903, you are advised that in accordance with the recommendation of this office of August 12th the Secretary of the Interior, on August 15, 1903, approved a deed dated July 6, 1903, from Andrew Barker as heir of Sarah Barker (alias Leda Black), deceased Sac and Fox allottee No. 533, conveying to Martin Thorpe, for $1304, lots 1 and 2 of the SE/4 of Section 25, Township 19 N., Range 5 'E., and lots 1, 2 and 3 of the SW/4 of Section 30, and lot 1 and the NW/4 of the NW/4 of Section 31, Township 19 N. Range 6 E., Oklahoma, containing 161.53 acres. The conveyance is made subject to the right of way granted the Atchison, Topeka & Santa Fe R. R. Company, and to the legal lease on the premises, the vendee to receive the benefits therefrom. A certificate of deposit dated July 15, 1903, for $1304, issued by the Farmers' a Merchants' Bank of Cushing, Oklahoma, to the order of Andrew Barker, the grantor, is attached to the deed.

    The deed has been recorded in Deed Book Inherited Indian Lands, volume 2, page 111.

    You are instructed to make proper delivery of the said deed to the grantee and of the consideration money to the grantor, taking receipts for the same in duplicate and transmitting one copy of each receipt to this office.

                      Very respectfully,
                        A.C. Tonner
                      Assistant Commissioner.

KBF/LKS.

Sac & Fox – Shawnee Estates
1885-1910 Volume I

Refer in reply to the following:
Land.
79986-1903.

Department of the Interior.

OFFICE OF INDIAN AFFAIRS

WASHINGTON,   December 23, 1903.

William C. Kohlenberg, Esq.,
 Supt. Indian School,
  Sac & Fox Agency, Okla.

Sir:

You are hereby advised that in accordance with the recommendation of this office of December 7, 1903, the Acting Secretary of the Interior on December 11, 1903, disapproved the following conveyances of inherited Indian lands within the jurisdiction of your agency.

1. Deed dated June 1, 1903, executed by Carrie J. Little Bear, et al., as heirs of Oliver P. Morton, deceased Sac and Fox of Oklahoma, allottee No. 303, conveying to J. F. Maxey, Jr., for $3,300.00, the SE/4 of Section 28, T. 11 N., R. 4 N., Oklahoma, containing 160 acres.

Three certificates of deposit numbered 1032, 1033 and 1034 issued by the First National Bank of Shawnee, Oklahoma, dated July 22, 1903, for $1100.00, $1466.67 and $733.33 representing the consideration money accompanying the said deed are returned herewith for delivery to the grantee, J. R. Maxey, Jr., upon his executing a receipt therefor in duplicate.

2. Deed dated June 22, 1903, executed by O-zha-ock-peese, as heir of Lucy Anderson Sherman, deceased Sac and Fox of Oklahoma allottee No. 146, conveying to J. F. Maxey, Jr., for $1,280.00, the S/2 of the NW/4 and N/2 of the SW/4, of Section 3, T. 11 N., R. 4 E., Oklahoma, containing 160 acres.

Certificate of deposit No. 1006 dated July 1, 1903, for $1280.00, issued by the First National Bank of Shawnee, Oklahoma, to the order of O-zha-ock-peese, is herewith enclosed. This certificate of deposit should be returned to J F. Maxey, Jr., upon his executing a receipt therefor in duplicate.

3. Deed dated July 27, 1903, executed by Thomas J. Buffalo-horn (and wife), as heir of Clara Buffalohorn (Quah-quah-che), deceased Sac and Fox of Oklahoma allottee No. 86, conveying to CC.[sic] W. Carpenter, for $1,500.00, the NE/4 of Section 17, T. 16 N., R. 6 E., Oklahoma, containing 160 acres.

Sac & Fox – Shawnee Estates
1885-1910 Volume I

Certificate of deposit No. 1006 dated July 28, 1903, for $1500.00, issued by Stroud State Bank of Stroud, Oklahoma, to the order of Thomas J. Buffalo-horn is herewith enclosed. This certificate should be delivered to C. W. Carpenter, the grantee upon his executing a proper receipt therefor in duplicate.

4. Deed dated June 29, 1903, executed by John McClellan, et al., as heirs of Rebecca McClellan (Nah-aw-ke-te), deceased Sac and Fox of Oklahoma allottee No. 485, conveying to C. W. Carpenter, for $900.00, the NE/4 of Section 27, T. 18 N., R. 6 E., Oklahoma, containing 160 acres.

Certificate of deposit No. 127 dated July 20, 1903, for $900.00, issued by the Stroud State Bank of Stroud, Oklahoma, to the order of the heirs of Rebecca McClellan is herewith enclosed. This certificate should be delivered to C. W. Carpenter upon his executing a receipt therefor in duplicate.

You are advised that these transactions were investigated by Supervisor E. L. Chalcraft, and that in his report dated December 2, 1903, it was shown that there was practically no competition among the bidders, and the appraisement and the consideration named in each deed were far below the actual market value of the lands. In view of said report, the Department disapproved the foregoing deeds.

The disapproved deeds will be retained in the files of this office.

Very respectfully,
A.C. Tonner
Act Commissioner.

EBF-CGC

****

Sac and Fox Agency, Oklahoma,
December 28, 1903.

Received from W. C. Kohlenberg, Supt. & Sp. Disb. Agent, certificate of deposit No. 1006 dated July 1, 1903, for $1280.00, issued by the First National Bank, Shawnee, Oklahoma, to the order of O-zha-ock-peese. The certificate of deposit was issued to purchase the S/2 of NW/4 and N/2 of SW/4 of section 3-11-4 E. The deed disapproved by the Department. Office letter dated December 23, 1903, "Land 79986-1903."

JF Maxey Jr

****

Sac & Fox – Shawnee Estates
1885-1910 Volume I

> Sac and Fox Agency, Oklahoma,
> December 28, 1903.
>
> Received from W. C. Kohlenberg, Supt. & Sp. Disb. Agent, three certificate of deposit Nos. 1032, 1033 and 1034 issued by the First National Bank, Shawnee, Oklahoma, dated July 22, 1903, for $1100.00, $1466.67 and $733.33. The certificates were issued to purchase the SE/4 of section 28-11-4 E. The deed disapproved by the Department. Office letter dated December 23, 1903, "Land 79986-1903."
>
> JF Maxey Jr

Refer in reply to the following:
Land.
80526-1903.

Department of the Interior.
OFFICE OF INDIAN AFFAIRS

WASHINGTON, December 28, 1903.

William C. Kohlenberg, Esq.,
   Supt. Indian School,
      Sac and Fox Agency, Okla.

Sir:

Referring to your letter dated December 1, 1903, enclosing a deed dated June 15, 1903, from the heirs of Fannie Randall (Kit-toe), deceased Sac and Fox allottee No. 422, conveying the NE/4 of Sec. 26, T. 16 N., R. 6 E., Oklahoma, to John Foster, for $1000.00, you are advised that the name of one of the grantors appears in the petition and the certificate of the Business Committee as Tom Pe-na-she, while in the deed the name appears as Pe-na-she without the given name Tom. If the name of this grantor is Tom Pe-na-she, he should so sign it in the deed.

The deed and all accompanying papers are herewith returned in order that the apparent defect above referred to may be cured.

                Very respectfully
                WA Jones
                Commissioner.

EBF-CGC

Sac & Fox – Shawnee Estates
1885-1910 Volume I

DEPARTMENT OF THE INTERIOR
UNITED STATES INDIAN SERVICE.

SAC AND FOX AGENCY, IOWA.
Toledo, Jan. 7, 1904.

Supt. & Spcl. Disb. Agent.
Sac and Fox Agency, Okla.

Sir:-

There are three Indians at this Agency, who claim to be the only heirs to the estate of Na-She-tah, deceased, who had an allottment[sic] of land at your agency. the[sic] said Na-she-tah, being sister to Wa-pa-na-see, who was father of Pa-phia-na, Ne-pau-sa-qua, ane Ma-ka-so-pe-at, who are the claimants to the said estate.

Will you please make the necessary investigation of this case, and inform me as to the status of the estate in question at your early convenience.

Very respectfully,
W^m G Malin
U.S. Indian Agent.

DEPARTMENT OF THE INTERIOR
UNITED STATES INDIAN SERVICE.

Nadean Kans
Jany 15th 1904

W. C. Kohlenberg Es
Sauk & Fox Agency Okl

Dear Sir:

Me jash kee a member of the Prairie Band of Pot. Indians but formerly a member of Sac Indians joined in a deed with the [Illegible] heirs in the sale of an estate under your jurisdiction. This sale was made early the past fall. Can you give me any information about this [illegible] if same has been returned.

Very respectfully
G. L. Williams
Supt & Spl Dis Agt

Sac & Fox – Shawnee Estates
1885-1910 Volume I

Refer in reply to the following:
Land.
4393-1904.

Department of the Interior.

OFFICE OF INDIAN AFFAIRS

Washington, January 25, 1904.

W. C. Kohlenberg, Esq.,
    Superintendent Indian School,
        Sac & Fox Agency, Okla.

Sir:

    Referring to your letter dated December 24, 1903, you are advised that on January 11, 1904, this office submitted to the Department a deed dated June 22, 1903, from Sarah Ellis et als., as heirs of Mabel Ellis (Waw-sah-que), deceased Sac and Fox allottee No. 357, conveying to C. W. Carpenter for $1650 the SE/4 of Sec. 12, T. 18 N., R. 5 E., Oklahoma, containing 160 acres, the conveyance being made subject to the lease on the land.

    In your letter you stated that this land was appraised by J. A. Tanksley, Appraising Clerk, at $1620 but that in your opinion the land is worth not less than $2000.

    In view of your statement the Department on January 18, 1904, returned the deed to this office without approval and with the suggestion that if Mr. Carpenter will increase his bit to $2000, the value placed upon the land by you, the deed may be resubmitted for approval, otherwise it will be disapproved and the land again advertised for sale if the heirs so desire.

    You are requested to notify Mr. Carpenter of the suggestion of the Department in order that he may deposit the additional amount required ($350) or notify you of his declination to do so. The deed and certificate of deposit for $1650 and accompanying papers will be retained in this office pending the receipt of information from you as to what steps Mr. Carpenter proposes to take in the premises.

                Very respectfully,
                        AC Tonner
                      Acting Commissioner.

EBF-E

Sac & Fox – Shawnee Estates
1885-1910 Volume I

DEPARTMENT OF THE INTERIOR
UNITED STATES INDIAN SERVICE.

SAC AND FOX AGENCY, IOWA.
Toledo, Jan. 26, 1904.

Hon. W. C. Kohlenberg,
    Supt. Spcl. Disb Agt.
        Sac and Fox Agency, Okla.

Sir:-

    Replying to you favor of the 20th, instant, relative to the heirs of Ah-squa-sup-pit (deceased), I have to say, that James Onawat, an Indian of the Sac and Fox Nation, who is enrolled as an annuitant at this Agency, claims to be the only true heir to the estate of the said Ah-squa-sup-pit, and that he can prove his contention, not only by the Business Committee at this Agency, but by a number of the Fox Tribe of Indians living in Oklahoma.

    I will send a report of the findings of the business committee at this Agency, in the near future.

                Very respectfully,
                    W^m G Malin
                    U. S. Indian Agent.

Refer in reply to the following:

Land. **Department of the Interior.**
4399-1904.   OFFICE OF INDIAN AFFAIRS
                WASHINGTON,   January 27, 1904.

W. C. Kohlenberg, Esq.,
    Superintendent Indian School,
        Sac & Fox Agency, Okla.

Sir:

    You are advised that on December 8, 1903, this office made a report to the Department respecting a deed dated August 24, 1903, from Henry Hunter, as heir of Bertha Hunter, formerly Bertha Wyman (Chuck-e-quah) deceased Sac and Fox allottee No. 415, purporting to convey the NW/4 of Sec. 11, T. 16 N., R. 6 E., Oklahoma, to Lee Patrick, the consideration be $1,000.

    This deed was originally submitted to the Department on September 30, 1903, with the recommendation that it be approved and it was approved by the Acting

Sac & Fox – Shawnee Estates
1885-1910 Volume I

Secretary of the Interior on October 19, 1903. It was recorded in the book of inherited lands in this office on October 29, 1903, and was sent to the supervisor in charge of the Sac and Fox agency on November 4, 1903, with instructions to make proper delivery of the deed to the grantee and of the consideration money to the grantor. On November 6, 1903, this office requested the supervisor not to deliver the deed or consideration but to return the same to this office. This action was taken because of the complaint by one, Arthur R. Johnson, complaining that he was the lessee of the land and that he had made valuable improvements thereon which he would lose if the sale in question were ratified. Upon investigation the supervisor reported November 21, 1903, that Johnson was on the land and had made the improvements there but that Patrick, the grantee, in said deed, has purchased said improvments[sic] and effected a settlement with Johnson. The supervisor, however, reported that the appraisement of the land in the sum of $960 made by appraising clerk J. S. Tanksley on August 17, 1903, was too low and that Patrick had contracted to sell the land for $2150 although there had been no perceptable[sic] rise in the value of lands in the vicinity since the appraisement was made.

In reporting the matter to the Department the office requested to be advised whether the delivery of the deed and consideration money should be made to the parties in interest.

In its letter of January 16, 1904, the Department refers to the act of May 27, 1902, (32 Stat. 275), which provides that the adult heirs of a deceased Indian to whom a trust or other patent containing restrictions upon alienation has been issued for land allotted to him may sell and convey lands inherited from such decedent with the condition that "all such conveyances shall be subject to the approval of the Secretary of the Interior and when so approved shall convey full title to the purchaser the same as if a final patent without restriction upon alienation had been issued to the allottee." The purpose of making such conveyance subject to the approval of the Secretary of the Interior was, as the Department states, to provide protection to the Indian and prevent the alienation of his land for an inadequate price; that the authority vested in the Secretary of the Interior by this provision of law carries with it the duty of fully protecting the Indians in the sale of their lands; that ordinarily where the duty of approval has devolved upon an executive officer he has the power and authority at all times before the matter has passed entirely out of his control to review and rescind any action taken by him and correct any mistake in the matter; that there is no reason why the same rule cannot be applied in cases like this; that before the deed has passed out of the control of this Department any mistake made in connection therewith whether occasioned by oversight or misinformation, as in this case, may be corrected; and that the deed here has never passed beyond the control of the Department it having at all times been in the hands of employees thereof.

Sac & Fox – Shawnee Estates
1885-1910 Volume I

Following the recommendation of this office, the Department directs that you be instructed to notify Mr. Patrick that the delivery of the deed to him will be withheld until he has deposited an additional sum sufficient to make the consideration represent the full value of the land to be ascertained by the reappraisement of the land subject to the approval of the department.

You are instructed to personally make a reappraisement of this land and then to notify Mr. Patrick of the additional sum, if any, it will be necessary for him to deposit with you to meet said reappraisement. You will then report all the facts to this office.

Very respectfully,

AC Tonner
Acting Commissioner.

EBF-E

DEPARTMENT OF THE INTERIOR
UNITED STATES INDIAN SERVICE.

SAC AND FOX AGENCY, IOWA.
Toledo, February 9, 1904.

Hon. W. C. Kohlenberg,
    Supt. & Spcl. Disb. Agt.
        Sac and Fox Agency, Okla.

Sir:-

John Leaves, (Tau-ta-pau-go), claims that there is due to his brother, to whose estate he is the sole heir, one annuity payment and some lease money, due on his land lease at the time of his death, or has subsequently fallen due. If this claim is founded on fact, and there is any money remaining due to the said decedent, which would rightfully fall to the heirs of said decedent, if you will so notify me, and sent[sic] receipts for his signature, I will see that said receipts are properly signed and witnessed, and return the same to you.

Very respectfully,
WG Malin
U. S. Indian Agent.

Sac & Fox – Shawnee Estates
1885-1910 Volume I

Shawnee OT, Feb 10, 1904.
W. C. KOHLENBERG
Received of Supt. & Spl. Disb Agent ~~U.S. Indian Agent~~
a warranty deed dated August 24th , 190 4 , given by
JF Kerker
Heirs Mamie Buffalohorn   to   Albert Gardiner
for the SE/4 Sec 20 -11 - 4 E   CF Kerker

Consideration, $ 2504   Kerker, Gardiner, Kerker
                                 for Albert Gardiner

****

C/D No. 1071 drawn on Bank of Commerce Shawnee, Okla.
$2504.00   March 1st, 1904.
    Received of W.C. Kohlenberg Supt & Spl Disb Agent Twenty five hundred four and 00/100 dollars consideration in deed dated August 24th, 1903 to J.F. Kirker[sic], Albert Gardner[sic] and C.F. Kirker for SE/4 20-11-4 his
                                                                    x
Witness   Thomas Jefferson Buffalohorn mark
  William [Illegible]
  Horace Guffin

****

Refer in reply to the following:
Land. **Department of the Interior.**
3686-1904.   OFFICE OF INDIAN AFFAIRS
                   WASHINGTON,   January 30, 1904.

W. C. Kohlenberg, Esq.,
    Superintendent Indian School,
        Sac and Fox Agency, Okla.
Sir:
    Referring to your letter dated December 1, 1903, you are advised that in accordance with the recommendation of this office of December 26, 1903, the Acting Secretary of the Interior on January 15, 1904, approved a deed dated August 24, 1903, from Thomas J. Buffalohorn and Grace, his wife, as heirs of Mamie Buffalohorn, deceased Sac and Fox allottee No. 87 conveying to J. F. Kerker, Albert Gardiner and C. F. Kerker for $2504 the SE/4 of Sec. 20, T. 11 N., R. 4 E., Oklahoma, containing

Sac & Fox – Shawnee Estates
1885-1910 Volume I

160 acres. The conveyance is make subject to the lease on the land, the grantee to receive the benefits therefrom.

A certificate of deposit No. 1071 dated August 25, 1903, for $2504 issued by the Bank of Commerce of Shawnee, Oklahoma, to the order of Thomas Jefferson Buffalohorn is attached to the deed.

The deed has been recorded in deed book of inherited Indian lands, Vol. 3, page 175.

You are instructed to make proper delivery of the deed to the grantee and of the consideration money to the grantors taking receipts for the same in duplicate and transmitting one copy of each receipt to this office.

Very respectfully,

AC Tonner
Acting Commissioner.

EBF-E

Refer in reply to the following:
Land.
8125-1904.

Department of the Interior.
OFFICE OF INDIAN AFFAIRS
WASHINGTON,

February 12, 1904.

W. C. Kohlenberg, Esq.,
    Supt. Indian School,
        Sac and Fox Agency, Okla.

Sir:

Referring to your letter dated December 28, 1903, you are advised that in accordance with the recommendation of this office of January 28th the Acting Secretart[sic] of the Interior on February 1, 1904, <u>disapproved</u> a deed dated October 5, 1903, from P. S. Hoffman, as guardian of Junitta Davis, as heir of George Washington (Pah-she-paw-ho), deceased Sac and Fox allottee No. 458. conveying to William B. DePue, for $1200.00, the NE/4 of Sec. 9, T. 17 N., R. 6 E., Oklahoma, containing 160 acres, for the reason that the consideration named in the deed is not deemed a fair price for the land, and is below the increased appraisement of $1600.00 made by you. A certificate of deposit No. 195, dated December 9, 1903, for $1200.00 issued by the Stroud State Bank of Stroud, Oklahoma, to the order of said Grantor is herewith enclosed.

Sac & Fox – Shawnee Estates
1885-1910 Volume I

You are requested to have this certificate properly endorsed to the order of Mr. DePue, and to deliver the same to him upon his executing a receipt therefor. The disapproved deed will be retained in the files of this office.

Very respectfully,
AC Tonner
Acting Commissioner.

EBF-CGC

****

Feb 23 1904

Received of W. C. Kohlenberg Supt. & Spl. Disb. Agent at Sac and Fox Agency Okla, certificate of deposit No. 195 drawn on the Stroud State Bank Stroud Okla in the amount of $1200 by W.B. Depue made payable to P.S. Hoffman, legal guardian of Junitta Davis upon approval of deed to NE/4 9-17-6, which deed was disapproved by the Acting Secretary of the Interior on February 1st, 1904.

W.B. DePue

Refer in reply to the following:
Land. 8123-1904.

Department of the Interior.
OFFICE OF INDIAN AFFAIRS
WASHINGTON,

February 12, 1904.

W. C. Kohlenberg, Esq.,
   Supt. Indian School,
      Sac and Fox Agency, Okla.

Sir:

    Referring to your letter dated December 27, 1904[sic], you are advised that in accordance with the recommendation of this office of January 28, 1904, the Acting Secretary of the Interior on February 1, 1904, disapproved a deed dated August 24, 1903, from Charles Nullake, as heir of Hester Anderson (Waw-waw-she), deceased Sac and Fox allottee No 153, conveying to John F. Kerker, Albert T. Gardiner and Charles F. Kerker, for $1601.00, lots 2 and 3 and the S/2 of NW/4 of Sec. 5, T. 11 N., R. 5 E., Oklahoma, containing 160 acres, more or less, for the reason that the consideration named in the deed is below the correct appraisement of $1680.00 made by you.

Certificate of deposit No. 1074 dated August 29, 1903, for $1601.00 issued by the Bank of Commerce of Shawnee, Oklahoma, to the order of said grantor is herewith enclosed. You are requested to have this certificate properly endorsed to the order of the grantees, and to deliver same to them upon their executing a proper receipt therefor.

The disapproved deed will be retained in the files of this office.

Very respectfully,
AC Tonner
Acting Commissioner.

KBF-CGC

****

May 18 1904

Received of W. C. Kohlenberg, Supt. & Spl. Disb. Agent at Sac and Fox Agency, Oklahoma, certificate of deposit No. [?]074 [illegible] the Bank of Commerce, Shawnee, Okla. for $1601.00 by John F. Kerker, Albert T. Gardiner and Charles F. Kerker, made payable to the order of Charles Nullake, consideration of deed dated August 24th, 1903, and [illegible...] the Acting Secretary of the Interior [illegible...]

Kerker, Gardiner & Kerker
per Albert Gardiner

Refer in reply to the following:

LAND.
10183-1904.

Department of the Interior.

OFFICE OF INDIAN AFFAIRS
WASHINGTON, February 23, 1904.

W. C. Kohlenberg, Esq.,
    Superintendent Sac and Fox Indian School,
        Sac and Fox Agency, Oklahoma.

Sir:

Referring to your letter dated January 18, 1904, you are advised that in accordance with the recommendation of this officer of February 5, 1904, the Acting

Sac & Fox – Shawnee Estates
1885-1910 Volume I

Secretary of the Interior on February 10, 1904, approved a deed dated December 7, 1903, from Henry C. Jones and Melissa Jones, his wife, as heirs of Emilie Jones, deceased Sac and Fox allottee #12, conveying to A. M. Largent for $2600.00 the NE/4 of Section 10, Township 11 North, Range 6 East, containing 160 acres.

A certificate of deposit (#26) dated December 26, 1903 for $2600.00, issued by the First State Bank of Prague, Oklahoma to the order of H. C. Jones is attached to the deed. The deed has been recorded in Deed Book, Inherited Indian Lands, volume 3, page 239.

You are instructed to make proper delivery of the deed to the grantee and of the consideration money to the grantors, taking receipt for the same in duplicate and transmitting one copy of each receipt to this office.

Very respectfully,
A C Tonner
Acting Commissioner.

FBF:LM

****

	W. C. KOHLENBERG	March 7<u>th</u>, *190* 4.
	Received of Supt. & Spl. Disb Agent	~~U. S. Indian Agent,~~
a warranty deed dated	December 7<u>th</u>	, *190* 3 , *given by*
heirs Emilie Jones	*to* A M Largent	
for the NE/4 10 - 11 - 6		
Consideration, $	A. M. Largent	

****

$2600.00   March 7th, 1904

Received of W.C. Kohlenberg Supt & Spl Disb Agent Twenty six hundred and 00/100 dollars consideration in deed dated December 7th, 1903 to A.M. Largent for NE/4 Sec. 10-11-6

Witnesses
    Horace Guffin   Henry C Jones
    HL Elmslee

Sac & Fox – Shawnee Estates
1885-1910 Volume I

Feb 23 - 1904

Received of W.C. Kohlenberg Supt & Spl Disb Agent at the Sac and Fox Agency, Okla two certificates of deposit Nos. 196 & 197 drawn on the Stroud State Bank Okla both in the like amount of $600 by W.B. Depue and made payable to Webster Smith and P.S. Hoffman as legal guardian of Juintta[sic] Davis respectively, upon approval of a deed to SE/4 9-17-6, which deed was disapproved by the Acting Secretary of the Interior on February 1st, 1904.

WB DePue

****

Refer in reply to the following:
Land.
8127-1904.

Department of the Interior.
OFFICE OF INDIAN AFFAIRS
WASHINGTON,

February 12, 1904.

W. C. Kohlenberg, Esq.,
    Supt. Indian School,
        Sac and Fox Agency, Okla.

Sir:

Referring to your letter dated December 28, 1903, you are advised that in accordance with the recommendation of this office of January 28, 1904, to the Acting Secretary of the Interior on February 1, 1904, <u>disapproved</u> a deed dated October 5, 1903, from Webster Smith and P. S. Hoffman, as guardian of Junitta Davis, as heirs of Albert Washington (Ne-po-pe), deceased Sac and Fox allottee No. 2159, conveying to William B. De Pue, for $1200.00, the SE/4 of Sec. 9, T. 17 N, R. 7 E., Oklahoma, containing 160 acres, for the reason that the consideration named in the deed is below the increased appraisement of $1520.00 as made by you.

Two certificates of deposit numbered 196 and 197, for $600.00 each, issued by the Stroud State Bank of Stroud, Oklahoma, on December 9, 1903, to the order of the respective grantors are herewith enclosed. You are requested to have these certificates

Sac & Fox – Shawnee Estates
1885-1910 Volume I

properly endorsed to the order of Mr. DePue, and to deliver the same to him upon his executing a receipt therefor.

The disapproved deed will be retained in the files of this office.

Very respectfully,

A.C. Tonner
Acting Commissioner.

KBF-CGC

Refer in reply to the following:

Department of the Interior.

LAND.
8178-1904.

OFFICE OF INDIAN AFFAIRS

WASHINGTON, February 23, 1904

W. C. Kohlenberg, Esq.,
    Superintendent Sac and Fox Indian School,
        Sac and Fox Agency, Oklahoma,

Sir:

Referring to your letter dated January 12, 1904, you are advised that in accordance with the recommendation of this office of January 29, 1904, the Acting Secretary of the Interior on February 2, 1904 approved a deed dated November 10, 1903 from Hiram Thorp and Julia his wife, and George Thorp, as heirs of Charlotte Thorp, deceased Sac and Fox allottee #240, conveying to J. H. Maxey, for $1602.00 the NW/4 of the NW/4 of Section 23 and 10 acres off the East side of the SW/4 of the SW/4 of Section 14, the said 10 acres being more particularly described as follows: beginning at the SE/4 (corner ?) of said SW/4 of the SW/4 of Section 14, and running thence North 80 rods; thence West 20 rods,; thence South 80 rods; thence East 20 rods to the place of beginning, all in Township 11 North of Range 5 East, Oklahoma.

Two certificates of deposit, #1164 and #1165 dated November 10, 1903 for $457.72 and $1144.28 respectively, issued by the First National Bank of Shawnee, Oklahoma to the order of the principal grantors are attached to the deed. The deed has been recorded in Deed Book Inherited Land Deeds, volume 3, page 232.

You are instructed to make proper delivery of the deed to the grantee and of the consideration money to the principal grantors, as the interest of each may appear, taking receipts for the same in duplicate and transmitting one copy of each receipt to this office.

Sac & Fox – Shawnee Estates
1885-1910 Volume I

Very respectfully,
AC Tonner
Acting Commissioner.

WBG:LM

****

March 7ᵗʰ, *190*4.

Received of ~~U. S. Indian Agent,~~
a warranty deed dated December 10ᵗʰ , *190* 4 , *given by*
heirs Charlotte Thorpe   *to*   J H Maxey
for the NW/4 NW/4 Sec 23 ten acres off East side
SW/4 SW/4 sec 14 twp 11 - 5 East
Consideration, $1602⁰⁰   J H Maxey

****

$457.72   March 14th. 1904
    Received of W.C. Kohlenberg Supt & Spl Disb Agent Four hundred fifty seven and 72/100 dollars my share of the consideration to deed date[sic] ~~June#28~~ November 10th.1903 to J.H. Maxey for NW/4 NW/4 Sec. 23 and 10 acres off the east side of the SW/4 SW/4 Sec. 14 all in twp 11-5 E.
Witnesses
   Horace Guffin
   HL Elmslee   George Thorp

****

$II44[sic]   March 2nd. 1904
    Received of W.C. Kohlenberg Supt & Spl Disb Agent Eleven hundred forty four and 28/100 dollars my share of the consideration money in deed dated November 10th.1903 to J. H. Maxey for NW/4 NW/4 Sec. 23 and 10 acres off the east side SW/4 SW/4 Sec. 14 all in twp 11 N. R.5 east.
Witnesses
   Horace Guffin   his
   HL Elmslee   Hiram Thorp x mark

Sac & Fox – Shawnee Estates
1885-1910 Volume I

Received of a warranty deed dated heirs George Grass *for the* NE/4 2 - 18 - 5

December 21st *to* A E Patrick

Feb 29 , *190*4.
~~U. S. Indian Agent,~~ , *190* 3 , *given by*

Consideration, $900^{00}

****

$450.00   March 4th. 1904
    Received of W.C. Kohlenberg Supt & Spl Disb Agent Four hundred and fifty and 00/100 dollars my share of the consideration deed dated December 21st. 1904 to A.E. Patrick for NE/4 2-18-5
Witnesses
    Alex Connolly   her
    Horace Guffin   Mary Grass   x mark

****

$450.00   March 5th. 1904
    Received of W.C. Kohlenberg Supt & Spl Disb Agent Four hundred fifty and 00/100 dollars my share of the consideration in deed dated December 21st. 1904 to A.E. Patrick for NE/4 2-18-5
Witnesses
    Horace Guffin   his
    William Hurr   Silas Grass   x mark

****

Sac & Fox – Shawnee Estates
1885-1910 Volume I

Refer in reply to the following:

LAND.
10179-1904.

Department of the Interior.
OFFICE OF INDIAN AFFAIRS
WASHINGTON, February 23, 1904

W. C. Kohlenberg, Esq.,
    Superintendent Sac and Fox Indian School,
    Sac and Fox Agency, Oklahoma,

Sir:
    Referring to your letter of January 23, 1904, you are advised that in accordance with the recommendation of this office of February 5, 1904, the Acting Secretary of the Interior on February 10, 1904, approved a deed dated December 21, 1903, from Mary Grass (nee Mary Hodge) and Silas Grass as heirs of George Grass (Pah-pas-ko-kuck) deceased Sac and Fox allottee #28, conveying to A. E. Patrick for $900.00 the NE/4 of Section 2, Township 18 North, Range 5 East, Oklahoma, containing 169.38 acres.

    Two certificates of deposit, #219 and #220 dated January 21, 1904 for $450.00 each, issued by the Stroud State Bank of Stroud, Oklahoma, to the order of the respective grantors are attached to the deed. The deed has been recorded in Deed Book Inherited Lands, volume 3, page 235.

    You are instructed to make proper delivery of the deed to the grantee and of the consideration money to the grantors as the interest of each may appear, taking receipts for the same in duplicate, and transmitting one copy of each receipt to this office.

                          Very respectfully,
                                 AC Tonner
EBF:LM   Acting Commissioner.

	Feb 5	, *190*4
Received of		~~U. S. Indian Agent,~~
a *warranty deed dated* October 26th		, *190* 3 , *given by*
heirs David Falls *to* A T McMillan		
for the SE/4 Sec 35 - 17 - 6		
Consideration, $182.5		A.T. McMillan

Sac & Fox – Shawnee Estates
1885-1910 Volume I

****

$608.33   March 2nd. 1904

Received of W.C. Kohlenberg Supt & Spl Disb Agent Six hundred Eight and 33/100 dollars my share of consideration in deed dated October 26th. 1903 to A.T. McMillan for SE/4 35-17-6

Witness
   Horace Guffin   his
   William Hurr   Grover Falls mark

****

$ 608 33/100   February 23, 1904.

Received of   ~~U.S. Indian Agent~~

Six hundred eight and 33/100   *Dollars,*

consideration in deed, dated   October 26   *190* 4,

to   A.T. McMillan   *for*   SE/4 - 35 - 17 - 6

WITNESS
   Harry L Elmslee
   Horace Guffin   Samuel Falls

****

$ 608 33/100   February 25th, 1904.

Received of   ~~U.S. Indian Agent~~

Six hundred eight and 33/100   *Dollars,*

consideration in deed, dated   October 26th   *190* 4

, *to*   A.T. McMillan   *for*   SE/4 - 35 - 17 - 6

WITNESS
   Harry L Elmslee   her
   Horace Guffin   Annie Smith x mark

****

Sac & Fox – Shawnee Estates
1885-1910 Volume I

Department of the Interior.

Refer in reply to the following:

LAND.
8128-1904.

OFFICE OF INDIAN AFFAIRS
Washington, Feb. 17, 1904

W. C. Kohlenberg, Esq.,
   Superintendent Indian School,
      Sac and Fox Agency, Oklahoma.

Sir:

   Referring to your letter dated December 28, 1903, you are advised that in accordance with the recommendation of this office of January 28, the Acting Secretary of the Interior on February 1, 1904, approved a deed dated October 26, 1903, from Grover Falls, Samuel Falls and Edna, his wife, and Annie Smith and Frank Smith, her husband, as heirs of David Falls. (Waw-me-ketch-tho-ko), deceased Sac and Fox allottee No. 273, conveying to A. T. McMillen for $1,825 the SE/4 of Section 35, township 17 north, range 6 east, Oklahoma, containing 160 acres.

   Certificate of deposit No. 198 dated December 9, 1903, for $1,825, issued by the Stroud State Bank, of Stroud, Okla., to the order of said grantors, is attached to the deed.

   The deed has been recorded in Deed Book Inherited Indian lands, volume 3, page 222.

   You are instructed to make proper delivery of the deed to the grantee, and of the consideration money to the grantors, as the interest of each may appear, taking receipts for the same in duplicate, and transmitting one copy of each receipt to this office.

                         Very respectfully,
                                AC Tonner

E.B.F.-L.C.   Acting Commissioner.

Sac & Fox – Shawnee Estates
1885-1910 Volume I

Received of		March 2$\underline{nd}$, *190* 4.
a warranty deed dated	August 24$\underline{th}$	*U. S. Indian Agent,* , 190 3 , *given by*
heirs Samuel Anderson	*to*	John F. Gardner
for the SW/4 5 - 11 - 5		Albert F. Gardner
		Chas F. Kirker
Consideration, $ 1450		[Name Illegible]
		[Name Illegible]

****

C/D N● 1072[sic] drawn on the Bank of Commerce Shawnee, Okla.
$1450.00   March 2nd. 1904
    Received of W.C. Kohlenberg Supt & Spl Disb Agent Fourteen
hundred and fifty and 00/100 dollars consideration in deed dated
August 24th. 1903 to John F. Kirker, Albert F. Gardner and Chas. F. Kirker
for SW/4 5-11-5
Witnesses   Charles Nullake
    Alex Connolly
    Horace Guffin

****

Refer in reply to the following: **Department of the Interior.**

LAND.   OFFICE OF INDIAN AFFAIRS
8177-1904.   WASHINGTON,   February 23, 1904

W. C. Kohlenberg, Esq.,
    Superintendent Sac and Fox Indian School,
            Sac and Fox Agency, Okla.

Sir:
    Referring to your letter of January 17, 1904, you are advised that in accordance
with the recommendation of this office of January 29, 1904, the Acting Secretary of
the Interior on February 2, 1904 approved a deed dated August 24, 1903 from Charles
Nullake, as heir of Samuel Anderson, (Me-saw-what-) deceased Sac and Fox allottee

Sac & Fox – Shawnee Estates
1885-1910 Volume I

#142, conveying to John F. Kerker, Albert F. Gardiner and Charles F. Kerker for $1450.00 the SW/4 of Section 5, Township 11 North, Range 5 East, Oklahoma, containing 160 acres, more or less, subject to the legal lease thereon.

Certificate of deposit #1072 dated August 29, 1903 for $1450.00 issued by the Bank of Commerce of Shawnee, Oklahoma to the order of Charles Nullake is attached to the deed. The deed has been recorded in Deed Book Inherited Indian Lands, volume 3, page 231.

You are instructed to make proper delivery of the deed to the grantee and the consideration money to the grantor, taking receipts for the same in duplicate, and transmitting one copy of each receipt to this office.

Very respectfully,
AC Tonner
Acting Commissioner.

EBF:LM

Received of ~~U. S. Indian Agent,~~ a warranty deed dated Aug 24th, 190 3, given by heirs Bertha Wyman to Lee Patrick for the NW/4 Sec 11 - twp 16 N R 6 East

March 7th, 190 4.

Consideration, $ 1000 & 320   Lee Patrick

****

1320.00   March 7th. 1904

Received of W.C. Kohlenberg Supt & Spl Disb Agent Thirteen hundred twenty and 00/100 dollars the increased consideration in deed dated August 24th. 1903 to Lee Patrick for NW/4 11-16-6

Witnesses
  Horace Guffin
  William Hurr   Henry Hunter his
                                                      x mark

****

Sac & Fox – Shawnee Estates
1885-1910 Volume I

Refer in reply to the following:

LAND.
13114-1904.

Department of the Interior.

OFFICE OF INDIAN AFFAIRS

WASHINGTON, March 2, 1904.

W. C. Kohlenberg, Esq.,
    Superintendent Indian School,
        Sac and Fox Agency, Oklahoma.

Sir:

    Referring to your letter dated February 3, 1904, you are advised that in accordance with the recommendation of this office of February 18, the Acting Secretary of the Interior on February 23, 1903, authorized the delivery to the grantee of a deed dated August 24, 1903, from Henry Hunter, as heir of Bertha Hunter, nee Bertha Wyman, (Chuck-e-quah), deceased Sac and Fox allottee No. 415, conveying to Lee Patrick, for the increased consideration of $1320, the northwest quarter of Section 11, township 16 north, range 6 east, Oklahoma, containing 160 acres.

    The records of this office show that this deed was submitted to the Department with recommendation for approval in office letter of September 30, 1903, the consideration then being $1,000, and that the deed as submitted was approved by the Acting Secretary of the Interior on October 19, 1903. Subsequent to said approval and before delivery of the deed to the grantee, Supervisor Chaloraft[sic], then in charge of your Agency, reported on November 21, 1903, that the appraisement of the land by former appraising clerk Tanksley in the sum of $960 was too low, and that the consideration of $1,000 was not a fair price for the land.

    The deed was therefore recalled by this office and was held pending a reliable reappraisement of the land, which reappraisement was made by you on January 31, 1904, in the sum of $1320, as shown by the certificate accompanying your letter of February 3, 1904.

    The grantee having deposited a certificate for the additional sum of $320, this office on February 18, 1904, recommended that your appraisement be approved and that authority be granted for the delivery of the deed. This authority, as was before stated, has been granted by the Department.

    The deed has been recorded in Deed Book Inherited Indian lands, volume 2, page 241.

    You are instructed to make proper delivery of the deed to the grantee and of the consideration money, $1320, to the grantor, taking receipts for the same in duplicate, and transmitting one copy of each receipt to this office.

Very respectfully,
AC Tonner
E.B.F.-L.C.   Acting Commissioner.

Refer in reply to the following:

Department of the Interior.

LAND.
13459-1904.
OFFICE OF INDIAN AFFAIRS
W<small>ASHINGTON</small>,   March 7, 1904.

W. C. Kohlenberg, Esq.,
    Superintendent Indian School,
        Sac and Fox Agency, Oklahoma.

Sir:

    Referring to your letter of February 16, 1904, transmitting a deed from the heirs of John J. Ingalls, (Waw-ko-mo) deceased Sac and Fox allottee #335, conveying to Lee Patrick for $1654.00 the NE/4 of Section 14, Township 17 North, Range 6 East, Oklahoma, you are advised that the affidavit of H. Josey as guardian of the minor grantor, as required by the second subdivision of paragraph 6 of section 3 of the amended rules is not with the papers. You are requested to furnish said affidavit.

Very respectfully,
AC Tonner
EBF:LM   Acting Commissioner.

Refer in reply to the following:

Department of the Interior.

Land.
14615-1904.
OFFICE OF INDIAN AFFAIRS
W<small>ASHINGTON</small>,   March 7, 1904.

W. C. Kohlenberg, Esq.,
    Superintendent Sac and Fox Indian School,
        Sac and Fox Agency, Oklahoma,

Sir:

    This office is in receipt of your letter of February 26, 1904, in which you report the attempted sale of Sac and Fox allotment #400, involving he NE/4 of Section 27, Township 16 North, Range 6 East, Oklahoma, to Joseph Pickard for $1700.00

    You state that the land was listed for sale upon the petition of J. Conger, who represented himself as the sole heir of the deceased allottee, Gabriel Marshall; that after the sale Conger refused to sign the deed and that upon investigation it was discovered that he does not inherit any share of the allotment, but that the sole heir of the allotted resides in Iowa.

In compliance with your request you are authorized to return to Mr. Pickard the certified check and to declare the sale off.

Very respectfully,
AC Tonner
Acting Commissioner.

EBF:LM

Department of the Interior.

Refer in reply to the following:
LAND.
8181/1904.

OFFICE OF INDIAN AFFAIRS
WASHINGTON, March 16, 1904.

W. C. Kohlenberg, Esq.,
    Superintendent Indian School,
        Sac and Fox Agency, Oklahoma.

Sir:

    Referring to your letter dated January 7, 1903, you are advised that in accordance with the recommendation of the office of January 29, 1904, the Acting Secretary of the Interior on February 2, 1904, approved a deed dated August 24, 1903, from Cora Ward, Frank Kent and Emma Kent, his wife, as heirs of Mock-e-naw, deceased Sac and Fox allottee No. 47, conveying to J. S. Custis[sic] for $850.00, the NW/4 of Sec. 15, T. 17 N, R. 6 E., Oklahoma, containing one hundred and sixty acres, subject to the lease of the land, the grantee to receive the benefits therefrom.

    Certificate of deposit No. 192, dated December 7, 1903, for $850.00 issued by the Stroud State Bank of Stroud, Oklahoma, to the order of the grantors, is attached to the deed.

    The deed has been recorded in Deed Book Inherited Indian Lands, Volume 4, Page 2.

    You are instructed to make proper delivery of the deed to the grantee and of the consideration money to the grantors, as the interest of each may appear, taking receipts for the same in duplicate and transmitting one copy of each to this office.

Very respectfully,
AC Tonner
Acting Commissioner.

EBF:H

Sac & Fox – Shawnee Estates
1885-1910 Volume I

Department of the Interior.

Refer in reply to the following:
Land.
18277-1904.

OFFICE OF INDIAN AFFAIRS

WASHINGTON, March 26, 1904.

W. C. Kohlenberg, Esq.,
    Superintendent Indian School,
        Sac and Fox Agency, Okla.

Sir:

    Referring to your letter dated March 12, 1904, there is returned herewith a deed dated February 1, 1904, from the heirs of Isaac Goodell, deceased Sac and Fox allottee No. 80 conveying the SE/4 of Sec. 35, T. 1[?] N., R. 6 E., Okla., to L. E. Clary, for $3500.00.

    Your attention is invited to the fact that the signatures of the grantors to said deed were not attested by the subscribing witnesses as is required by Par. 1 of Sec. 2, Amended Rules. The acknowledgement of Mary Goodell and Fannie and James Curtis before Mary Antoine, notary public, was not signed and sealed by the notary, and the acknowledgement before you was not dated.

    It is requested that these defects be supplied and the deed returned to this office for appropriate action.

                Very respectfully,
                      AC Tonner
                      Acting Commissioner.

EBF-E

                              March 30th, 1904

    Received of W.C. Kohlenberg Supt & Spl Disb Agent a warranty deed dated February 15th, 1904 given by the heirs of Moses Keokuk to Lee Patrick conveying the SW/4 NE/4, NW/4 SE/4, NE/4 SW/4, SE/4 NW/4 consideration $2100.00

                                Lee Patrick

****

Sac & Fox – Shawnee Estates
1885-1910 Volume I

$1050.00　　　　　　　　　　　March 30th. 1904
　　Received of W.C. Kohlenberg Supt & Spl Disb Agent Ten hundred and fifty ($1050) and 00/100 my share of the consideration in deed dated February 15th, 1904 to Lee Patrick for SW/4 NE/4 NW/4 SE/4 NE/4 SW/4 SE/4 NW/4
Witnesses
　　Horace Guffin　　　　　　　　Charles Keokuk
　　[Name Illegible]

****

$1050.00　　　　　　　　　　　March 30th. 1904
　　Received of W.C. Kohlenberg Supt & Spl Disb Agent Ten hundred and fifty ($1050.00) and 00/100 my share of the consideration in deed dated February 15th, 1904 to Lee Patrick for SW/4 NE/4, NW/4 SE/4, NE/4 SW/4, SE/4 NW/4
Witnesses
　　Horace Guffin　　　　　　　　Mary A Keokuk
　　[Name Illegible]

****

Refer in reply to the following:

Department of the Interior.

Land.
17927-1904.

OFFICE OF INDIAN AFFAIRS
　　　　WASHINGTON,　　March 24, 1904.

W. C. Kohlenberg, Esq.,
　　Superintendent Indian School,
　　　　Sac & Fox Agency, Okla.

Sir:

　　Referring to your letter dated February 27, 1904, you are advised that in accordance with the recommendation of this office of March 8th the Acting Secretary of the Interior on March 15, 1904, approved a deed dated February 15, 1904, from Mary A. Keokuk, and Charles Keokuk, as heirs of Moses Keokuk, deceased Sac and Fox allottee No. 260, conveying to Lee Patrick, for $2100, the SW/4 NE/4, NW/4 SE/4, NE/4 SW/4, SE/4 NW/4 of Sec. 21, T. 15 N., R. 5 E., Oklahoma, containing 160 acres, subject to the legal lease on the land, the grantee to receive the benefits therefrom.

Sac & Fox – Shawnee Estates
1885-1910 Volume I

Two certificates of deposit, No. 255 and 256, dated February 25, 1904, for $1050 each, issued by the Stroud State Bank, of Stroud, Okla., to the order of the respective grantors are attached to the deed.

The deed has been recorded in deed book, Inherited Indian Lands, Vol. 5, p 68.

You are instructed to make proper delivery of the deed to the grantee and of the consideration money to the grantors, as the interest of each may appear, taking receipts for the same in duplicate and transmitting one copy of each receipt to this office.

Very respectfully,

AC Tonner
Acting Commissioner.

EBF-E

Sugar Grove Ark.
March 31, '04

W.C. Kohlenberg,
    Sac & Fox Okla.

Dear Sir:-

Yours of the 22nd inst received and we – my sister & I have carefully noted the contents: We must acknowledge that we are not satisfied with the arrangement.

In consulting with a lawyer, we learn that Jennie Hall and Rachel are not entitled to any share whatever in our mother's land. But from our point of view we wish to understand more fully why. If Jennie or Rachel Hall are entitled to a third of our mother[sic] land cannot we four children receive a share in any property of Henry Hall according to your arrangement? Which I must say is puzzling! and according to the amt. of lease money we do not wish it paid us until we feel better informed. One thing more please –

If Jennie and Rachel Hall are entitled to 1/3 of our mother's land. Cannot we request the sale ~~ore~~ or advertisement of Henry Hall's land stopped through the same arrangement of inheritance?

If you think it necessary we can come to the Agency and consult with you.

Please let us hear from you.

Yours truly
Mrs. Fannie Banister
Mrs. Julia Brown
Sugar Grove,
Arkansas.

Sac & Fox – Shawnee Estates
1885-1910 Volume I

April 2nd. 1904
Received of W.C. Kohlenberg Supt & Spl Disb Agent a warranty deed given by the heirs of Eva Wheeler to J. H. Maxey conveying the S/2 NW/4 & N/2 SW/4 Sec. 1-11-4. Deed dated December 28th. 1903.
JH Maxey

****

$325.00 April 4$\underline{th}$. 1904
Received of W.C. Kohlenberg Supt & Spl Disb Agent Three hundred twenty five ($325.00) and 00/100 dollars my share of the consideration in deed dated December 28th, 1903 for S/2 NW/4 N/2 SW/4 Sec. 1-11-4 E. to J.H. Maxey.
Witnesses
  William Hurr
  Horace Guffin   Chief McKosito his X mark

****

$325.00 April 4th. 1904
Received of W.C. Kohlenberg Supt & Spl Disb Agent Three hundred twenty five ($325.00) and 00/100 dollars my share of the consideration in deed dated December 28th, 1903 to J.H. Maxey for S/2 NW/4 N/2 SW/4 Sec. 1-11-4 E.
Witnesses
  William Hurr
  Horace Guffin   David Wakolle his X mark

****

Sac & Fox – Shawnee Estates
1885-1910 Volume I

$325.00   April 4th. 1904

    Received of W.C. Kohlenberg Supt & Spl Disb Agent Three hundred twenty five ($325.00) and 00/100 dollars my share of the consideration in deed dated December 28th, 1903 to J.H. Maxey for S/2 NW/4 N/2 SW/4 Sec. 1-11-4 E.

    Witnesses
        William Hurr
        Horace Guffin   Edgar Mack   his X mark

****

$325.00   Sac and Fox Agency, Oklahoma Territory,
                                 March 30, 1904

    Received from W. C. Kohlenberg, Supt. & Sp. Disb. Agent, Three Hundred Twenty Five and 00/100 dollars my share of the consideration in deed dated December 28, 1903 to J. H. Maxey for the S/2 of the NW/4 and the N/2 SW/4 of Sec. 1-11-4 E.

    Witnesses:
  Mary Antoine
  William Hurr   Judith Houston   her X mark

****

Refer in reply to the following:
Land.
14617-1904.
17929 - 04

Department of the Interior.

OFFICE OF INDIAN AFFAIRS
                    WASHINGTON,   March 25, 1904.

W. C. Kohlenberg, Esq.,
    Superintendent Indian School,
        Sac and Fox Agency, Okla.

Sir:

    Referring to your letter dated February 25, 1904, you are advised that in accordance with the recommendation of this office of March 8 the Acting Secretary of the Interior on March 15, 1904, approved a deed dated December 28, 1903, from Chief McKosito, Edgar Mack, David Wakolle and Judith Houston, as heirs of Eva

Sac & Fox – Shawnee Estates
1885-1910 Volume I

Wheeler, deceased Sac and Fox allottee No. 448, conveying to J. H. Maxey, for $1300, the S/2 NW/4 and N/2 SW/4 of Sec. 1, T. 11 N., R. 4 E., Okla., containing 160 acres.

Four certificates of deposit numbered 1281 to 1284, inclusive, dated January 28, 1904, for $325 each, issued by the First National Bank of Shawnee, Okla., to the order of the respective grantors, are attached to the deed.

The deed has been recorded in deed book, Inherited Indian Lands, Vol. 5, p. 70.

You are instructed to make proper delivery of the deed to the grantee and of the consideration money to the grantors, as the interest of each may appear, taking receipts for the same in duplicate, and transmitting one copy of each receipt to this office.

Very respectfully,
AC Tonner
Acting Commissioner.

EBF-E

April ~~Feb~~ 2, 1904

Received of W.C. Kohlenberg Supt & Spl Disb Agent at Sac and Fox Agency, Okla three certificates of deposit Nos. 170, 171 & 172 drawn on the Stroud State Bank in the respective amounts, $333.34, 333.33 and $333.33 by Jacob Puckett and made payable to John Foster legal guardian of Isadore Neal, Victor Neal and Jesse Carter respectively upon approval of deed to NE/4 29-18-6, which deed was disapproved by the Acting Secretary of the Interior Secretary of the Interior on February 1st, 1904.

Jacob Puckett

****

Refer in reply to the following:
Land.
8130-1904.

Department of the Interior.
OFFICE OF INDIAN AFFAIRS
WASHINGTON,

February 11, 1904.

W. C. Kohlenberg, Esq.,
   Supt. Indian School,
      Sac and Fox Agency, Okla.

Sac & Fox – Shawnee Estates
1885-1910 Volume I

Sir:

You are advised that in accordance with the recommendation of this office of January 28th, the Acting Secretary of the Interior on February 1, 1904, disapproved a deed dated August 24, 1903, from Jessie Carter, et al., as heirs of Mary Neal (We-ke-ah), deceased Sac and Fox allottee No. 462, conveying to Jacob Puckett, for $1,000.00, the NE/4 of Sec 28, T. 18 N., R. 6 E., Oklahoma, containing 160 acres, for the reason that the consideration named in the deed is not deemed a fair price for the land and is below the increased appraisement of $1300.00 made by you.

Three certificates of deposit numbered 170, 161 and 172, for $333.34, $333.33 and $333.33 respectively, issued by the Stroud State Bank, Oklahoma, on November 18, 1903, to the order of said grantors are herewith enclosed. You are requested to have these certificates properly endorsed to the order of Mr. Puckett and to deliver the same to him upon his executing a receipt therefor.

The disapproved deed will be retained in the files of this office.

Very respectively,
AC Tonner
Acting Commissioner.

EBF-CGC

April 6th. 1904

Received of W.C. Kohlenberg Supt & Spl Disb Agent a warranty deed dated February 24, 1904 given by the heirs of John G. Carlisle to E. L. Conklin conveying the SE/4 Sec. 7-17-6
Consideration $1610.^{00} E L Conklin

****

$1610.00 April 13th. 1904

Received of W.C. Kohlenberg Supt & Spl Disb Agent Sixteen hundred and ten ($1610.00) and 00/100 dollars consideration in deed dated February 24, 1904 to E.L. Conklin for SE/4 7-17-6 E.

Witnesses
  Horace Guffin   his
  [Name Illegible   Tah-tup-Puck-ko x mark

****

Sac & Fox – Shawnee Estates
1885-1910 Volume I

Department of the Interior.

OFFICE OF INDIAN AFFAIRS

Refer in reply to the following:
LAND.
17930-1904

Washington, March 29, 1904

W. C. Kohlenberg, Esq.,
    Superintendent Indian School,
        Sac and Fox Agency, Oklahoma,
Sir:

    Referring to your letter of February 27, 1904, you are advised that in accordance with the recommendation of this office of March 8, 1904, the Acting Secretary of the Interior on March 15, 1904, approved a deed dated February 24, 1904, from Tah-tup-puck-ko, as the heir of John G. Carlisle, (Pah-she-sha-she) deceased Sac and Fox allottee #55, conveying to E. L. Conklin for $1630.00 the SE/4 of Section 7, Township 17 North, Range 6 East, Oklahoma, containing 160 acres.

    A certificate of deposit (No. 254) dated February 25, 1904, for $1610.00 issued by the Stroud State Bank of Stroud, Oklahoma, payable to the order of the grantor is attached to the deed.

    The deed has been recorded in Deed Book, Inherited Indian Lands, volume 5, page 71.

    You are instructed to make proper delivery of the deed to the grantee and of the consideration money to the grantor, taking receipts for the same in duplicate, and transmitting one copy of each receipt to this office.

                    Very respectfully,
                      AC Tonner
EBF:LM   Acting Commissioner.

                      April 15th. 1904
    Received of W.C. Kohlenberg Supt & Spl Disb Agent a warranty deed dated December 14th, 1903 given by the heirs of Horace Ingalls to Lee Patrick conveying the Lot 7 of the NW/4 Lots 8 & 9 of SE/4 and lots 5 & 6 of the SW/4 Sec. 27-11-4 E.
Consideration $ 1854.00   Lee Patrick

****

Sac & Fox – Shawnee Estates
1885-1910 Volume I

$618.00　　　　　　　　　　　　　　April 18th. 1904
　　Received of W.C. Kohlenberg Supt & Spl Disb Agent Six hundred Eighteen and 00/100 dollars my share of the consideration in deed dated December 14, 1903 given by the heirs of Horace Ingles to Lee Patrick for Lot 7 of the NW/4 Lots 8 & 9 of SE/4 Lots 5 & 6 of the SW/4 Sec. 27-11-4 E.

Witnesses
　HL Elmslee　　　　　　　　　　Mattie Ingalls　her X mark
　William Hurr

****

$1236.00　　　　　　　　　　　　　April 16th. 1904
　　Received of W.C. Kohlenberg Supt & Spl Disb Agent Twelve hundred thirty six and 00/100 dollars the share of the minor heir, Sadie Ingalls of the consideration mentioned in deed dated December 14th. 1903 given by the heirs of Horace Ingalls to Lee Patrick for Lot 7 of the NW/4 Lots 8 & 9 of the SE/4 and Lots 5 & 6 of the SW4 of Sec. 27-11-4 E.

　　　　　　　　　　　　　　　　　　H Josey
Certificate of guardianship attached　　Legal Guardian

****

Refer in reply to the following:　　**Department of the Interior.**

LAND.　　　　　OFFICE OF INDIAN AFFAIRS
13832-1904.　　　　Washington,　　April 8, 1904.

W. C. Kohlenberg, Esq.,
　　Superintendent of Sac and Fox School,
　　　　Sac and Fox Agency, Oklahoma.

Sir:
　　Referring to your letter of February 4, 1904, you are advised that in accordance with the recommendation of this office February 20, the Acting Secretary of the Interior Secretary of the Interior on February 26, 1904 approved a deed dated December 14, 1903, from Mattie Ingalls and H. Josey as guardian of Sadie Ingalls a

Sac & Fox – Shawnee Estates
1885-1910 Volume I

minor, as heirs of Horace Ingalls (Pe-shaw-kaw) a deceased Sac and Fox allottee number 338, conveying to Lee Patrick for $1,854.00 Lot 7 of the NW/4, Lots 8 and 9 of the SE/4 and Lots 5 and 6 of the SW/4 of Sec. 27, T. 11 N., R. 4 E., Oklahoma, containing 162.48 acres.

Two certificates of deposit dated January 26, 1904, for $618.00 and $1,236.00 respectively, issued by the Stroud State Bank of Stroud, Oklahoma, to the order of the respective grantors are attached to the deed.

The deed has been recorded in Deed Book, Inherited Indian Lands, Volume 4, Page 39.

You are instructed to make proper delivery of the deed to the grantee and of the consideration money to the grantors as the interest of each may appear, taking receipts for the same in duplicate, and transmitting one copy of each receipt to this office.

Very respectfully,
AC Tonner
Acting Commissioner.

EBF:LM

DUPLICATE

Received of FRANK A. THACKERY, Supt. & Spl. Disb, APR 18 1905, 190 U. S. Indian Agent, a warranty deed dated September 6, 190 4, given by Heirs of Black Wing to W C Robinson for the NW4 of 4-9-16

****

Duplicate

$89^{18}

Received of FRANK A. THACKERY, Supt. & Spl. U. S. Indian Agent, MAY 2, 190 4.

a warranty deed dated The sum of Eighty-nine and $^{18/}$100 Dollars, 190 , given by

for the this being the remainder of her share of the estate of Black Wing

Consideration, $ [Illegible] Wilson

****

Original

$89<u>18</u> MAY 2, 1904.

Received of FRANK A. THACKERY, Supt. & Spl. Disb. *U. S. Indian Agent,*

a warranty deed dated The sum of ~~, 190 , given by~~

Eighty-nine and 18/100 Dollars

for the this being the remainder of her share of

the Black Wing estate

~~Consideration, $~~ Naura Wilson

****

$ 20.00 Feb 10, 1904.

Received of FRANK A. THACKERY, Supt. & Spl. Disb. *U.S. Indian Agent,*

Deposit for Twenty and no/100 *Dollars,*

consideration in ^unapproved *deed, dated* May 18 *190* 3, *to* five

heirs of Black Wing *for* NW4 of Sec 4

Town. 9 N, Range 1 E.

WITNESS

John Studholme William C Robinson

****

$ 700.00 Feb 10, 1904.

Received of FRANK A. THACKERY, Supt. & Spl. Disb. *U.S. Indian Agent,*

Eight certificates of deposit conveying a total of Seven hundred and no/100 *Dollars,*

consideration in ^unapproved *deed, dated* May 18 *190* 3, *to* five

heirs of Black Wing *for* NW4 of Sec 4

Town. 9 N, Range 1 E.

WITNESS

Arthur Long William C Robinson

****

Sac & Fox – Shawnee Estates
1885-1910 Volume I

>   Feb 22   , 190 4
> Received of FRANK A. THACKERY, Supt. & Spl. Disb U. S. Indian Agent,
> unapproved
> a warranty ^ deed dated   May 18   , 190 3 , given by
> Abs. Shawnee Allottee #441   to   W. C. Robinson
> for the NW4 of Sec 4 Town 9 N, Range 1 E.
>   Witnesses   her
> Consideration, $ 720⁰⁰   to mark   Tip-kaw-we X
>   WA Dickens   mark
>   Louis Trombla

> April 19th. 1904
> Received of W.C. Kohlenberg Supt & Spl Disb Agent a warranty deed dated December 14th, 1903 given by the heirs of John J. Ingalls to Lee Patrick for the NE/4 14-17-6 E.
> Consideration $1654.00

****

> $275.66   April 16th. 1904
> Received of W.C. Kohlenberg Supt & Spl Disb Agent Two hundred seventy five and 66/100 dollars my share of the consideration in deed dated December 14th, 1903 given by the heirs of John J. Ingalls to Lee Patrick for NE/4 14-17-6 E.
>   her
> Witnesses   X
>   HL Elmslee   Mattie Ingalls   mark
>   William Hurr

****

$1378.34　　　　　　　　　　　　April 16th. 1904
　　Received of W.C. Kohlenberg Supt & Spl Disb Agent Thirteen hundred seventy eight and 34/100 dollars the share of the minor heir, Sadie Ingalls of the consideration mentioned in deed dated December 14th, 1903 given by the heirs of John J. Ingalls to Lee Patrick for NE/4 14-17-6 E.

　　　　　　　　　　　　　　　　　　　H Josey
Certificate of guardianship attached　　Legal Guardian

　　　　　　　　　　**********

Refer in reply to the following:
　　LAND.　　**Department of the Interior.**
　20029-1904.
　　　　　　　OFFICE OF INDIAN AFFAIRS
　　　　　　　　　Washington,　　April 12, 1904.

W. C. Kohlenberg, Esq.,
　　Superintendent Sac & Fox Agency,
　　　　Sac & Fox Agency, Oklahoma.

Sir:

　　Referring to your letter dated February 16, 1904, you are advised that in accordance with the recommendation of this office of March 19th, the Acting Secretary of the Interior on March 23, 1904, approved a deed dated December 14, 1903, from Mattie Ingalls and H. Josey, as guardian of Sadie Ingalls, as heirs of John J Ingalls, (Waw-Ko-mo), deceased Sac and Fox allottee No. 325, conveying to Lee Patrick for $1,654.00, the NE/4 of Sec. 14. T. 17 E., R. 6 E., Oklahoma, containing 160 acres, subject to the legal lease on the land, the grantee to receive the benefits therefrom.

　　Two certificates of deposit dated January 30, 1904, for $275.66 and $1, 378.34 issued by the State Bank of Stroud, Oklahoma, to the order of the respective grantors are attached to the deed.

　　The deed has been recorded in Deed Book Inherited Indian Lands, Volume 5, Page 122.

　　You are instructed to make proper delivery of the deed to the grantee and of the consideration money to the grantors, as the interest of each may appear, taking receipts for the same in duplicate and transmitting one copy of each receipt to this office.

Sac & Fox – Shawnee Estates
1885-1910 Volume I

EBF-H

Very respectfully,
AC Tonner
Acting Commissioner.

Sac and Fox Agency, Oklahoma Territory,
April 20, 1904

Received from W. C. Kohlenberg, Supt. & Sp. Disbg. Agent, certified check for $500.00 payable to the order of the Commissioner of Indian Affairs, drawn on the First National Bank, Shawnee, Okla.

JH Maxey Jr

110

****

Sac and Fox Agency, Okla.
April 20, 1904

Received from W. C. Kohlenberg, Supt. & Sp. Disbg. Agent, a warranty deed dated May 4, 1903, given by the heirs of Cassie Eaton, deceased, to J. H Maxey, Jr. conveying the NE/4 of section 17-11-4 E.

JH Maxey Jr

111

****

$2000.00   April 20th, 1904

Received of W.C. Kohlenberg, Supt & Spl Disb Agent Two thousand and 00/100 dollars consideration mentioned in deed dated May 4th, 1903 given by the heir of Cassie Eaton to J.H. Maxey Jr. for NE/4 Sec. 17-11-4 east.

Witnesses.   Cassie Tribble
Horace Guffin
Mary Antoine

****

Sac & Fox – Shawnee Estates
1885-1910 Volume I

Refer in reply to the following:
Land.
20858-1904.

Department of the Interior.
OFFICE OF INDIAN AFFAIRS
WASHINGTON, April 13, 1904.

W. C. Kohlenberg, Esq.,
    Superintendent Indian School,
        Sac and Fox Agency, Okla.

Sir:

    Referring to agency letters dated May 20 and October 31, 1903, you are advised that in accordance with the recommendation of this office of March 24, 1904, the Acting Secretary of the Interior on March 28, 1904, approved a deed dated May 4, 1903, from Cassie Tribble (formerly Cassie Eaton) as heir of Cassie Eaton, deceased Sac and Fox allottee No. 264., conveying to J. H. Maxey, Jr., for $2,000 the NE/4 of Sec.. 17, T. 11 N., R. 4 E., Oklahoma, containing 160 acres.

    A certified check for $500 dated May 2, 1903, drawn by J. H. Maxey, Jr., on the First National Bank of Shawnee, Okla., to the order of the Commissioner of Indian Affairs and made payable to your order by endorsement and certificate of deposit No. 436, not dated, for $2,000, issued by said bank to the order of Cassie Tribble, are attached to the deed.

    The deed is recorded in deed book, Inherited Indian Lands, Vol. 5, p 125.

    You are instructed to make proper delivery of the deed to the grantee and of the consideration money to the grantor, taking receipts in duplicate for the same and transmitting one copy of each receipt to this office.

    It will be observed that the check and certificate of deposit transmitted herewith represent in the aggregate $2500, being $500 in excess of the consideration named in the deed. It is therefore presumed that the check for $500 should be returned to Mr. Maxey. In order that you may make proper disposition of this check it has been endorsed payable to your order.

                    Very respectfully,

                            W.A. Jones
                            Commissioner.

EBF-E   ACT

Sac & Fox – Shawnee Estates
1885-1910 Volume I

PETITION FOR SALE OF INHERITED INDIAN LAND.

To the HONORABLE ROSS GUFFIN,
  U. S. Indian Agent,
    Sac and Fox Agency, Oklahoma.

The petition of Gertrude Brown, Isaac Givens, Eveline Givens, Henry Hunter, Lydia Grant and Lucy Thurman respectfully represent and show that they are members of the Sac and Fox tribe of Indians and reside in Lincoln County, Oklahoma Territory; that your petitioners are the owners, by inheritance from Ah-quaw-saw deceased, a member of the Sac and Fox tribe of Indians, who died Feb 10th 1891, of the following described lands, situated and being in Lincoln County, Oklahoma Territory, to-wit:

  The South West quarter of section fourteen (14) township sixteen (16) North of range six (6) East of the Indian Meridian

 Your petitioners further represent that they inherit respectively as follows: Gertrude Brown, 1/3 interest, Isaac Givens, 2/15 interest, Eveline Givens, 2/15 interest, Henry Hunter 2/15 interest, Lydia Grant 2/15 interest, Lucy Thurman 2/15 interest.

 That the above named heirs, your petitioners, are the sole and only heirs left surviving the said Ah-quaw-saw deceased.

 Your petitioners further represent that said land is subject to sale under Section Seven of the Act of Congress of May 27th, 1902; that said land does not constitute any part of, and was never used as a homestead of said deceased or heirs.

 Wherefore your petitioners pray that the above described land be listed and sold as authorized and according to the rules and regulations applicable thereto.

Signed in the presence of
 Edna Falls
 E L Conklin

Gertrude Brown her X mark
Eveline Givens her X mark
Lucy Thurman X mark
Lydia Grant her X mark
Henry Hunter his X mark
Isaac Givens

Sac & Fox – Shawnee Estates
1885-1910 Volume I

DEPARTMENT OF THE INTERIOR
UNITED STATES INDIAN SERVICE.

SAC AND FOX AGENCY, IOWA.
Toledo, May 10, 1904.

Hon. W. C. Kohlenberg,
　Supt. & Spc'l. Disb. Agt.
　　Sac and Fox Agency, Okla.

Sir:-

　Your communication under date of the 3rd, instant, relative to a woman by the name of Me-ka-taw, who is an enrolled annuitant at this Agency, is at hand, and after calling the business committee together, with the said Ma-ka-taw[sic], I have elicited the following information from them, relative to the relationship of the said Indian woman, and Maw-waw-she, deceased.

　Ma-squa-ta and Qua-squa-sa, were the father and mother of Me-wa-pe-ka-so, and Ka-ke-pa-no, thus making them full brothers.,

　Ke-wa-pe-ka-so was the father of Me-ka-taw.

　Ka-ke-pa-no, was the father of Maw-waw-she.

　It appears from the above, that the said Maw-waw-she, and Me-ka-taw, are first cousins in direct line. Me-ka-taw says that Aw-ko-see is related to her, but from the best understanding I was able to obtain from her, or the Committee, the said relationship was not so direct as that between Maw-waw-she and Me-ka-taw, but runs as follows;

　Ne-ma-ko-wa was the father of Aw-ko-see, and by marriage, the nephew of Maw-waw-she, but there was no blood relationship existing between them. The business committee and the woman, Me-ka-taw agree upon the above relationship, as existing between her and Maw-waw-she, deceased, also, as that existing between her and Aw-ko-see.

　Me-ka-taw admits, that she told Aw-ko-see to sell the land, but did not say what disposition he should make of the money received therefor. Ma-ka-taw would not say whether she would authorize the selling of the hay or not, if she was adjudged the heir of the said land, but I should think it the proper thing to do, and when the matter was settled as to the heirship, the rental, or sale money could be turned over to the person rightfully entitled to it. If the above is sufficient to settle the claim of Me-ka-taw to the land, or if further evidence is required in the matter, and if I can be of further use in the final adjustment of this business, do not fail to command me, and I will again call the committee together, and go over the case again.

Sac & Fox – Shawnee Estates
1885-1910 Volume I

Quin-E-pah, an old man who is enrolled at this Agency, requested me to make inquiry concerning the estate of Ma-na-ka-wa, deceased, who he claims was his niece, and who died some time ago. Of course this is rather indefinite, but it was all that I could get from him.

Very respectfully,

Wm G. Malin
U. S. Indian Agent.

Refer in reply to the following:
Land.
21450-1904.
21449-1904.

Department of the Interior.

OFFICE OF INDIAN AFFAIRS

WASHINGTON,   May 11, 1904.

W. C. Kohlenberg, Esq.,
   U. S. Indian Agent,
     Sac and Fox Agency, Okla.

Sir:

   Referring to your two communications of March 12, 1904, enclosing conveyances covering inherited Indian lands, you are advised that the Acting Secretary of the Interior, upon the recommendation of this office dated March 26 approved the following deeds:

   1.- Deed dated February 1, 1903, from Amanda Nullake and Walter Nullake, as heirs of Henry Nullake, (Tah-paw-she-pah-me-hot), deceased Sac and Fox allottee No. 178, conveying to H. Josey, for $1200, the S/2 of NW/4 and N/2 of SW/4 of Sec. 2, T. 11 N., R. 4 E., containing 160 acres.

   Attached to this deed are two certified checks made by H. Josey to the Stroud State Bank. They are dated March 11; the first, No. 258, payable to Amanda Nullake, is for $600; the second, No. 259, payable to Walter Nullake, is for a like sum.

   2.- Deed dated February 22, 1904, from Webster Smith as heir of Ida Smith, deceased Sac and Fox allottee No. 34, conveying to Joseph Pickard, for $1800, the SE/4 of Sec. 2, T. 16 N., R. 6 E., containing 160 acres.

   Attached to this deed is a certificate of deposit No. 425, made by Joseph Pickard in favor of Webster Smith, for $1800.

Sac & Fox – Shawnee Estates
1885-1910 Volume I

You will please deliver these deeds to the proper parties and the consideration to the respective grantors, as their interest may appear, taking receipts therefor in duplicate and transmitting one copy of each receipt to this office, retaining the other for your files.

>Very respectfully,
>AC Tonner
>Acting Commissioner.

MG-E

****

Nov. 14, 1904
Received of W.C. Kohlenberg Supt & Spl Disb Agent a warranty deed dated February 22nd. 1904 given by the heir of Ida Smith to Joseph Pickard conveying SE/4 Sec. 2-16-6 East
Consideration $1800.00   Joseph Pickard

****

$1800.00   May 16, 1904
Received of W.C. Kohlenberg Supt & Spl Disb Agt. at Sac and Fox Agency, Okla., Eighteen hundred dollars, being the consideration in the deed from the heir of Ida Smith to Joseph Pickard, for the SE/4 of section 2,- 16,-6 E. deed dated Feb 22, 1904
  Witnesses:
  Horace Guffin   Webster Smith   his x mark
  HL Elmslee

****

May 19 1904
Received of W.C. Kohlenberg Supt. & Spl. Disb. Agt., a warranty deed dated February 1, 1904, given by the heirs of Henry Nullake, (Tah-taw-she-pah-me-hot) to H. Josey for the S/2 of the NW/4 and the N/2 of the SW/4 of section 2,-11,-4 E.
Consideration, - $1200.00   H. Josey

****

Sac & Fox – Shawnee Estates
1885-1910 Volume I

$600.00　　　　　　　　　　　　　　May 19, 1904
　　Received of W.C. Kohlenberg, Supt. & Spl. Disb. Agt. at Sac and Fox Agency, Okla., Six hundred dollars being my share of the consideration in the deed dated February 1, 1904, from the heirs of Henry Nullake (Tahtaw-she-me-hot) to H. Josey, for the S/2 of the NW/4 and the N/2 of the SW/4 of section 2-11-4 E.

Alex Connolly　⎫　　　　　　Amanda Nullake　　her
Horace Guffin　⎬ Witnesses　　　　　　　　　　　x
　　　　　　　⎭　　　　　　　　　　　　　　　mark

****

$600.00　　　　　　　　　　　　　May 26th. 1904
　　Received of W.C. Kohlenberg Supt & Spl Disb Agent Six hundred and 00/100 dollars my share of the consideration in deed dated February 1st 1904 given by the heirs of Henry Nullake to H. Josey for $1200.00 conveying N/2 SW/4 S/2 NW/4 Sec, 2-11-4 E.

Witnesses　　　　　　　　　　　Walter Nullake
　Horace Guffin
　Harry L Elmslee

Department of Justice.

Office of the United States Attorney.
District of Oklahoma.
Guthrie.

　　　　　　　　　　　　　　　　May 24th, 1904.
W. C. Kohlenberg, Esq.,
　Supt. & Spec. Disb. Agent,
　　Sac & Fox Agency, Oklahoma.

Sir:-
　　Your letter of the 17th inst., asking as to the heirship of the property of John I. Ingalls, a Sac & Fox Indian who died February 20th, 1892, is received, and the same

Sac & Fox – Shawnee Estates
1885-1910 Volume I

has been referred to the Commissioner of Indian Affairs. When an answer is received from him, it will be immediately transmitted to you.

> Very respectfully,
> Horace Speed
> U. S. Attorney.

Refer in reply to the following: **Department of the Interior.**
LAND.
32562/1904.   OFFICE OF INDIAN AFFAIRS
                 WASHINGTON,   May 26, 1904.

W. C. Kohlenberg, Esq.,
    Superintendent Sac and Fox Agency,
        Oklahoma.

Sir:

There is enclosed herewith a letter from Millie Tohee, of Perkins, Oklahoma. She writes in reference to her rights as heir to the land of her father, Daniel Tohee, asserting that a former wife of Tohee by Indian custom is claiming a share in her deceased father's allotment. She claims that this woman, Julia Small, voluntarily deserted her father, and married another Indian by name Robert Small, and that there are only two that are legal heirs of Daniel Tohee, herself and Robert Tohee, and asks help from the Department in the matter.

You will please investigate the statements contained in this communication and report thereon, returning the enclosure.

> Very respectfully,
> AC Tonner
> Acting Commissioner.

MG-H

Mayetta, Kansas, May 30, 1904.
Supt or Indian Agent, Sac and Fox Agency, O.T.
    Dear Sir:

RECEIVED
NOV 16 1904
SAC & FOX AGENCY,
OKLAHOMA.

Tapsey, an Indian living in the reservation near by, asked me to write concerning the allotment made to a certain half Sac and half Pottawatomie Indian woman by the name of Kee-wan-mo-qua who he says died here about two years ago.

Sac & Fox — Shawnee Estates
1885-1910 Volume I

Tapsey claims this woman was his neice[sic]- as a child of a sister now long since dead. He wants to get the benefit of said womans[sic] lands when the same shall be sold.

                Very respectfully
                Joseph Moose
      In Kansas (?)

R E WOOD   W I WILLIAMS
WOOD & WILLIAMS
LAWYERS
SHAWNEE OKLAHOMA

                Shawnee, Okl. Ter.
                June 13, 1904.

Hon. W.C. Kohlenberg,
    Sac and Fox Agency,
        Okl. Ter. Dear sir:-We herewith inclose you certified check, Venlee's affidavit, and we will look after the Probate proceedings for Mr. Mead. WE[sic] would like to know the name of the alottee[sic], and the relationship between the Allottee and these minors. Are they minor children of the allottee, or are they collateral heirs?

    Was Mr. H.C. Brunt, of Chandler, appointed guardian by the Probate court of Lincoln county[sic]? When you have the deeds signed up please forward them to us, so we may proceed with the matters in Probate Court.

            Very truly yours,
                Wood & Williams

DEPARTMENT OF THE INTERIOR
UNITED STATES INDIAN SERVICE.

                Nadeau Kansas,
                June 27th. 1904.

W.C. Kohlenberg,
    Supt. & Spcl Disb. Agent.
        Sac and Fox Agency,
            Oklahoma.
Dear sir:-
        In reply to your letter of June 22nd, 1904, I beg to state that Nam-aht is enrolled on the annuity rolls at this Agency as Wish-te-yah, and is 20 years of age. Wish-te-yah, is the son of a deceased sister of Kan-keh-o-qua-hit also deceased and

they were brother and sister of Ship-she-wahn-o. I have consulted with one or two of the Business Committee, and they agree that Ship-she-wahn-o and Wish-te-yah, are the only heirs to this estate. There may be other distant relatives but if so they are too far removed to have any interest in this estate.

Very respectfully,
G. L. Williams
Supt. & Spcl. Disb. Agent.
By Scott

Refer in reply to the following:
LAND.
35544-1904.

Department of the Interior.
OFFICE OF INDIAN AFFAIRS
WASHINGTON, July 1, 1904.

W. C. Kohlenberg, Esq.,
    Superintendent Indian School,
        Sac and Fox Agency, Oklahoma.

Sir:

This office is in receipt of your letter of May 17, addressed to the United States Attorney at Guthrie, Oklahoma, and was referred here by the Hon. Horace Speed under date of May 24, 1904.

You enclose a family tree and a certificate of the business committee, relative to the heirship of John J. Ingalls, the question raised being the proper disposition of the portion of the estate vesting in William Ingalls at his death. You seem to think that it should go to Sadie Ingalls rather than to be divided between her and her mother relying upon paragraph 7, of Section 3, Article 4, Succession, - Statutes of Oklahoma, 1893.

This question was raised before by you in a letter addressed to this office. The conclusion reached here is that under such conditions the estate descends not only to the brothers and sisters of the deceased child of the deceased heir, but to the mother as well, if she survives.

The object of the section quoted by you is to cut off half brothers and sisters born of a marriage contracted by the surviving parent after the decease of the father of the heir through whom the estate is derived by the deceased child mentioned in the Statutes, and in this case William Ingalls.

You have also been advised that this is not a Probate Court and that no decision from this Department can positively determine the heirs of any person. That alone is the function of the court having jurisdiction of the property where the question arises.

Very respectfully,
AC Tonner
Acting Commissioner.

MG-WDW

Refer in reply to the following: Land.

Department of the Interior.

39,130-1904.   OFFICE OF INDIAN AFFAIRS

Washington,   July 2, 1904.

W. C. Kohlenberg, Esq.,
    Superintendent in charge,
        Sac and Fox Agency, Oklahoma.

Sir:

    I am in receipt of your letter, dated June 8, 1904, in reference to the heirs of Nellie Mason. Your communication is in answer to office letter of June 3, 1904, stating that in the opinion of this office the determination of the proper heirs, as shown by the application for the sale of the lands in question, was erroneous in some respects.

    It is proper to state here that this office is not a probate court and cannot determine who are the heirs in an estate where there is a controversy in reference thereto. The only object in calling your attention to what is believed to be a misconstruction of the laws of Oklahoma in reference to heirship is to protect the Department, yourself and the parties of interest. It may be laid down as a safe rule, however, so far as the Department is concerned, that a deed where the purchaser is satisfied that the proper parties have conveyed, will be approved by the Department, as it cannot undertake to guarantee the correctness of any findings of this sort. Such matters belong wholly to the proper courts, but at the same time it is very desirable that the heirs be determined without resort to the courts in order that the proceeds from these sales may not be dissipated in useless litigation to the detriment of the claimants.

    The only difference between your conclusions and that of the office arises over the disposition of the interest of Rufus Hall in the case now pending. Your conclusion is that the 7th paragraph, section 3, article 4, under the subject "Succession", in the Statutes of Oklahoma, is such that his father is not his heir and that his brothers and sisters of the whole and half blood are, because the estate is one of inheritance and should go to those brothers and sisters of the same blood as that of the ancestor

Sac & Fox – Shawnee Estates
1885-1910 Volume I

through whom the estate is derived. The view of the Indian Office is that said 7th paragraph is intended to meet a situation where the deceased child of the deceased ancestor has half brothers and half sisters on the parent's side through whom the estate is not derived.

In this case Harry Hall, father of Rufus Hall, survived him and also survived Eudora Hall, his wife and Rufus Hall's mother, and afterwards married Jennie Hall who survived him, but left no children. Without this paragraph had Harry Hall been the father of other children by Jennie Hall they would have inherited as half brothers or sisters of Rufus Hall. The 4th paragraph is as follows: "If decedent leave no issue, nor husband nor wife, the estate must go to the father". In other words the 7th paragraph quoted is only supplemental to and explanatory of paragraph 12, in reference to kindred of the half and whole blood. However, if the purchaser is satisfied with a deed from the parties you have named and the parties deeding are satisfied with the compensation divided as you have divided it, there can be no valid objection raised hereto such a transfer.

Very respectfully,

AC Tonner
Acting Commissioner.

(M.G.) P.

Refer in reply to the following:
Land.
42309 -1904.

Department of the Interior.
OFFICE OF INDIAN AFFAIRS
Washington,   July 9, 1904.

W. C. Kohlenberg, Esq.,
   Superintendent Indian School,
      Sac and Fox Agency, Oklahoma.

Sir:

This office is in receipt of your communication of June 22, 1904, in which you enclose a letter from A. B. Ward of Tecumseh, Oklahoma, relative to the allotment of F.V. Powers, Sac and Fox allottee No. 548.

You state that as near as you are able to determine, F.V. Powers was a white woman now dead, and that the Indians who are familiar with her history informed you that she left no heirs, but that before her death she made a will, leaving her allotment to Mary Clothier (Barnes), but you are doubtful as to the validity of such will. Mary Barnes is living upon and receiving the benefits of the land. You are of the opinion that under the laws, of Oklahoma, the allotment would go to the Territory, the decedent having no heirs surviving her. You also state that there is on deposit with

Sac & Fox – Shawnee Estates
1885-1910 Volume I

the assistant treasurer at St. Louis $295.00 to the credit of "F.V. Powers' heirs", which was derived from rental of the land, $150.00, and from railroad right of way, $135.00. Since there are no heirs you are unable to determine to whom the amount should be paid and ask as to the proper disposition to be made of the allotment and the funds on deposit to her credit.

In reply you are advised that under date of October 26, 1899 this office addressed a communication to Lee Patrick, then United States Indian Agent in charge of the Sac and Fox Agency, in reply to a communication from Moses Keokuk, chairman and Charles Keokuk, secretary of the Sac and Fox Council, dated October 13, 1899 as to the inheritance of this allotment.

In said letter it was stated that Jennie V. Powers several years before allotments were made, adopted by Indian custom two white children, and two half blood Sac and Fox children, to wit: Frank W. Hamblin and his sister, Mrs. Johnson, (whites), and Gilbert White and Mary Barnes (nee Clothier) half bloods, and by will recognized them as her heirs, giving to the two males money, proceeds of her personal property, and to the females her allotment. The council requested a decision as to the rights of these adopted children, principally the half bloods in and to the said allotment, as in case they could not inherit, it would, by the laws of Oklahoma revert to the territory. Agent Patrick was advised that as the adoption of the children appeared to have been had before the Sac and Fox Indians became citizens of the United States, it was advisable that said adoption take place before the passage of section 3571 of the statutes of Oklahoma, 1893, in which case it might be that adoption according to the Indian custom was valid, but that this was a question that could be determined by a proper court alone.

He was further advised that in case there were no legal heirs of Jennie V. Powers in existence, the land would escheat to the territory, but that such fact would have to be determined by proper judicial proceedings to be instituted by the proper authorities of the territory. He was also advised that in the meantime the land might be leased and the proceeds retained to be disposed or as the court might thereafter determine.

Under date of September 30, 1901, the Department returned to this office certain papers in connection with a contest against the allotment of Mrs. Powers made by Albert McPherson, together with a report dated September 24, 1901, from Inspector Cyrus Beede, to whom the matter had been referred by the Department.

The Inspector reported that Mrs. Powers remained a member of the Sac and Fox tribe from the date of her adoption in Kansas until her death. The Acting Secretary in transmitting the papers remarked that Keokuk's affidavit which accompanied the Inspector's report showed that the Sac and Fox Council in considering the matter of Mrs. Powers[sic] heirs decided that the property could descend to the two children of Mr. and Mrs. Powers and to a niece and nephew of George Powers.

Sac & Fox – Shawnee Estates
1885-1910 Volume I

As stated by you, the will of Mrs. Powers so far as the same relates to the allotment is void and of no effect. It would however pass personal property if properly made and executed.

It is suggested that Mrs. Barnes or one of the other parties interested should apply for letters of administration on the estate of Mrs. Powers with a view of determining to whom the rents and others moneys to the credit of Mrs. Powers belongs. The county attorney should also be notified of the situation in order that he may look into the matter and bring suit for the allotment as the property of the Territory of Oklahoma, if in his opinion, after investigation, the facts warrant such proceedings.

Very respectfully,
AC Tonner
Acting Commissioner.

J.F.A-L.M.

****

ROY HOFFMAN　　　　　　　　JOHN EMBRY
HOFFMAN & EMBRY
ATTORNEYS AND COUNSELORS AT LAW.
CHANDLER, OKLA.

8-13-1904

Hon. W. C. Kohlenberg,
　　Special Disbursing Agt.,
　　　　Sac and Fox, O.T.

Friend Kohlenberg:-
　　　　Pursuant to my phone conversation Miss Clark, our stenographer, accompanying Mrs. Barnes, will call on you today for the payment of the lease and right of way money in the Mrs. Powers estate. I am taking the future disposition of this estate up in the Probate court along the lines of the letter of which you so kindly gave me a coy and will call on the county attorney in your name as the letter advises, asking him to appear and represent the interests of the territory. This matter has been much mixed up and I want to get it determined one way or the other by the proper tribunal in accordance with the suggestion of the Department.

Thanking you for the courtesy shown, I am,

Very truly,
Roy Hoffman

****

Sac & Fox – Shawnee Estates
1885-1910 Volume I

The UNITED STATES,
To May Barnes, administratrix of the estate of F. V. Powers *Dr.*

DATE			DOLLARS	CTS
1904				
August	13	To Individual Indian Money		
		unapproved lease 117.50		
		" " 42.50		
		R.R.Right of way 135.00	295	00

Letters of Administration with original

RECEIVED, at Sac and Fox Agency, Oklahoma   August 13, 1904   , 190 ,
of W. C. KOHLENBERG   Two Hundred Ninety Five ($295.00) & 00/100   dollars,
Supt. & Spl. Disb Agent
in full of the above account.

* *Witness:* Lucy Clark
* *Witness:* Mary Antoine

May Barnes
Administratrix of the estate of F.V. Powers

I certify, on honor, that the above account is correct and just, and that I have actually, this 13th day of August, 1904 , *190* paid the amount thereof.

W.C.Kohlenberg
Supt. & Spl. Disb Agt.

NOTES.— All vouchers must show a sufficient explanation of the objects and necessity of the expenditure, and be made in triplicate. The dates, rates, and places at which services were rendered must, in all cases, be stated.

* All signatures by mark must be witnessed by two witnesses.

****

Sac & Fox – Shawnee Estates
1885-1910 Volume I

TRIPLICATE.

C A S H.

VOUCHER No. 9
INDIVIDUAL INDIAN MONEY.

First Quarter, 1905

May Barnes
Administratrix of Estate of
$ 295⁰⁰ F.V. Powers

Paid in or by Check No. 366549

DRAWN ON

U. S.,
St. Louis, Missouri

IN FAVOR OF
May Barnes

Adm. of Estate of F.V. Powers

State whether paid in cash or by check; if by check, give the number and date of the check and the name of the bank or institution upon which and in whose favor it is drawn.

Section 297 Regulations of Indian Department 1894.

Any disbursing or other officer of the United States or other person who shall knowingly present, or cause to be presented, any voucher, account, or claim to any officer of the United States for approval or payment, or for the pur-pose of securing a credit in any account with the United States, relating to any matter pertaining to the Indian Service, which shall contain any material misrepresentation of fact in regard to the amount due or paid, the name or character of the article furnished or received, or of the service rendered, or to the date of purchase, delivery, or performance of service, or in any other particular, shall not be entitled to payment or credit for any part of said voucher, account, or claim; and if any such credit shall be fiven or received, or payment made, the United States may recharge the same to the officer or person receiving the credit or payment and recover the amount from either or both, in the same manner as other debts due the United States are collected; PROVIDED, That where an account contains more than one voucher the foregoing shall apply only to such vouchers as contain the misrepresentation; AND PROVIDED FURTHER, That the officers and persons by and between whom the business is transacted shall be presumed to know the facts in relation to the matter set forth in the voucher, account, or claim; AND PROVIDED FURTHER, That the foregoing shall be in addition to the penalties now prescribed by law, and in no way to affect proceedings under existing law for like offenses. That, where practicable, this section shall be printed on the blank forms of vouchers provided for general use. (Act March 1, 1883 § 8, 22 Stat., 451; Ace July 4, 1884, § 8; Cir. 113 Ind. O.)

DEPARTMENT OF THE INTERIOR
UNITED STATES INDIAN SERVICE.

SAC AND FOX AGENCY, IOWA.
Toledo, August 23, 1904.

Hon. W. C. Kohlenberg,
    Supt. & Spl. Dis. Agt.
        Sac and Fox Agency, Okla.

Sir:-

Sac & Fox – Shawnee Estates
1885-1910 Volume I

Cha-ka-ta-co-see, husband of Qua-che-we, was in my office yesterday, and requested me to write you concerning the estate of Ah-ko-see, deceased. She claims that Ah-ko-see was a brother of the father of Qua-che-we, and she wants to know if Ah-ko-see had direct heirs, who would of course have prior claim to his estate. Please inform me as to the status of the case.

        Very respectfully,
           Wm G. Malin
           Supt. &. Spl. Dis. Agt.

Refer in reply to the following:
Land.
55416-1904.

Department of the Interior.
OFFICE OF INDIAN AFFAIRS
W<small>ASHINGTON</small>, September 1, 1904.

W. C. Kohlenberg, Esq.,
 Superintendent Sac and Fox Indian School,
  Sac and Fox Agency, Oklahoma.

Sir:
 This is to acknowledge receipt of your letter of August 10th. You transmit a deed from the heirs of Lucille Ingalls, deceased Sac and Fox allottee No. 336 to H. P. Carpenter. With these papers you transmit a copy of the court procedure showing that the court holds that the mother does not share the interest of the deceased child, which was inherited from the father. In this case the mother, being Mattie Ingalls does not inherit from her son, William Ingalls the 1/6 interest of the original allotment which the said William inherited from his father, but she does inherit part of the interest the said William inherited from his aunt Bessie. To this however the office cannot agree. If the mother is entitled to inherit 1/2 of the portion of William's estate derived from his aunt, Bessie Ingalls, she is clearly entitled to inherit 1/2 of the interest he derived from his father, the estate all coming from his grandmother on his father's side.
 The decision of the court increases the amount of money which the guardian will have in his hands, but according to the view entertained here, it does so at the expense of the mother. The deed will not be recommended for approval unless it can be shown that a like question has been decided upon appeal from some probate court of Oklahoma.

        Very respectfully,
          W.A. Jones
MG:LM   Commissioner.

Sac & Fox – Shawnee Estates
1885-1910 Volume I

Department of the Interior.

Refer in reply to the following:
Land.
57495-1904.

OFFICE OF INDIAN AFFAIRS
WASHINGTON, September 9, 1904.

W. C. Kohlenberg, Esq.,
    Superintendent Indian School,
        Sac and Fox Agency, Oklahoma.

Sir:

    There is enclosed herewith a copy of a communication dated August 19, 1904, from Superintendent O. C. Edwards of the Kickapoo Training School, Horton, Kansas, concerning the estate of Henry Davis or Henry Sha-quin consisting of a tract of land on the Sac and Fox Reservation in Kansas described as Lots 3 and 4 and the SW/4 of Sec. 10, T. 1, R. 17, in which the heirs of Moses Keokuk now residing within the Sac and Fox Agency Oklahoma claim an interest. There are also forwarded herewith the enclosures of said letter.

    You are requested to examine the same and make further report to this office concerning the claim of the heirs of Moses Keokuk. The deed covering the land in controversy will be held in this office pending the receipt of your report. You will please return the communication and its enclosures with your report.

                      Very respectfully,
                      W.A. Jones
CFH:E   Commissioner.

DEPARTMENT OF THE INTERIOR
UNITED STATES INDIAN SERVICE.

Winnebago, Nebraska, October 20, 1904.

W. C. Kohlenberg,
    Sup't. & Sp'l. Disb. Agent.
        Stroud, Oklahoma.

Sir:-

    I am requested by Frank Ewing, a Winnebago Indian, to inquire of you concerning certain land in which he thinks he has an interest. The land in question he states is the allotment of his aunt, sister of his father, and is on your reservation. The aunt's name was Black Hawk Woman, and she was the wife of John Ford. Ewing

Sac & Fox – Shawnee Estates
1885-1910 Volume I

states that he has been informed the land has been sold by Ford and wishes to inquire if this is correct.

       Very respectfully,

TS   Sup't & Sp'l Disb. Agent.

Refer in reply to the following:
LAND.
684507-1904.

Department of the Interior.

OFFICE OF INDIAN AFFAIRS
    W<small>ASHINGTON</small>, December 9, 1904.

W. C. Kohlenberg, Esq.,
 Superintendent Indian School,
  Sac and Fox Agency, Oklahoma.

Sir:

 There is enclosed herewith a communication dated November 29, 1904 from Levi W. Jones. He complains concerning the action taken in the matter of dividing the allotment made to Henry Jones, deceased. He asserts that the widow received much the bet of the division and that the minor heir was thereby injured. He makes some other allegations to the effect that the division was made in order that a creditor of the widow and also of the guardian of the minor child should be benefitted. He asserts that this creditor has purchased the land and that it was paid for prior to the sale and intimates that the transaction is bad.

 You will please report upon the statements made, returning the enclosure with your reply.

        Very respectfully,
        AC Tonner
M.G.-L.M.   Acting Commissioner.

Sac & Fox – Shawnee Estates
1885-1910 Volume I

Refer in reply to the following:
Land.
88814-1904.
88816- "
2414-05

Department of the Interior.

OFFICE OF INDIAN AFFAIRS

WASHINGTON, January 19, 1905.

W. C. Kohlenberg, Esq.,
   Superintendent Sac and Fox School,
      Sac and Fox Agency, Oklahoma.

Sir:

    Under date of January 9, 1905, the Acting Secretary of the Interior approved the conveyance of the following inherited Indian lands, the deeds and relative papers of which you transmitted to this office December 16, 1904.

    Deed dated November 14, 1904, from Mary Miller Gokey and Paul Gokey, her husband, as heirs of Henry Miller, deceased Sac and Fox allottee 325, conveying to Lee Patrick of Stroud, Oklahoma for $1354.00, the S/2 of the SE/4 Sec. 3, T. 11 SN., R. 5 E., containing 80 acres. The consideration is attached to the deed and is in the form of a certificate of deposit o the Stroud State Bank, dated November 25, 1904, for $1354.00 This is payable to the Commissioner or Indian Affairs and is now endorsed for deposit account of the grantor.

    The affidavit of the business committee states that Mary Miller Gokey and her daughter, Ruth Gokey, are the sole heirs of Henry Miller, deceased, while all of the proceedings relative to the partition of the land, including the decree of the court giving Mary Miller Gokey as her share of the estate the entire interest in the S/2 of the SE/4 Sec 3, T. 112 N., R. 5 E., refer to the daughter as Ida Miller. It is presumed that Ruth Miller and Ida Miller are one and the same person. If they are not, the deed should not have been approved and is not to be delivered, as the proceedings of the court would be void and further action necessary. Kindly advise the office in regard to this matter.

    Deed dated November 28, 1904, from Thomas Penashe as the sole heir of Ida White, deceased Sac and Fox allottee 327, conveing[sic] to Lee Patrick of Stroud, Oklahoma, for $2000.00, lots 3 and 4 and the S/2 of the NW/4 Sec 2, T. 13 N., R. 6 E., containing 158.31 acres. The consideration is attached to the deed and is in the form of a certificate of deposit from the Stroud State Bank for $2000.00 dated December 13, 1904. This is payable to the Commissioner of Indian Affairs and is now endorsed for deposit account of the grantor.

    You will dispose of the consideration and deeds in accordance with the amended rules, approved September 19, 1904, and the instructions contained in the letter transmitting the same, dated September 30, 1904. Forward to this office the notice

Sac & Fox – Shawnee Estates
1885-1910 Volume I

received from the bank showing collection, and a receipt for the deeds. A copy of the former should be retained in the Agency files.

        Very respectfully,
            C F Larrabee
            Acting Commissioner.

RMS
C

****

        Sac and Fox Agency, Okla.
          February 6th, 1905

Received of W.C. Kohlenberg Supt & Spl Disb Agent a warranty deed dated November 28th, 1904 given by the heir of Ida White to myself conveying Lots 3 & 4 and the S/2 of the NW/4 of Sec. 2 Twp 13 Range 6 E.
Consideration $ 2000.00   Lee Patrick

****

        Sac and Fox Agency, Okla.
          February 6th, 1905

Received of W.C. Kohlenberg Supt & Spl Disb Agent a warranty deed dated November 14th, 1904 given by the heirs of Henry Miller to myself conveying the S/2 of the SE/4 of Section 3 Twp 11 N. R. 5 E.
Consideration $ 1354.00   Lee Patrick

Refer in reply to the following:
Land.
3205-1905.

Department of the Interior.

   OFFICE OF INDIAN AFFAIRS
     W<small>ASHINGTON</small>, January 19, 1905.

W. C. Kohlenberg, Esq.,
  Superintendent Sac and Fox Agency,
    Sac and Fox Agency, Oklahoma.

Sac & Fox – Shawnee Estates
1885-1910 Volume I

Sir:

I herewith transmit a copy of the decree of the Probate Court of Lincoln County, Oklahoma, in the case as to the heirs of James Black, deceased Sac and Fox allottee 213. This decree gives the heirs as Benjamin Franklin, William Parkinson, Tom Pe-na-she, Amos Black, Leona Franklin, Stephen Harrison, and Paul Randell, while the deed shows that Benjamin Franklin is the husband of Leona Franklin, but not an heir, and states the heirs as follows: William Parkinson and wife, Benjamin Harrison and wife, Tom Pe-na-she and wife, Amos Black and wife, Leona Franklin and wife[sic], Stephen Harrison, and Paul Randell. As presumably there is an error in the decree and Benjamin Franklin, William Parkinson, etc., should read Benjamin Harrison, William Parkinson, etc., it is requested that the papers be corrected and returned to this office at your earliest convenience.

Very respectfully,

RMS
C F Larrabee
Acting Commissioner.

Winnebago Agency, Neb.
Feb. 10, 1905

Mr. W. C. Kohlenberg
    Supt & Sp'l Disb Agent
    Sac and Fox Agency, O.T.
Sir:

Rec'd your letter dated Jan. 23, and contents noted.

Please let me know what Fannie Gilbert a Winnebago Indian woman has said to you relative to that heirship money, which an Iowa man told us about last summer. My aunt (Nee-pash-nee-win-kar) Winnebago pronunciation, etc. married an Iowa man over twenty years ago but as I am not very old, I could not tell you the Iowa man's name.

My aunt's brother Blackhawk also died there while visiting at her house.

This Nee-pash-nee-win-kar is my own aunt. Fannie Gilbert, who is trying to claim to be the sole heir is my own first cousin, as our fathers twere[sic] brothers. If this said Winnebago woman has left any property (land) and if it is sold, please let me know. An Iowa man told me so last summer.

As I desire to get my share of the said money I ms'r[sic] to send you an affidavit stating I am - Nee-pash-nee-win-kar's niece, etc, if there is such money held by you to pay to her relatives.

I could not say what her name was down there but Mr. Kohlenberg you can easily make inquiries or it will be recorded in the office. Please let me hear from you at once, and let me know what her name is down at Iowa Agency.

Sac & Fox – Shawnee Estates
1885-1910 Volume I

Very Respectfully,
Judith Gilbert

****

Winnebago Agency, Neb.
Feb. 14, 1905

W. C. Kohlenberg
Sac and Fox Agency, O.T.

Sir:-
I will write to you again today. My aunt was called "Blackhawk Woman", and it seems as though she had an allotment down there. She died and her "Iowa" husband sold the land for $3800, and the agent asked if she had any heirs living among the Winnebago's. So one Iowa man rose up in the crowd before quite a number of Iowas and said "Blackhawk Woman" had heirs living here etc.

So now Mr. Kohlenberg if this is the case, I wish to know the facts from you so I may put in my claim.

Please let me hear from you at once, and advise me in the matter have to proceed in this case in order to get my share of said money

Very Resp'tfully
Judith Gilbert

****

Winnebago Agency, Neb.
Jan 16, 1905

To the Agent
Iowa Agency
Okla.

Sir:-
Fannie Gilbert a member of this Winnebago tribe has gone to get heirship money left by a Winnebago woman, who had been married into the Iowa tribe for over thirty years. She died and left no children.

I am a cousin of Fannie Gilbert's, our fathers were first cousins (their parents) were our brothers so we are descended from the same people. I Fannie is to draw this money please look into the matter before you pay her a cent for I don't like to be left out as I am heir to said money if there is such money coming to this deceased Winnebago woman's heirs, etc.

Please let me hear from you at once and don't –pay Fannie Gilbert any of that money unless it is probated etc.

Sac & Fox – Shawnee Estates
1885-1910 Volume I

Very Respectfully,
Judith Gilbert

Refer in reply to the following:
Land.
17,942-1905.

Department of the Interior.
OFFICE OF INDIAN AFFAIRS
WASHINGTON,

March 13, 1905.

W.C. Kohlenberg, Esq.,
  Superintendent in charge,
    Sac and Fox Agency and School,
      Oklahoma.

RECEIVED
MAR 17 1905
SAC & FOX AGENCY,
OKLAHOMA.

Sir:

    Referring to your communication dated February 15, 1905, inviting the attention of this Office to the claims of Jennie and Farrah Roubideaux to an interest in the estate of Sarah Roubideaux, deceased, which said estate is located in the State of Kansas, and was sold to W.A. Margrave, for $4700, you are advised that this Office upon receipt of your said communication, forwarded the same to Superintendent O.C. Edwards, having charge of the Iowa Reservation, in Kansas, for report relative to the matter.

    Reporting under date of March 3, 1905, Superintendent Edwards states as follows:

> "I have the honor to acknowledge the receipt of Office letter 'Land-13828-1905' dated February 23, 1905, inclosing communication from W.C. Kohlenberg, Supt. and Spl. Disb. Agent of the Sac and Fox Agency, Oklahoma, dated February 15, 1905, requiring immediate report.
>
> I would respectfully say that the delay in making immediate answer has occasioned by the fact that I was away at White Cloud, Kansas, under orders of Special Agent W.L. Miller relative to investigating certain charges made against me by George Nuzum.
>
> I learned of these other so-called heirs to the Sarah Roubidoux estate sometime since but after the payment of the $4700 to Joseph, Antoine, and Maggie Roubideaux. My information is this, that the father of these children, Joseph, Antoine, and Maggie Roubideaux[sic], was married Indian fashion to a Sauk woman and to an Iowa woman;

that some Agent several years ago, before his death, required that he should take one or the other of these women as his legal wife; that he selected the Sauk woman. If this be true, it would appear that these other children have no legal right as heirs. Farrah Roubidoux came to my office some time last fall and laid the matter before me. I told him[sic] that if there was any way in which I could help him I would be glad to do so. Mr. Margrave told me at that time that he was willing to pay them some to satisfy them rather than to go into law over the matter, no amount was mentioned and I have no knowledge of any amount having been paid. I am writing to Mr. Margrave this date requesting him to inform me as to what amounts if any, he has paid to these other heirs and will forward his answer thereto as soon as received."

The Office makes no comment with respect to the conclusions reached by Mr. Edwards as to the interests of Jennie and Farrah Roubideaux in the estate. According to their statement, as set forth in your report of February 15, 1905, they are entitled to share equally with Joseph, Antoine and Maggie Roubideaux. Their claim, therefore, would be for a one-fifth interest each, in and to the estate, or the proceeds derived from the sale thereof. The estate sold for $4700, and each of their interests would be of the value of $940. It would further appear from the fact that the purchaser, W.A. Margrave, has paid them some money in consideration of which they executed certain instruments, presumably quit-claim deeds, that there is some foundation to their claim. It is suggested that you advise these heirs in Oklahoma to place their claims in the hands of some reputable attorney with the purpose in view of having the claims adjusted by the purchaser, Mr. Margrave, and the other heirs residing in Kansas.

In selecting an attorney for these claimants, you should exercise great care in securing one who will not demand exorbitant fees and who bears a good reputation for honesty in dealing with Indians. It is thought the fee should be a contingent one, and agreed upon prior to the employment of the attorney.

Very respectfully,
C F Larrabee
Acting Commissioner.

(C.F.H.) P.

Sac & Fox – Shawnee Estates
1885-1910 Volume I

Refer in reply to the following:
Land.
14279-1905.

Department of the Interior.

OFFICE OF INDIAN AFFAIRS

WASHINGTON, March 23, 1905.

RECEIVED
MAR 27 1905
SAC & FOX AGENCY,
OKLAHOMA.

W. C. Kohlenberg, Esq.,
   Superintendent of Indian School,
      Sac and Fox Agency, Oklahoma.

Sir:

    With your letter of February 17, 1905, you transmitted, with other accounts, a statement presented by P. S. Hoffman, legal guardian of Junitta Davis, of the court costs amounting to $33.75, and the attorney fee amounting to $100.00 making a total of $133.75. You state that this allotment had been sold, court proceeding had, and the deed disapproved once before, and that Junitta Davis also has another allotment, in which she was the sole heir, which was sold twice and the deed disapproved both times; that there have been practically proceedings on four tracts, while she is charged with but one and you believe the attorney fees of $100.00 in proceedings of the single tract of land are excessive, and are more than the amounts allowed in Payne County, but in view of the fact that he received no compensation for the proceedings in the three other deeds disapproved, you recommend that this be allowed.

    You are advised that the Department has ruled that $25.00 is a reasonable attorney fee for any ordinary case of probate proceedings. The fact that the attorney has rendered services in other cases where the deeds were not approved does not justify charging the whole amount in this one case. It is presumed where the deeds have heretofore been disapproved that the land will eventually be sold and the attorney will be allowed his reasonable fee at such time.

    You also present the amount of John Foster, legal guardian in the estate of Frank Falk Springer, amounting to $43.85, court costs, and $50.00, attorney fee, making a total of $93.85. Referring to the voucher for the costs in the Probate Court, there appears an item for publication notice, hearing petition for approval $3.75, and publication notice of sale $7.00, making a total of $10.75, which seems to be an unusual and unnecessary charge, as in other cases no such items have been charged. Unless the guardian can show some ruling of the court requiring this item of expense, it can not be allowed. The attorney fee of $50.00 for probating is also considered excessive, and only $25.00 will be allowed in this case.

    Your attention is also called to the fact that the Secretary has ruled that all costs in probating a case should be charged up to all of the heirs in proportion to their respective shares in the estate. Therefore, you are directed to apportion the costs in these two cases to the several heirs and not charge the whole account to the minor heirs.

You will take up these matters with the legal guardians and advise them of the rulings of the Department in regard to the amount of attorney fee allowed. You will also present a statement showing the amount of the costs to be allowed that is to be charged to each of the heirs in these cases.

Very respectfully,
C F Larrabee
Acting Commissioner.

TBW-WDW

March 24, 1905

Received of W. C. Kohlenberg, Supt. & Spl. Disb. Agent, certified check for 801\underline{50}$ deposited with my successful bid on SW^4 Sec 23-18-6 E

[Name Illegible]

****

601$\underline{00}$ Dec 5 4   12-5-04

Six hundred one and 00/100
601$\underline{00}$

SW^4 23-18-6

Albert Kenworthy

SUPPLEMENT TO PETITION OF HEIRS, FLORA DAVIS (MC,CLELLAN[sic])
Dated Sept. 5th, 1904.

In event of the sale of the allotment of Flora Davis, SW/4 Sec. 23-18-6 E., advertised to be sold December 5th, 1904, we, the undersigned sole and only heirs of the said Flora Davis, deceased, do hereby agree that the consideration received therefor shall be deposited to our respective credits in the correct proportionate amounte[sic] with some United States depository subject to our checks not in excess of $10.00 per month after the same has first been approved by the Supt & Spl Disb Agent of Sac and Fox Agency, Okla., and in excess of $10.00 per month only upon special authority of the Commissioner of Indian Affairs when it is shown that the

Sac & Fox – Shawnee Estates
1885-1910 Volume I

money will be used judiciously for that we are capable of taking proper care of the same and we fully agree to the conditions stipulated in the Amendment to Section I, approved Sept., 19, 1904 to the Amended rules for the conveyance of Inherited Indian land approved Oct. 4, 1902.

Witnesses
  WC Kohlenberg
  Horace Guffin

              his
Frank Davis x mark
John Foster
Legal guardian

      I hereby certify that I have explained the nature of the above agreement to the parties thereto and am satisfied that they understand the purport of the same fully.

Dated at Sac and Fox Agency, Okla.
     Nov. 10   1904

           WC Kohlenberg
           Supt & Spl Disb Agent

                        Mar 24 1905
     Received of W. C. Kohlenberg Supt. & Spl. Disb. Agt., at Sac and Fox Agency, Oklahoma, a warranty deed from the heir of Anna Senache to W. J. Riggs, for the N/2 of the SE/4 and the S/2 of the NE/4 of Section 22 township 14, north of range 6 E.
Consideration $1340.00   W. J. Riggs

          ****

                        Mar 24 1905.
     Received of W. C. Kohlenberg Supt. & Spl. Disb. Agt., at Sac and Fox Agency, Oklahoma, a warranty deed from the heirs of Moses McKosito to Harry Mead for the SE/4 of section 6-11-5 E., for the consideration of $1850.00.
                                 Harry Mead

          ****

Sac & Fox – Shawnee Estates
1885-1910 Volume I

Department of the Interior.

OFFICE OF INDIAN AFFAIRS

WASHINGTON, March 18, 1905.

Refer in reply to the following:
Land.
15606-1905.

RECEIVED
MAR 23 1905
SAC & FOX AGENCY,
OKLAHOMA.

W. C. Kohlenberg, Esq.,
    Superintendent Sac and Fox Indian School,
        Sac and Fox Agency, Oklahoma.

Sir:

    Under date of February 24, 1905, the Acting Secretary of the Interior approved the conveyance of two tracts of land, the deeds and accompanying papers of which were transmitted by you for the consideration of the Department, February 9, 1905, and are described as follows:

    Deed dated September 12, 1904, from Leo Walker, Ben Walker, Guy Walker, Chief McKosito, as legal guardian of Ira Walker, and Edgar Mack as legal guardian of Elmer Walker, as sole heirs of Moses McKosito, a deceased Sac and Fox allottee, to Harry Mead of Shawnee, Oklahoma, conveying for $1850.00, the SE/4 of Sec. 6, T. 11 N., R. 5 E., containing 160 acres. The consideration is attached to the deed and is in the form of certificate of deposit No. 2568 from the Oklahoma National Bank of Shawnee, Oklahoma, payable to the Commissioner of Indian Affairs and now endorsed for deposit account of the grantors.

    Deed dated October 17, 1904, from Wiley Uribes and wife as sole heir of Anna Senoche, a deceased Sac and Fox allottee, to W. J. Riggs of Shawnee, Oklahoma, conveying for $1340.00, the N/2 of the SE/4 and the S/2 of the NE/4 of Sec. 22, T. 14 N., R. 6 E., containing 160 acres. The consideration is attached to the deed and is in the form of certificate of deposit No. 1619, from the First National Bank of Shawnee, Oklahoma, which is payable to W. J. Riggs and endorsed to the Commissioner of Indian Affairs, and is now prepared for deposit account of the grantor.

    You will dispose of the deeds and the considerations in accordance with the amended rules approved September 19, 1904, and the instructions contained in the letter transmitting the same dated September 30, 1904. Forward to this office the receipts for the deeds and the notices received from the bank showing collection. A copy of the latter should be retained in the Agency files.

                Very respectfully,
                      C.F. Larrabee
                      Acting Commissioner.

RMS
  C

Sac & Fox – Shawnee Estates
1885-1910 Volume I

> Mar 24 1905.
> Received of W. C. Kohlenberg Supt. & Spl. Disb. Agt., at Sac and Fox Agency, Oklahoma, a warranty deed from the heirs of Rebecca McClellan to A. Grimm Jr., for the NE/4 of section 27-18-6 E, for the consideration of $1085.00
>
> A. Grimm Jr

****

Refer in reply to the following:
Land.
17123-1905.

Department of the Interior.

OFFICE OF INDIAN AFFAIRS

WASHINGTON, March 18, 1905.

RECEIVED
MAR 21 1905
SAC & FOX AGENCY,
OKLAHOMA.

W. C. Kohlenberg, Esq.,
    Superintendent Sac and Fox Indian School,
        Sac and Fox Agency, Oklahoma.

Sir:

    Under date of March 2, 1905, the Acting Secretary of the Interior approved a conveyance of inherited Indian land, the deed and accompanying papers of which were forwarded by you for the consideration of the Department September 8, 1904.

    This deed is dated July 5, 1905, from John McClellan and wife, Edward McClellan and wife, Frank Davis, and John Foster, legal guardian of Frank B. Davis and Harry Davis, as sole heirs of Rebecca McClellan, a deceased Sac and Fox allottee, to A. Grim[sic], Jr. of the Sac and Fox Agency, Oklahoma, conveying for $1035.00, the NW/4 of Sec. 27, T. 18 N., R. 6 E., containing 160 acres. The consideration is attached to the deed and is in the form of certificates of deposit No. 318, 319, 320 and 321, for $241.12, $120.56, $361.66 and $361.66, payable to the grantors of the deed, and you are instructed to obtain their endorsements and deposit the certificates in accordance with the amended rules. Authority is also hereby granted you to liquidate the costs of the Probate Court incurred in having the interest of the minor heirs probated, in accordance with the agreement forwarded by you January 24, 1905, whereby the adult heirs agree to pay their proportionate shares of the costs.

    You will dispose of the deed in accordance with the amended rules approved September 19, 1904, and the instructions contained in the letter transmitting the same dated September 30, 1904. Forward to this Office the receipt for the deed and the notice from the bank showing collection. A copy of the latter should be retained for the Agency files.

Sac & Fox – Shawnee Estates
1885-1910 Volume I

Very respectfully,
C.F. Larrabee
Acting Commissioner.

RMS
C

Department of the Interior.

Refer in reply to the following:
Land.
19541-1905.

OFFICE OF INDIAN AFFAIRS
WASHINGTON, March 28, 1905.

W. C. Kohlenberg, Esq.,
    Superintendent Indian School,
        Sac and Fox Agency, Oklahoma.

SAC & FOX AGENCY,
OKLAHOMA.

Sir:

    Having further reference to your communication dated October 3, 1904, concerning certain claimants in Oklahoma Territory to the estate of Moses Keokuk, deceased, and to your further communication dated December 28, 1904, with which you transmitted a copy of proceedings had in the probate court of Lincoln County, Oklahoma Territory, in the matter of the said estate, you are advised that a copy of the said proceedings was forwarded to Superintendent Edwards, of the Kickapoo Training School, Horton, Kansas, under date of January 13, 1905, and reply thereto was received from Superintendent Edwards under date of March 9, 1905, enclosing a communication received by him from James Falloon, the attorney representing the heirs of Moses Keokuk residing in the State of Kansas.

    Copies of this communication and its enclosure are herewith.

Very respectfully,
C.F. Larrabee
Acting Commissioner.

CFH-Ma

****

19541-1905   -Copy-

Hiawatha, Kansas, Feb. 3, 1905.

O. C. Edwards, Esq.,
    Germantown, Kans.

Sac & Fox – Shawnee Estates
1885-1910 Volume I

Dear Sir:

Mr. Margrave was in here day before yesterday and requested that I explain to you the status of that suit to quiet title to land in case of Wa-tha-tha, vs. Moses Keokuk and others. I think I explained this to you once before and perhaps the matter is not distinct to you at present. He also said that the authorities at Washington stated that Moses Keokuk had two years within which to open up the suit. The statute provides for three years, but makes provision that the party applying must file an affidavit stating that they had not sufficient notice prior to the judgment within which to appear and defend.

The agent down in the Territory, while the suit was pending, wrote to the clerk of the District Court, R. W. Hicks, and inquired of the status of the case. He could not have done this without some conversation with Moses Keokuk, and I think that Moses Keokuk had notice and went to the agent and made his representations. It would be well for you to get a certified copy of this letter from Mr. Hicks, and present it to the Secretary of the Interior or who ever has immediate charge of this matter, with a statement of what the law is in that respect. I think a certified copy of all the proceedings should be had for the Secretary, so as to show that the decree in our District Court is effectual to vest the title in Wa-tha-tha.

Yours truly,
Jas. Falloon.

****

19541-1905   -Copy-

DEPARTMENT OF THE INTERIOR,
United States Indian Service.
Kickapoo Training School,
Horton, Kansas, March 9, 1905.

Hon. Commissioner of Indian Affairs
Washington, D. C.

Sir:

I have the honor to respectfully reply to "Land 57493-1904, 69673-1904, 90231-1904, 336-11905", dated January 13, 1905 inclosing a copy of a decree of Probate Court in Lincoln County Oklahoma Territory in the matter of the estate of Moses

Sac & Fox – Shawnee Estates
1885-1910 Volume I

Keokuk deceased which appears to vest a title to the allotment of Shiquine in Moses Keokuk. Wa-so-sa who advertised this land as heir of Henry Shaquine resides near Tama, Iowa, she is quite old, does not understand English very well and probably has no means for presenting additional testimony in this matter. I inclose herewith a letter from Jas. Faloon[sic], attorney, to the suit had in Hiawatha, Kansas, to quite title to this land, he appears to believe that the matter is settled in favor of Wa-so-sa and that a copy of the records in the District Court would corroborate him.

       Very respectfully,
        O. C. Edwards,
       Supt. & Spl. Disb. Agent.

Refer in reply to the following: **Department of the Interior.**

Land.   OFFICE OF INDIAN AFFAIRS
21369-1905.   WASHINGTON, March 30, 1905.

W. C. Kohlenberg, Esq.,
 Superintendent Indian School,
  Sac and Fox Agency, Okla.

Sir:

 Having further reference to the subject matter of Office letter dated March 13, 1905, concerning the estate of Sarah Roubidoux, deceased, you are informed that the Office is in receipt of a more recent report from the Superintendent of the Kickapoo Training School, at Horton, Kansas, dated March 16, 1905, enclosing a letter from Mr. W. A. Margrave, the purchaser of the estate of Sarah Roubidoux, deceased. A copy of the said report and the Communication of Mr. Margrave are enclosed herewith for your further information.

       Very respectfully,
        C. F. Larrabee
        Acting Commissioner

CFH-Ma
      ****

21369-1905   -COPY-
   DEPARTMENT OF THE INTERIOR.
    United States Indian Service,
     Kickapoo Training School,
      Horton, Kansas. March 16, 1905.

Sac & Fox – Shawnee Estates
1885-1910 Volume I

Hon. Commissioner of Indian Affairs,
Washington, D.C.
Sir:-

I have the honor to further reply to "Land- 13828-1905" dated February 23, 1905, which I answered in part March 3, 1905, relative to communication from W.C. Kohlenberg, Supt. of the Sac and Fox Okla. school dated February 15, 1905 presenting the claims of certain Indians under his jurisdiction to an interest in the estate of Sarah Roubidoux deceased, which said estate is located under my jurisdiction and was recently sold to W.A. Margrave for $4700, the proceeds arising from said sale having been paid to Joseph, Antoine and Maggie Roubidoux as the sole heirs of the deceased allottee.

I enclose herewith reply of W.A. Margrave relative to having paid money on certain claims made by the Oklahoma claimants.

Very respectfully,
O.C. Edwards
Supt. & Spl. Disb. Agent.

****
-COPY-

21369-1905.

Reserve, Kans. March 7, 1905.

O.C. Edwards Supt.
Horton Kans.

Dear Sir:- I was well acquainted with Joe Roubidoux the Father of Joseph, Maggie, Antoine and Sarah Roubidoux.

Old Mr. Roubidoux lived here on the Sac and Fox of Mo. Reservation and raised the family above mentioned. He like the most of these Indians made frequent visits to the Indian Territory.

Since the Sarah Roubidoux allotment has been sold two people have appeared and claim to be children of the above Joe Roubidoux, which is a matter which I am not prepared to affirm or deny. I only know of my own knowledge acquired by a residence of forty years among these people that Joe Roubidoux lived with a Sac and Fox woman and raised the four children above mentioned. If he was ingaged[sic] in the same occupation during his trips to the Territory I cannot say. However to avoid trouble I have given $250.00 to each of these supposed heirs and they have given me a quit claim deed.

The above Five hundred dollars was paid in cash and I have their receipts for same.

Sac & Fox – Shawnee Estates
1885-1910 Volume I

Respectfully yours
W.A. Margrave

Refer in reply to the following:
Land.
30675-1905.

Department of the Interior.
OFFICE OF INDIAN AFFAIRS
WASHINGTON, April 26, 1905.

RECEIVED
SAC & FOX AGENCY, OKLAHOMA.

W. C. Kohlenberg, Esq.,
    Superintendent in charge,
        Sac and Fox Agency, Oklahoma.

Sir:

    This Office is in receipt of your letter of April 18, 1905, relative to the accounts presented by P. S. Hoffman, legal guardian of Junitta Davis, and also the accounts of John Foster, legal guardian of Frank Falk Springer.

    Referring to the accounts presented by Mr. Hoffman, you say the costs in this case will be $58.75, which is to be divided between Webster Smith and Junitta Davis; that in the estate of which John Foster is legal guardian, the costs amount to $58.10, and that the heirs to this tract of land are Julia Tohee, Millie Tohee, and Frank Falk Springer, each of whom should pay one-third of the costs.

    In accordance with your request you are hereby authorized to approve the check of Webster Smith for the sum of $29.87, and the check of P.S. Hoffman as legal guardian for Junitta Davis for the sum of $29.88. You are also authorized to approve the checks of Julia Tohee and Millie Tohee for $19.37 each, and the check of John Foster as legal guardian for Frank Falk Springer for the sum of $19.37.

Very respectfully,
CF Larrabee
Acting Commissioner.

TBW-WDW

REFER IN REPLY TO THE FOLLOWING:
Land.
69572-1905.

DEPARTMENT OF THE INTERIOR,
OFFICE OF INDIAN AFFAIRS,
WASHINGTON, October 4, 1905.

R
9 1905
SAC & FOX AGENCY, OKLAHOMA

W. C. Kohlenberg, Esq.,
    Supt. in Charge of Sac and Fox Agency,
        Oklahoma.

Sac & Fox – Shawnee Estates
1885-1910 Volume I

Sir:

You are hereby authorized to approve the checks of the several heirs of the Vetter estate, to the amount of $56.50 in proportion to their several shares in said estate, to pay the Probate Court costs and the attorney's fees in the matter of the guardianship of Mary, Fred and Lucy Vetter, minors interested in said estate, as requested and for the reasons stated in your letter of May 24, 1905.

       Very respectfully,
       CF Larrabee
       Acting Commissioner.

TBW-Y.

REFER IN REPLY TO THE FOLLOWING: **DEPARTMENT OF THE INTERIOR,**
Land.
97194 - 1905. **OFFICE OF INDIAN AFFAIRS,**
      WASHINGTON, December 8, 1905.

Superintendent in Charge,
 Sac and Fox Agency, O. T.

Sir:

In compliance with your request of December 2, 1905, you are hereby advised that Office letter of October 4, 1905, authorizing you to approve the check of certain parties to pay court costs is hereby revoked and authority granted you to approve the checks of Frank Davis, Frank B. Davis and Harry Davis, for the sum of $20.58 each, to pay the expense incurred in probating the estate, as set forth in the itemized statement which is returned herewith for file in your office.

       Very respectfully,
       C.F. Larrabee
       Acting Commissioner.

TBW-Y.

REFER IN REPLY TO THE FOLLOWING: **DEPARTMENT OF THE INTERIOR,**
Land.
33601-1905. **OFFICE OF INDIAN AFFAIRS,**
      WASHINGTON, August 10, 1905.

Sac & Fox – Shawnee Estates
1885-1910 Volume I

laW. C. Kohlenberg, Esq.,
Superintendent,
Sac and Fox Agency, O. T.

Sir:

In accordance with your request of April 26, 1905, you are hereby authorized to approve the checks of Birdie DeRoin and Nettie Whitewater, for the sum of $12.50 each, to pay the attorney's fee of J. Jensen, legal guardian for Nettie Whitewater, in having the estate probated.

Very respectfully,
C.F. Larrabee
Acting Commissioner.

TBW-Y.

SUPPLEMENT TO PETITION OF HEIRS, BETSEY MANSUR
Dated August 15th, 1904.

In event of the sale of the allotment of Betsey Mansur, NE/4 Sec. 35 18-8 E., advertised to be sole Nov. 14, 1904, we, the undersigned, sole and only heirs of the said Betsey Mansur, deceased, do hereby agree that the consideration received therefor shall be deposited to our respective credits in the correct proportionate amounts with some United States depository subject to our checks not in excess of $10.00 per month after the same has first been approved by the Supt & Spl Disb Agent at the Sac and Fox Agency, Okla., and in excess of $10.00 per month only upon special authority of the Commissioner of Indian Affairs when it is shown that the money will be used judiciously or that we are capable of taking proper care of the same and we fully agree to the conditions stipulated in the Amendment to Section I, approved Sept. 19, 1904 to the Amended rules for the conveyance of Inherited Indian land, approved Oct. 4, 1902.

Witnesses
   Harry L Elmslee
   Horace Guffin

$425.00 Frank Smith his x mark
159.31 Ida Mansur her x mark
John Foster
Legal guardian

I hereby certify that [sic] have explained the nature of the above agreement to the parties thereto and am satisfied that they understand the purport of the same fully.

W.C. Kohlenberg
Supt. & Spl Disb Agent

Dated at Sac and Fox Agency, Okla.
Nov 14 1904

Sac & Fox – Shawnee Estates
1885-1910 Volume I

****

May 4th **1905**
Received of WC Kohlenberg Supt & Spl Disb Agent
My Certificate for 212\frac{50}{}$ **Dollars**
For deposited with my bid on the NE/4 35 – 18 – 6 E
No. 44 Lee Patrick

Department of the Interior.

Refer in reply to the following:
Land.
27115-1905.

OFFICE OF INDIAN AFFAIRS
WASHINGTON, May 22, 1905.

RECEIVED

W. C. Kohlenberg, Esq.,
  Superintendent Sac and Fox Agency,
    Sac and Fox Agency,
      Oklahoma.

SAC & FOX AGENCY,
OKLAHOMA.

Sir:

Under date of April 8, 1905, the Acting Secretary of the Interior Secretary approved a deed to inherited Indian land dated March 13, 1904, from May Barnes (nee Cluthier) as the sole heir of F. V. Powers, a deceased Sac and Fox allottee, to Lucy Clark, of Chandler, Oklahoma, conveying for $2500.00, the SW/4 of the SW/4 of Sec. 11, the NW/4 of the NW/4 of Sec. 14, the NE/4 of the NE/4 of Sec. 15, and the SE/4 of the SE/4 of Sec. 10, all in T. 11 N., R. 4 E, containing 160 acres. The consideration is attached to the deed and is in the form of certificate of deposit No. 2059, from the Union National Bank of Chandler, Oklahoma Territory, which is payable to the Commissioner of Indian Affairs and is now endorsed for deposit account of the grantor.

You will dispose of the deed and the consideration in accordance with the amended rules, approved September 19, 1904, and the instructions contained in Office letter dated September 30, notifying you of their adoption. Forward to this Office the receipt for the deed and the notice from the bank showing deposit. A copy of the latter should be retained in the Agency files.

The deed should bear the date of March 13, 1905, instead of March 13, 1904, and you are requested to have the correction made and notify this Office immediately so a similar correction can be made on the records.

Sac & Fox – Shawnee Estates
1885-1910 Volume I

Very respectfully,
CF Larrabee
Acting Commissioner.

RMS

****

Chandler, Okla   June 6   1905

Received of W.C. Kohlenberg, Supt. & Spl. Disb. Agent at Sac and Fox Agency, Okla., warranty deed to SW/4 of SW/4 section 11; NW/4 of NW/4 of section 14; NE/4 of NE/4 of section 15; SE/4 of SE/4 of section 10—all in Township 12 Range 4 East., recently purchased by me for the consideration of $2500.00

Lucy Clark

****

M. L. TURNER
PRESIDENT

F. R. HOER
CASHIER

C. M. DUNWORTH
ASST. CASHIER

No. 5159

WESTERN NATIONAL BANK.

CAPITAL AND PROFITS $200,000.00   MA 30 1905

UNITED STATES DEPOSITORY

RECEIVED
SAC & FOX AGENCY,
OKLAHOMA.

Oklahoma City, Okla.   5/29/05

W. C. Kohlenberg, Supt. & S. D. A.,
  Sac and Fox Agency, O. T.

Dear Sir:
  In accordance with yours under date of May 26, we are today crediting your account as follows:

  MAY BARNES, $2,500.00.

Respectfully yours,   Copy
F. R. Hoer
Cashier.

REFER IN REPLY TO THE FOLLOWING

DEPARTMENT OF THE INTERIOR,
OFFICE OF INDIAN AFFAIRS,

LAND.
33599-1905.

WASHINGTON,   July 6, 1905.

W. C. Kohlenberg, Esq.,
  Superintendent Indian School,
    Sac and Fox Agency, Oklahoma.

Sac & Fox – Shawnee Estates
1885-1910 Volume I

Sir:

This Office is in receipt of your letter of April 26, 1905, enclosing the account of J. B. A. Robertson, attorney at law, for $150.00, for professional services rendered the heirs of James Black, deceased, in the suit against one Ah-na-wit.

In[sic] appears that this was an ex-parte suite, and that the sum charged for legal services rendered is exorbitant. From the information now at hand, the Office is of the opinion that $50.00 would be a reasonable fee for the services rendered, and until it is clearly shown that the matter was of greater importance than now appears, the Office will not approve the claim for more than $50.00, and you will so advise Mr. Robertson of this fact.

Very respectfully,
CF Larrabee
Acting Commissioner.

T.B.W.
LC . .[sic]

Copy to Western National
7-27-1905

REFER IN REPLY TO THE FOLLOWING:

DEPARTMENT OF THE INTERIOR,

Land.
46967 - 1905.

OFFICE OF INDIAN AFFAIRS,

WASHINGTON, July 22, 1905.

F. A. Thackery, Esq.,
Superintendent Shawnee School,
Shawnee, O. T.

Sir:

This office is in receipt of your letter of June 13, 1905, requesting that you be authorized to approve the checks of Se - so - tay - se, Nannie Bobb and Nah - so - pea - se, for $35 each. These parties are the heirs of Miles - se - so - tay - se, absentee Shawnee allottee No. 542, who, as such heirs, conveyed to W. A. Ruggles for $400 the S/2 of the NE/4 of Sec. 2, T. 9 N., R. 2 E.

In your application for authority you state that each of these parties are Indian women with families and are in very poor circumstances. They are full bloods and speak only in the Indian language but they are in urgent need of the amount named for clothing and subsistence.

In compliance with your recommendation you are hereby authorized to approve checks for $35 to each of said three heirs.

Sac & Fox – Shawnee Estates
1885-1910 Volume I

RFT-Y.

Very respectfully,
CF Larrabee
Acting Commissioner.

****

REFER IN REPLY TO THE FOLLOWING:

Land.
50271 - 1905.

Copy to Western National
7-27-1905
DEPARTMENT OF THE INTERIOR,
OFFICE OF INDIAN AFFAIRS,
WASHINGTON,   July 22, 1905.

F. A. Thackery, Esq.,
 Superintendent Shawnee School,
  Shawnee, O. T.

Sir:

In compliance with your recommendation of June 26, 1905, you are authorized to approve the check of Charley Bobb, one of the heirs of Miles - se - so - tay - se, Absentee Shawnee allottee No. 542, for $50, to be used by him in repairs and in making an addition to his house on his own allotment out of the consideration money arising from the sale of the land to W. A. Ruggles.

Very respectfully,
CF Larrabee
Acting Commissioner.

RFT-Y.

Shawnee, Pottawatomie County Oklahoma.

I, Frank A Thackery, Superintendant[sic] and Special Disbursing Agent, in charge of the Shawnee and Pottawatomie Agencies in Oklahoma Territory, do hereby certify that the records of my office show that a CERTIFICATE of ALLOTMENT, number 143 was issued to THOMAS GOODBOO, a member of the Citizens and of Pottawatomie Indians residing upon the " Thirty mile square tract " Reservation in the Indian Territory, in accordance with an Act of Congress approved May 23rd. 1872., that said Certificate of Allotment covered the following described land to-wit:-

The south half of the North-east quarter of section twenty-two (22) and the North-west quarter of the south-east quarter of said section twenty-two (22) all in

Sac & Fox – Shawnee Estates
1885-1910 Volume I

Township Ten (10) North, Range three (3) East of the I. M. in Pottawatomie County Oklahoma containing 119.70 acres, said Certificate being dated January 16th. 1895 and is the only Allotment Certificate, or patent, issued by the United States Government for the above described land.

The records of my office also show that, the above described land was sold and conveyed to L. N. Ogee, under the direction of the U. S. Indian Agent, Lee Patrick, and said sale approved by the Hon. Secretary of the Interior on May 29th. 1901 and said records also show that, prior to the approval of said [paper torn] to L. N. Ogee, said land was appraised by the Gover[paper torn] [sic]prasing official, and the amount of said [paper torn] said Government appraiser was $2500^{00} The recor[paper torn] office also show that the widow, Sophia Lafalier, fo[paper torn] Goodboo and the following named five children, Mary [paper torn] Frank, Josie and Thomas Goodboo, were the sole and [paper torn] ving heirs at law of the said Thomas Goodboo deceased [paper torn]

The record or evidence in this office of any will hav[paper torn] made or left, or any unpaid debts against the estate of the said Thomas Goodboo deceased that would in any way be liens against the real-estate above described. That so far as the records of this office show, the sale of said land to the said L. N. Ogee was in all respects regular, was conducted in accordance with the rules and regulations of the Department of the Interior and to my knowledge there is no claims[sic] of any character against the said estate.

Dated this ____ day of August, A. D. 1905.

Supt. and Spl. Disb. Agt.

REFER IN REPLY TO THE FOLLOWING: **DEPARTMENT OF THE INTERIOR,** R E C E I V E D

Land.   **OFFICE OF INDIAN AFFAIRS,**   SEP 1 1905

61624 - 1905.   WASHINGTON,   August 28, 1905 OX AGENCY, OKLAHOMA

W. C. Kohlenberg, Esq.,
    Superintendent Sac and Fox Agency,
        Oklahoma Ter.

Sir:
    This Office is in receipt of a letter from Annie Longshore, formerly Annie McKinney, dated at Sparks, O. T., August 1st, 1900, stating that Wilson McKinney died December 25th, 1904, and left six heirs, all of whom are of age; that these heirs

Sac & Fox – Shawnee Estates
1885-1910 Volume I

have divided the land, consisting of 320 acres, amicably among themselves, and desire some action taken to confirm their titles to the land.

You are requested to make an investigation of this matter to see whether or not all of the heirs have agreed upon the division of the land and whether or not such division is equitable, and if so, you will render them such assistance as may be necessary to make the required deeds. All of the heirs should join in deeds to each other, and when they have been properly executed, you will forward them to this Office for approval.

        Very respectfully,
        F. E. Leupp
TBW-Y.   Commissioner.

Sac & Fox – Shawnee Estates
1885-1910 Volume I

****

PLAT

SHOWING LOCATION OF PROPERTY IN QUESTION,
and
Manner of Division of the NE Quarter of

SECTION 35 and 36   TOWNSHIP 13 N   RANGE 4 E

with location of the different heirs own allotment

Tract No 1 goes to Martha Comalis
  " " 2 "   Mary Comalis
  " " 3 "   Lizzie McKinney
  " " 4 "   Lucy Chuyon
  " " 5 "   Anna Longshon
  " " 6 "   Aaron McKinney

[Copy of original plat]

224

Sac & Fox – Shawnee Estates
1885-1910 Volume I

10-7-1905

PLAT
SHOWING LOCATION OF PROPERTY IN QUESTION,
and
Names of Division of the NE Quarters of

SECTIONS 35 and 36   TOWNSHIP 13 N   RANGE 4 E
with the location of the different heirs own allotments

Inside Quadrant of Plat:
    Mary McKinney Connalis
    Anna McKinney Longshore
Lucy McKinney O'Brien
Lizzie McKinney
Martha McKinney Connalis

Bottom:
    Tract No. 1 goes to Martha Connalis
    " " 2 " " Mary Connalis
    " " 3 " " Lizzie McKinney
    " " 4 " " Lucy O'Brien
    " " 5 " " Anna Longshore
    " " 6 " " Aaron McKinney

Right Side:
    NE/4 Sec 36 is allotment of Wilson McKinney (deceased) #247
    NE/4 Sec 35 "   "   " Jefferson McKinney   "   #248
    Aaron McKinney's allotment located 30 miles from this locality

[Transcription of Plat on page 224]

****

Sac & Fox – Shawnee Estates
1885-1910 Volume I

☞ Acknowledgments must be in accordance with the forms prescribed by the State or Territory in which the land is situated.

Territory of Oklahoma
Sac and Fox Agency } ss:

Be it remembered, That on this 7th day of October, A.D. 190 5 before the undersigned, a Supt. & Spl. Dis. Agent in and for the Agency aforesaid, personally appeared Lizzie McKinney, a single person, Mary Connalis, Lucy O'Brien, Anna Longshore, Chas. Longshore, Aaron McKinney, Cedro Connalis and Daniel O'Brien, and Emma McKinney

to me personally known to be the identical persons who executed the within instrument of writing, and such persons duly acknowledged the execution of the same.

In testimony whereof, I have hereunto subscribed my name xxxxxxxxxxxx xxxx on the day and year last above written.

W.C. Kohlenberg
Supt. & Spl. Dis. Agent

****

☞ Acknowledgments must be in accordance with the forms prescribed by the State or Territory in which the land is situated.

Territory of Oklahoma
County of Lincoln } ss:

Be it remembered, That on this 7th day of October, A.D. 190 5 before the undersigned, a Notary Public in and for the County and aforesaid, personally appeared Lizzie McKinney, a single person, Mary Connalis, Lucy O'Brien, Anna Longshore, Chas. Longshore, Aaron McKinney, Cedro Connalis and Daniel O'Brien, and Emma McKinney

to me personally known to be the identical persons who executed the within instrument of writing, and such persons duly acknowledged the execution of the same.

In testimony whereof, I have hereunto subscribed my name xxxxxxxxxxxx xxxx on the day and year last above written.

N. Whitacre
Notary Public
My commission expires Mch. 3 1906

****

Sac & Fox – Shawnee Estates
1885-1910 Volume I

WARRANTY DEED

FROM

The Heirs of Wilson McKinney

....

....

TO

Martha Connalis

....

.....................OF.............................

....COUNTY.

This instrument was filed for record on the............day of....................., 190 at..............o'clock..........M., and duly recorded in Book..........., on page............

....
Register of Deeds.

Department of the Interior,

OFFICE OF INDIAN AFFAIRS,

..................................., 190

The within deed is respectfully submitted to the Secretary of the Interior, with the recommendation that it be approved.

Commissioner.

Department of the Interior,

..................................., 190

The within deed is hereby approved.

....
Secretary.

Office of Indian Affairs,

LAND DIVISION.

..................................., 190

Recorded in Deed Book, Inherited Indian Lands, Vol.   , page

****

Sac & Fox – Shawnee Estates
1885-1910 Volume I

INDIAN DEED INHERITED LANDS.

This Indenture, Made and entered into this 7th day of October one thousand nine hundred and five , by and between Anna Longshore and Chas. Longshore, her husband, Lucy O'Brien and Daniel O'Brien, her husband, Aaron McKinney and Emma McKinney, his wife, Martha Connalis and Joe Connalis her husband, and Lizzie McKinney,

of   Sac and Fox Agency, Oklahoma
heirs of   Wilson McKinney
deceased, a   Sac and Fox   Indian, part ies of the first part, and Mary Connalis of Sac and Fox Agency, Okla. , part y of the second part:

Witnesseth, That said part ies of the first part, for and in consideration of the sum of One -- dollars, in hand paid, the receipt of which is hereby acknowledged, do hereby grant, bargain, sell, and convey unto said part y of the second part the following described real estate and premises situated in Lincoln County, Territory of Oklahoma , to wit:

Fifty-three and one third (53-1/3) acres of land in the Northeast Quarter (NE 1/4) of section thirty six (36) township thirteen (13) North, of Range four (4) East of the Indian Meridian, more particulary[sic] described as follows: Beginning at the northwest corner of the Northeast Quarter (NE 1/4) of the Northeast Quarter (NE 1/4) of section thirty six (36), township thirteen (13) north, of Range four (4) East of the I.M., thence twenty-six and two-thirds (26-2/3) rods east, thence one hundred and sixty (160) rods south, thence fifty three and one third (53-1/3) rods west, thence one hundred and sixty (160) north, thence twenty-six and two thirds (26-2/3) rods east to place of beginning, containing fifty-three and one third acres.

together with all the improvements thereon and the appurtenances thereunto belonging, and warrant the title to the same.

To have and to hold said described premises unto the said part y of the second part, her heirs, executors, administrators, and assigns, forever.

In witness whereof, The said part ies of the first part ha ve hereunto set their hand s, and seal s the day and year first above written.   Lizzie McKinney
                                                                     Lucy O'Brien
        WITNESSES   Anna Longshore   [SEAL]
N. Whitacre   Martha Connalis
W.C. Kohlenberg   Chas Longshore   [SEAL]

Sac & Fox – Shawnee Estates
1885-1910 Volume I

          Aaron McKinney   [SEAL]
          Joe Connalis   his x mark
                 his [SEAL]
          Daniel O'Brien x mark
          Emma McKinney   [SEAL]

☞ Acknowledgments must be in accordance with the forms prescribed by the State or Territory in which the land is situated.

Territory of Oklahoma ⎫
Sac and Fox Agency   ⎬ ss:
         ⎭

Be it remembered, That on this 7th day of October , A.D. 190 5 before the undersigned, a Supt. & Spl. Dis. Agent in and for the Agency aforesaid, personally appeared Lizzie McKinney, a single person, Mary Connalis, Lucy O'Brien, Anna Longshore, Chas. Longshore, Aaron McKinney, Cedro Connalis and Daniel O'Brien, and Emma McKinney

to me personally known to be the identical persons who executed the within instrument of writing, and such persons duly acknowledged the execution of the same.
 In testimony whereof, I have hereunto subscribed my name xxxxxxxxxxxxx xxxx on the day and year last above written.
            W.C. Kohlenberg
            Supt. & Spl. Dis. Agent

        ****

INDIAN DEED INHERITED LANDS.

This Indenture, Made and entered into this 7th day of October one thousand nine hundred and five , by and between Aaron McKinney and Emma McKinney his wife, Martha Connalis and Joe Connalis her husband, Mary Connalis and Cedro Connalis her husband and Lizzie McKinney and Anna Longshore and Chas. Longshore her husband.

of Sac and Fox Agenxy[sic], Oklahoma
heirs of Jefferson McKinney
deceased, a Sac and Fox Indian, part ies of the first part, and
    Lucy O'Brien

Sac & Fox – Shawnee Estates
1885-1910 Volume I

of Sac and Fox Agency, Okla. , part y of the second part:

Witnesseth, That said part ies of the first part, for and in consideration of the sum of
One -- dollars,
in hand paid, the receipt of which is hereby acknowledged, do hereby grant, bargain, sell, and
convey unto said part y of the second part the following described real estate and premises
situated in Lincoln County, Territory of Oklahoma , to wit:

Fifty-three and one third acres of land off the north side of the Northeast
Quarter (NE 1/4) of section thirty five (35) township thirteen (13) north of range four
(4) east of the Indian Meridian, more particularly described as follows:

Beginning at the Northeast corner of the Northeast quarter (NE 1/4) of section
thirty five (35) township thirteen (13) north of range four (4) east of the I.M., thence
fifty-three and one-third (53-1/3) rods south thence one hundred and sixty rods west
(160) thence fifty three and one third (53-1/3) rods north thence one hundred and sixty
(160) rods east to the place of beginning, containing fifty-three and one third (53-1/3)
acres.

together with all the improvements thereon and the appurtenances thereunto belonging, and
warrant the title to the same.

To have and to hold said described premises unto the said part y of the second part, her
heirs, executors, administrators, and assigns, forever.

In witness whereof, The said part ies of the first part ha ve hereunto set their
hands and seal s the day and year first above written. Lizzie McKinney

	Mary Connalis	
WITNESSES	Anna Longshore	[SEAL]
N Whitacre	Martha Connalis	
W.C. Kohlenberg	Chas. Longshore	[SEAL]
	Aaron McKinney	
	Cedro Connalis his	[SEAL]
	Joe Connalis x mark	
		[SEAL]

☞ Acknowledgments must be in accordance with the forms prescribed by the State or Territory in which the land is situated.

Territory of Oklahoma ⎫
Sac and Fox Agency ⎬ ss:
                     ⎭

Be it remembered, That on this 7th day of October , A.D. 190 5 before the
undersigned, a Supt. & Spl. Dis. Agent in and for the Agency aforesaid,
personally appeared Lizzie McKinney, Mary Connalis, Anna Longshore,
Mary Connalis, Chas. Longshore, Aaron McKinney, Cedro Connalis and Joe Connalis
and Emma McKinney

Sac & Fox – Shawnee Estates
1885-1910 Volume I

to me personally known to be the identical persons who executed the within instrument of writing, and such persons duly acknowledged the execution of the same.

In testimony whereof, I have hereunto subscribed my name xxxxxxxxxxxxx xxxx on the day and year last above written.

        W.C. Kohlenberg
        Supt. & Spl. Dis. Agent
    My commission expires March 3 190 6

☞ Acknowledgments must be in accordance with the forms prescribed by the State or Territory in which the land is situated.

Territory of Oklahoma } ss:
County of Lincoln

Be it remembered, That on this 7th day of October, A.D. 190 5 before the undersigned, a Notary Public in and for the County and Territory aforesaid, personally appeared Lizzie McKinney, Mary Connalis, Anna Longshore, Martha Connalis, Chas. Longshore, Aaron McKinney, Cedro Connalis and Joe Connalis and Emma McKinney

to me personally known to be the identical persons who executed the within instrument of writing, and such persons duly acknowledged the execution of the same.

In testimony whereof, I have hereunto subscribed my name and affixed my Notarial seal on the day and year last above written.

        N. Whitacre
        Notary Public
    My commission expires Mch. 3 1906.

****

Sac & Fox – Shawnee Estates
1885-1910 Volume I

WARRANTY DEED

FROM

The Heirs of Jefferson McKinney

....

....

TO

Lucy O'Brien

....

....

....................OF............................

....COUNTY.

This instrument was filed for record on the .... day of ...., 190 at .... o'clock .... M., and duly recorded in Book ...., on page ....

....
Register of Deeds.

Department of the Interior,

OFFICE OF INDIAN AFFAIRS,

...., 190

The within deed is respectfully submitted to the Secretary of the Interior, with the recommendation that it be approved.

Commissioner.

Department of the Interior,

...., 190

The within deed is hereby approved.

....
Secretary.

Office of Indian Affairs,

LAND DIVISION.

...., 190

Recorded in Deed Book, Inherited Indian Lands, Vol.   , page

****

Sac & Fox – Shawnee Estates
1885-1910 Volume I

INDIAN DEED INHERITED LANDS.

This Indenture, Made and entered into this   7th   day of   October   one thousand nine hundred and   five , by and between   Aaron McKinney and Emma McKinney his wife, Martha Connalis and Joe Connalis her husband, Mary Connalis and Cedro Connalis her husband and Lizzie McKinney and Lucy O'Brien and Daniel O'Brien her husband.

of   Sac and Fox Agency, Oklahoma
heirs of   Jefferson McKinney
deceased, a   Sac and Fox   Indian, part ies   of the first part, and
Anna Longshore
of   Sac and Fox Agency, Okla.   , part y   of the second part:

Witnesseth, That said part ies of the first part, for and in consideration of the sum of
One -- dollars, in hand paid, the receipt of which is hereby acknowledged, do   hereby grant, bargain, sell, and convey unto said part y   of the second part the following described real estate and premises situated in   Lincoln   County,   Territory   of   Oklahoma   , to wit:

Fifty-three and one third acres of land situated in the Northeast quarter of section thirty five (35) township thirteen (13) north of range four(4) east of the Indian Meridian, more particularly described as follows: Beginning at the Southeast corner of the Northeast quarter (NE 1/4) of the northeast quarter (NE 1/4) of section thirty five (35) township thirteen (13) north of range four (4) east of the Indian Meridian, thence south twenty six and two-thirds (26-2/3) rods, thence west one hundred and sixty (160) rods, thence north fifty-three and one-third (53-1/3) rods thence east one hundred and sixty (160) rods, thence south twenty-six and two-thirds (26-2/3) rods to place of beginning containing fifty-three and one-third acres.

together with all the improvements thereon and the appurtenances thereunto belonging, and warrant the title to the same.

To have and to hold said described premises unto the said part y   of the second part,   her heirs, executors, administrators, and assigns, forever.

In witness whereof, The said part ies   of the first part ha ve   hereunto set their hand s and seal s the day and year first above written.   Lizzie McKinney
Mary Connalis
WITNESSES   Lucy O'Brien   [SEAL]
N Whitacre   Martha Connalis
W.C. Kohlenberg   Aaron McKinney   [SEAL]
Cedro Connalis

Sac & Fox – Shawnee Estates
1885-1910 Volume I

Joe Connalis his x mark [SEAL]
Daniel O'Brien his x mark [SEAL]

☞ Acknowledgments must be in accordance with the forms prescribed by the State or Territory in which the land is situated.

Territory of Oklahoma } ss:
Sac and Fox Agency

Be it remembered, That on this 7th day of October , A.D. 190 5 before the undersigned, a Supt. & Spl. Dis. Agent in and for the Agency aforesaid, personally appeared Lizzie McKinney, Mary Connalis, Lucy O'Brien, Mary Connalis, Aaron McKinney, Cedro Connalis, Joe Connalis and Daniel O'Brien and Emma McKinney to me personally known to be the identical persons who executed the within instrument of writing, and such persons duly acknowledged the execution of the same.

In testimony whereof, I have hereunto subscribed my name xxxxxxxxxx xxx on the day and year last above written.

W.C. Kohlenberg
Supt. & Spl. Dis. Agent

****

☞ Acknowledgments must be in accordance with the forms prescribed by the State or Territory in which the land is situated.

Territory of Oklahoma } ss:
County of Lincoln

Be it remembered, That on this 7th day of October , A.D. 190 5 before the undersigned, a Notary Public in and for the County and Territory aforesaid, personally appeared Lizzie McKinney, Mary Connalis, Lucy O'Brien, Martha Connalis, Aaron McKinney, Cedro Connalis and Joe Connalis and Daniel O'Brien and Emma McKinney to me personally known to be the identical persons who executed the within instrument of writing, and such persons duly acknowledged the execution of the same.

In testimony whereof, I have hereunto subscribed my name and affixed my Notarial seal on the day and year last above written.

N. Whitacre
Notary Public
My commission expires Mch. 3 1906.

Sac & Fox – Shawnee Estates
1885-1910 Volume I

WARRANTY DEED

FROM

**The Heirs of
Jefferson McKinney**

....

....

TO

Anna Longshore

....

..................OF..............................

....COUNTY.

This instrument was filed for record on the................day of........................, 190 at..................o'clock...........M., and duly recorded in Book............., on page.............

....
Register of Deeds.

Department of the Interior,

OFFICE OF INDIAN AFFAIRS,

...., 190

The within deed is respectfully submitted to the Secretary of the Interior, with the recommendation that it be approved.

Commissioner.

Department of the Interior,

...., 190

The within deed is hereby approved.

....
Secretary.

Office of Indian Affairs,

LAND DIVISION.

...., 190

Recorded in Deed Book, Inherited Indian Lands, Vol.   , page

Sac & Fox – Shawnee Estates
1885-1910 Volume I

INDIAN DEED INHERITED LANDS.

This Indenture, Made and entered into this 7th day of October one thousand nine hundred and five, by and between Anna Longshore and Chas. Longshore, her husband, Lucy O'Brien and Daniel O'Brien, her husband, Aaron McKinney and Emma McKinney, his wife, Martha Connalis and Joe Connalis her husband, Mary Connalis and Cedro Connalis, her husband

of   Sac and Fox Agency, Oklahoma
heirs of   Wilson McKinney
deceased, a   Sac and Fox   Indian, part ies of the first part, and Lizzie McKinney of Sac and Fox Agency, Okla. , part y of the second part:

Witnesseth, That said part ies of the first part, for and in consideration of the sum of One -- dollars, in hand paid, the receipt of which is hereby acknowledged, do hereby grant, bargain, sell, and convey unto said part y of the second part the following described real estate and premises situated in Lincoln County, Territory of Oklahoma , to wit:

Fifty-three and one third (53-1/3) acres of land off the west side of the Northeast quarter (NE 1/4) of section thirty six (36) township (13) of range four (4) east of the Indian Meridian.

More particularly described as follows: Beginning at the Northwest corner of the NE 1/4 of section 36, Twp. 13 N., of range 4 E, thence one hundred and sixty (160) rods south, thence fifty three and one third (53-1/3) rods east, thence one hundred and sixty (160) rods north, thence fifty-there and one third (53-1/3) rods west to place of beginning. Containing fifty three and one third (53-1/3) acres.

together with all the improvements thereon and the appurtenances thereunto belonging, and warrant the title to the same.

To have and to hold said described premises unto the said part y of the second part, her heirs, executors, administrators, and assigns, forever.

In witness whereof, The said part ies of the first part ha ve hereunto set their hand s, and seal s the day and year first above written.   Mary Connalis
                                                                                          Lucy O'Brien

WITNESSES		
N. Whitacre	Anna Longshore	[SEAL]
W.C. Kohlenberg	Martha Connalis	
	Chas Longshore	[SEAL]
	Aaron McKinney	

Sac & Fox – Shawnee Estates
1885-1910 Volume I

                       Cedro Connalis   [SEAL]
                       Joe Connalis   x mark
                       Daniel O'Brien x his mark [SEAL]

☞ Acknowledgments must be in accordance with the forms prescribed by the State or Territory in which the land is situated.

Territory of Oklahoma } ss:
Sac and Fox Agency

Be it remembered, That on this 7th day of October, A.D. 190 5 before the undersigned, a Supt. & Spl. Dis. Agent in and for the Agency aforesaid, personally appeared Mary Connalis, Lucy O'Brien, Anna Longshore, Martha Connalis, Chas. Longshore, Aaron McKinney, Cedro Connalis, Joe Connalis, and Daniel O'Brien and Emma McKinney
to me personally known to be the identical persons who executed the within instrument of writing, and such persons duly acknowledged the execution of the same.

In testimony whereof, I have hereunto subscribed my name xxxxxxx xxx on the day and year last above written.

                       W.C. Kohlenberg
                       Supt. & Spl. Dis. Agent

****

☞ Acknowledgments must be in accordance with the forms prescribed by the State or Territory in which the land is situated.

Territory of Oklahoma } ss:
County of Lincoln

Be it remembered, That on this 7th day of October, A.D. 190 5 before the undersigned, a Notary Public in and for the County and Territory aforesaid, personally appeared Mary Connalis, Lucy O'Brien, Anna Longshore, Martha Connalis, Chas. Longshore, Aaron McKinney, Cedro Connalis, Joe Connalis and Daniel O'Brien and Emma McKinney
to me personally known to be the identical persons who executed the within instrument of writing, and such persons duly acknowledged the execution of the same.

In testimony whereof, I have hereunto subscribed my name and affixed my Notarial seal on the day and year last above written.

                       N. Whitacre
                       Notary Public
             My commission expires Mch. 3   1906.

WARRANTY DEED

FROM

The Heirs of Wilson McKinney

....

....

TO

Lizzie McKinney

....

...................OF..................................

....COUNTY.

This instrument was filed for record on the............day of..............................., 190 at ....o'clock...........M., and duly recorded in Book ...., on page ....

....
Register of Deeds.

Department of the Interior,

OFFICE OF INDIAN AFFAIRS,

...., *190*

The within deed is respectfully submitted to the Secretary of the Interior, with the recommendation that it be approved.

Commissioner.

Department of the Interior,

...., *190*

The within deed is hereby approved.

....
Secretary.

Office of Indian Affairs,

LAND DIVISION.

...., *190*

Recorded in Deed Book, Inherited Indian Lands, Vol.   , page

Sac & Fox – Shawnee Estates
1885-1910 Volume I

[Letter below typed as given]

Mr frank A Thackry
   kind sir
i have made appilacathion for my pattent and sent you all the papers that you told me to have made witch i hope is all i need. [illegible] heare if i need any more please let me no at once and if that will do i hope that you will helpe will you please sine the rest that i need you told me last fall that you would help me all that you could and i think you will do all that you can for me please sine my applackthon or what papers that you think that i need and send them to ous that me and my son glean [illegible] if you please by so doing you will oblige me very mutch

                    Victoria ezell

               ****

                    INDIAN [Illegible]
                    SHAWNEE, OKLA
Received   November 6-1905
Answered   "   6-1905
                         From
   Victoria Ezell
      of   Shawnee
              O.T.5

[Illegible] to removing restriction
from her allotment.

239

Sac & Fox – Shawnee Estates
1885-1910 Volume I

DEPARTMENT OF THE INTERIOR
UNITED STATES INDIAN SERVICE.

Sac and Fox School, Iowa.
Toledo, November 15, 1905.

Hon. W. C. Kohlenberg,
Supt. & Spl. Disb. Agt.
Sac and Fox Agency, Okla.

Sir:-

Replying to your letter of May 22, 1905, I have to say, that I have consulted with the business committee of the Sac and Fox Indians in Iowa, regarding the Abby Redrock matter, with the following result.

It appears to be conceded by Ko-naw-paw-kah, that John Canoe was the rightful heir of Abbey[sic] Redrock, hence, it is not worth while going back of a point, already admitted. While the said John Canoe was unmarried, and had neither brother or sister living at the time of his death/[sic] he had an aunt who was a full sister of his mother, whose name was Pau-au-che-qua, and who was living at the date of Canoe's death, who, being the nearest of kin, and most directly related to Canoe, was his rightful and legal heir. Pau-Au-Che-Qua was a married woman and at her decease, left a husband, one son, and two daughters who are living at this date. It is clear, that according to law, this living husband is entitled to a one third interest in the estate of his wife and the three children are entitled to the residue, whatever it may be. It seems clear, that the property having passed in regular descent the point where Ko-Naw-Paw-Ka claims heirship because of his relationship to former owners, his claim to heirship is faulty, and has no base in fact, upon which it can be legally predicated.

Very respectfully
W. G. Malin
Supt. & Spl. Disb. Agent

Sac & Fox – Shawnee Estates
1885-1910 Volume I

Abstract of Disbursements: Voucher No. 2—Lease money.

Allot No.	Roll No.	
189	6	Guy, Leo, Ben, Ira, and Elmer Walker are the sole heirs of Lidie[sic] Walker, each sharing a one-fifth interest in her estate, as her children.
307	10	John Earle Keokuk, Frank Keokuk, Peyton Keokuk, and Fannie Keokuk, are the sole heirs of Charles Keokuk, deceased, each sharing a one-fourth interest, as his children.
238	41	Edward Butler, George Butler, and Jane Butler are the sole heirs of Jim Bear, deceased, each sharing a one-third interest. Mollie Bear was married to Jim Bear and at his death he left his estate to her. At her death it went to her brothers and sister, Edward, George and Jane Butler.
247	59	Lucy O'Brien, Mary Connalis, Martha Connalis, Aaron McKinney, Annie Longshore and Lizzie McKinney are the sole heirs of Wilson McKinney, each sharing a one-sixth interest in his estate, as his children.

We, the undersigned members of the Sac and Fox National Council hereby certify that the above heirship determinations are true and correct.

Witnesses: Ulyses S. Grant his x mark
Horace Guffin   Alex Connolly
Charles F Welles

I hereby certify that the above statements have been explained to the persons signing this certificate and that they understood same.

Sac and Fox Agency, Okla.   William Hurr
    November 25, 1905.   Interpreter.

****

Abs. Disb. Voucher 3   No. 224

We, the undersigned members of the Sac and Fox tribe of Indians, hereby certify that Annie McKosito is the mother and natural guardian of Grover Wakolle, and the proper person to receive and receipt for his share of the lease money accrued on the allotment of Rufus Wakolle, to which he is an heir.

Witnesses: Ulyses S. Grant his x mark
Horace Guffin   Alex Connelly
Charles F Welles

Sac & Fox – Shawnee Estates
1885-1910 Volume I

I hereby certify that the above statement is correct, to the best of my knowledge and belief.

> W. C. Kohlenberg
> Supt. & Spl. Dis. Agent.

Sac and Fox Agency, Okla.
Nov. 27, 1905

****

Sac and Fox Agency, Okla.

Authority setting forth that Annie McKosito is the mother and Natural Guardian of Grover Wakolle and entitled to receipt for his lease money.

    Cash Voucher #3,
    First Quarter, 1906.

    Inclosure No 7.

REFER IN REPLY TO THE FOLLOWING:
Land.
94396-1905.

DEPARTMENT OF THE INTERIOR,
OFFICE OF INDIAN AFFAIRS,
WASHINGTON, November 29, 1905.

Copy to Western Nation & First National
of Tecumseh, 12/4/05.

Superintendent Indian School,
    Shawnee, Okla.

Sir:

As recommended in your letter of November 20, 1905, you are hereby authorized to make payment of the full amount of the money due the heirs of Ash-nick Person, alias Mrs. Otwas, Citizen Pottawatomie allottee No. 299, arising from the sale of the NW/4 of Sec. 39, T. 9 N., R. 1 E., to C. W. Miller, for $800, as recommended in your letter of October 21, and which recommendation you now repeat.

> Very respectfully,
> CF Larrabee
> Acting Commissioner.

RFT-D

Sac & Fox – Shawnee Estates
1885-1910 Volume I

Abstract of Disbursements: Voucher No. 3—Lease money.

Allot No.	Roll No.	
373	115	Linda Messawat is the sole heir of Alma Messawat and inherits the whole of her estate, as her only surviving sister.
386	156	Andrew Conger is the sole heir of Hattie Conger, deceased, and inherits the whole of her estate, as her only surviving brother.
105	163	Liza, Moses, and Mary Harris are the sole heirs of Joseph Harris, deceased, and inherit a one-third interest each, as his surviving wife and children.
210	164	Agnes Long at her death left her husband Thomas Long and her brother, George Manatowa, each sharing a one half interest in her estate. George Manatowa died, leaving his half-interest to his wife, (now Laura Carter) one-sixth; and to his three children Elmer, Lorina, and Bertha Manatowa, each a one-ninth interest in the original estate of Agnes Long.

Thomas Long, husband of Agnes Long, died, leaving his half-interest to David Pennock, who was a grandson of his deceased brother and who shares a one-sixth interest; and to M-jish-ke, who is a granddaughter of a deceased brother, sharing a one-sixth interest. The remaining one-sixth interest goes to John Brown, one-eighteenth; Thomas, Harry, Mary & Beulah, each share a one-thirty-sixth interest, as the husband, and the children of a deceased granddaughter of the brother to Thomas Long. The heirs are therefore

> Laura Carter..................................1/ 6
> Elmer Manatowa........................... 1/ 9
> Lorina Manatowa...........................1/ 9
> Bertha Manatowa...........................1/ 9
> David Pennock..............................1/ 6
> John Brown...................................1/18
> Thomas Brown.............................1/36
> Harry Brown................................1/36
> Mary Brown.................................1/36
> M-jish-ke.....................................1/ 6

224	165	George Manatowa at his death left Laura Carter, his wife, sharing a one-third interest; Elmer, Lorina and Bertha Manatowa, his children, each sharing a two-ninths interest in his estate as his sole heirs.
201	168	Jennie Hall heirs. Sarah Bigwalker is the mother of Jennie Hall; Esther, Maud, Lelia, and Margaret Bigwalker, Dollie McClellan and Mamie Morton, are sisters and half-sisters of Jennie Hall, deceased, each sharing a one-seventh interest in her estate as the sole and only heirs.

Sac & Fox – Shawnee Estates
1885-1910 Volume I

287 169   Harry Hall heirs. Harry Hall at his death left his entire estate to his wife, Jennie Hall, and to his daughter, Rachel Hall (by a former wife), each sharing a half-interest in his estate. Jennie Hall died, leaving her half-interest in this estate to her mother, Sarah Bigwalker, and to her sisters and half-sisters, Esther, Maud, Lelia, and Margaret Bigwalker, Dollie McClelln[sic] and Mamie Morton, each sharing one-seventh of her half interest as the sole and only heirs.

261 170   Phoebe Keokuk heir. Phoebe Keokuk at her death left Marie Fear and Alice Lee, her sisters, each sharing a one-third interest, and Moses Keokuk, her husband, sharing a one-third interest. Moses Keokuk died, leaving his one-third interest to Mary A. Keokuk and Charles Keokuk, each sharing half of his third, or one-sixth interest each. Charles Keokuk died, leaving his sixth interest to his four children, John Earle Keokuk, Frank Keokuk, Peyton Keokuk, and Fannie Keokuk, each sharing one-fourth of one-sixth, or a one-twentyfourth[sic] interest in the original estate of Phoebe Keokuk.

356 171   Maw-mel-lo-haw heirs. Maw-mel-lo-haw at his death left his wife Sarah Ellis, sharing a one-third interest, and his children Annie McKosito and Katie Ellis, each sharing one-seventh of two-thirds, or two-twentyfirsts[sic] interest each. Katie Ellie[sic] died, leaving her 2/21 interest to her husband Jesse Kakaque, and her daughter Maud Kakaque, each sharing one-half of two-twentyfirsts or one-twenty-first interest in the original estate of Maw-mel-lo-haw.
The above are the sole and only heirs.

209 174   Thomas Long heirs. Thomas Long at his death left no wife, no children, no father nor mother. He had one brother, Meno-quot, who died before him. Meno-quot had one son who was the grandfather of David Pennock, who shares a one-third interest. He also left a daughter who was the mother of M-jish-ke, who shares a one-third interest. He also had a daughter who was the moh her[sic] of Josephine Brown, who shared one-third interest. Josephine Brown died, leaving her third to John Brown, her husband, who shares a one-ninth interest; Thomas, Harry, Beulah and Mary E Brown, who each share a 1/18 interest in the original estate of Thomas Long. The heirs therefore are
        David Pennock......................1/3 interest
        John Brown...........................1/9   "
        Thomas Brown......................1/18 "
        Harry Brown..........................1/18 "
        Beulah Brown.........................1/18 "
        Mary N. Brown.......................1/18 "
        M-jish-ke................................1/3   "

240 175   Charlotte Thorp heirs. Mary Thorp, Adaline Thorp, Edward Thorp, and James Thorp are the sole and only heirs of Charlote[sic] Thorp entitled to

Sac & Fox – Shawnee Estates
1885-1910 Volume I

176 176   share in the balance of the allotment, which has been partitioned and the remaining heirs' part old.

176 176   Hiram Nullake heirs. Amania Nullake is the wife of, and Walter Nullake a son of Hiram Nullake, deceased, each sharing a half-interest, and are his sole and only heirs.

85 177   Jennie Buffalohorn heirs The heirs of Jennie Buffalohorn are Margaret Bigwalker, George Appletree, Francis Martin and Julia Parkinson, children of Jennie Buffalohorn, each sharing a one-fourth interest in her estate, and are her sole and only heirs.

158 179   Flora Mokohoko heirs. at her death Flora Mokohoko left her daughter, Louisa Mack, and her son, Dickson Duncan as her sole and only heirs, each sharing a one-half interest.

207 180   James Wolf heirs. at his death he left George W. Pattock, a second cousin, and his sole and only heir at law, inheriting his entire estate.

504 181   Egbert Mitchell heir. Minnie Plumb is the sister of Egbert Mitchell, deceased, and his sole and only heir at law, inheriting his entire estate.

233 185   Joseph Fox heirs. Joseph Fox at his death left his wife, Bettie Fox, sharing a half-interest, and Kate Ellis, Sargent Ellis, Frank Ellis, and Mary Pappan, sharing the other half interest in the said estate of Joseph Fox; Bettie Fox sold her half of the allotment of Joseph Fox partitioned to her; therefore the remainder (Lots 1&2 of NE/4 of Sec. 11-18-5, belongs solely to the remaining heirs, who are as stated above, the sole and only heirs to the estate of the said Joseph Fox set apart for them by the court.

473 186   Francis Harris heirs. Francis Harris at his death left his entire estate to Mary Harris, his half sister; and Moses Harris, half brother, each sharing a half-interest in his estate as his sole and only heirs.

471 192   Richard Hawk at his death left his father, Samuel Hawk, as his sole heir. Samuel Hawk died, Nov. 17, 1899, leaving as his sole heir Eunice Hawk, his daughter Stella Hawk, and his son James Hawk, each sharing a one-third interest in the estate of Richard Hawk; James Hawk, died, leaving his one-third interest in the Richard Hawk estate to his children Silas Hawk and Ida Mansur, each sharing a half of his third, or a one-sixth interest. The sole and only heirs therefore are
     Eunice Hawk..................1/3
     Stella Hawk..................1/3
     Silas Hawk...................1/6
     Ida Mansur...................1/6

276 194   Beaver Falls heirs. Samuel Falls and Annie Smith are the sole and only heirs of Beaver Falls, being his brother and sister, and inheriting the whole of his estate.

Sac & Fox – Shawnee Estates
1885-1910 Volume I

139	195	**Robert Duncan heirs.** Robert Duncan at his death let his half brother, Richard Duncan, and his sister, Alice Duncan, as his sole and only heirs, each sharing a half-interest in his estate. Alice Duncan died, subsequently, leaving her half to Richard Duncan (her brother) and William Bear, (her husband, each sharing a half of her half or a one-fourth interest. Richard Duncan therefore inherits a three-fourths interest, and William Bear a one-fourth interest in the estate of Robert Duncan.
102	197	<u>Barbara McKosito</u> heirs. Barbara McKosito at her death left her husband, Chief McKosito, and a son, who each inherited a half interest in her estate. This son died, leaving his half interest to Dickson Duncan and Allen C. Thurman, who each share a one-fourth interest in the estate of Barbara McKosito.
434	198	<u>Charlotte Givens heirs</u>. Charlotte Givens at her death left as her sole and only heirs Gertrude Givens, (mother), Eveline and Isaac Givens, (brothers), and Lydia Grant and Lucy Thurman, (sisters), each sharing a one-fifth interest in her estate.
229	199	Lizzie <u>Rice</u> at her death left as her sole and only heirs her son, Edward Rice, and her daughter, Cora Bear, each sharing a half-interest in her estate.
413	200	<u>Ruth Miller heirs</u>. Ruth Miller at her death left her father, Henry Miller, who inherited her entire estate; Henry Miller died, leaving the entire estate to his wife, Mary Gokey (nee Miller) and to his daughter, Ida Miller, each sharing a half-interest in the original estate of Ruth Miller as the sole and only heirs.
52	203	<u>Josephine Brown heirs</u>. Josephine Brown at her death left her estate to John Brown, husband, sharing a one-third interest; Thomas, Harry, Beulah and Mary E. Brown, her children, each sharing a one-sixth interest, as her sole and only heirs.
390	204	<u>Hiram Gibbs heirs.</u> Hiram Gibbs at his death left his wife, Dosh Gibbs, sharing a one-third interest and his children Amanda Scott, Gilbert Gibbs, Alice Gibbs, Linda Rogers, and Mary Black, each sharing a 2~~1~~/15 interest in his estate as his sole and only heirs at law.
248	205	<u>Wilson McKinney heirs</u>. Wilson McKinney at his death left his estate to his children, Lucy O'Brien, Mary Connalis, Martha Connalis, Aaron McKinney, Lizzie McKinney, and Annie Longshore, each sharing a one-sixth interest in his estate as his sole and only heirs.
382	221	<u>Julia Messawat heir.</u> Linda Messawat is the sole and only heir of Julia Messawat, inheriting her entire estate as her daughter.
20	224	<u>Rufus Wakolle heir.</u> Rufus Wakolle at his death left his estate to Annie McKosito, wife, and Grover Wakolle, son, each sharing a half-interest as the sole and only heirs.
271	230	<u>Grover Falls heirs.</u> Grover Falls at his death left his estate to his sister, Annie Smith, and his brother, Samuel Falls, each sharing a half-interest as his sole and only heirs.
278	232	<u>Sarah Hall heirs.</u> Sarah Hall at her death left the following heirs:

Sac & Fox – Shawnee Estates
1885-1910 Volume I

    Fannie Banister, daughter, inherits a 2/15 interest
    Julia Brown,   "   "   2/15 "
    Benjamin Harris, Son   "   2/15 "
    David Harris,   "   "   2/15 "
    Irene Harris   daughter, inherited 2/15 "
    which at her death went to her son
       William H. Jefferson.
    Harry Hall (husband of Sarah Hall-) formerly Sarah Harris) inherited a one-third interest, which at his death went to his subsequent wife, Jennie Hall (Bigwalker), and his daughter, Rachel Hall, each sharing a half of his third or a 1/6 interest each.
    Jennie Hall at her death left her 1/6 interest to her mother Sarah Bigwalker and her sisters and half-sister, Esther, Maud, Lelia and Margaret Bigwalker, Dollie McClellan and Mamie Morton, each sharing 1/7 of her 1/6 or a 1/42 interest each in the original estate of Sarah Hall.

229 234   Lizzie Rice heirs. Lizzie Rice at her death left as her sole and only heirs Edward Rice, her son, and Cora Bear, her daughter, as her sole and only heirs, each sharing a half-interest in her estate.

232 235   William Nahmoswe heirs. William Nahmoswe at his death left his entire estate to his daughter, Lizzie Rice, as his sole and only heir: Lizzie Rice at her death left as her sole and only heirs her son, Edward Rice and her daughter, Cora Bear, each sharing a half-interest in the original estate of William Nahmoswe.

509 245   Robert Hunter heirs. Robert Hunter at his death left his children, Henry, Harrison, Emma, Gertrude and Daniel S. Hunter, as his sole and only heirs, each sharing one-fifth interest in his estate.

163 247   Mamie Pattequa heirs. Mamie Pattequa at her death left as her sole and only heirs Bertha and Addie Pattequa, her daughters, each sharing a half-interest in her estate.

45 254   Levi Barker heirs Levi Barker, at his death, left his entire estate to his father, Andrew Barker, as his sole and only heir.

340 255   William Ingalls heirs. William Ingalls at his death left his estate to his mother, Hattie Ingalls, and to his sister, Sadie Ingalls, and his half-brother, Henry Ingalls, each sharing a one-third interest as his sole and only heirs.

302 266   Kate Guthrie heirs Kate Guthrie at her death left her estate to her sister, Leona Grayeyes, and her half-sister, Shela Guthrie, each sharing a half interest in her estate as her sole and only heirs.

334 267   Cora Shaquequot heirs Cora Shaquequot at her death left her brother Wah-pah-ne-se, as her sole and only surviving heir. Wah-pah-ne-se died, leaving as his sole heirs, his wife, Pone-way-tah, sharing a one-third interest, and his children, Make-so-pe-at, Pa-phia,naw[sic], and Ne-pau-se-qua, each sharing a 2/9 interest in the original estate of Cora Sha-que-quot as the sole and only heirs.

206 171   John Wolf heir. John Wolf at his death left his entire estate to his son, James Wolf; James Wolf died, leaving as his sole heir, George W. Pattock,

Sac & Fox – Shawnee Estates
1885-1910 Volume I

second cousin, who inherits the whole of the estate.

208 172 Jane Wolf heir. Jane Wolf at her death left her husband, John Wolf, and her son, James Wolf, each sharing a half-interest in her estate as the sole and only heirs. John Wolf died, leaving his half-interest to his son, James Wolf, as his only heir, who thus inherited the whole of the estate. James Wolf died, leaving George W. Pattock, second cousin, as his sole and only heir at law, who thus inherits the whole of the original estate of Jane Wolf.

436 276 Ah-quah-sah heirs Ah-quah-sah at his death left his mother, Gertrude Givens, and his brothers and sisters, Isaac Givens, Eveline Givens, Lydia Grant and Lucy Thurman, each sharing a one-fifth of his estate as his sole and only heirs.

460 280 Mary Washington at her death left her estate to her son, George Washington, as her sole and only heir. George Washington at his death left Junitta Davis, his granddaughter (daughter of his deceased son Albert) as his sole and only heir, inheriting the whole of the original estate of Mary Washington.

27 281 Mah-tah-pwa heir. Mah-tah-pwa at his death left his estate to his father, Hugh Wakolle as his sole and only heir, who inherits the whole of the estate.

158 284 Flora Mokohoko heirs. Flora Mokohoko at her death left her daughter, Louisa Mack, and her son, Dickson Duncan, as her sole and only heirs, each inheriting a half-interest in her estate.

303 288 Oliver P. Morton heirs. Oliver P. Morton at his death, left his wife (now Carrie J. Littlebear) sharing a one-third interest, his children Clifford, George O. and Mamie Morton, each sharing a 2/9 interest in his estate. Clifford Morton died, leaving his 2/9 interest to his brother and sister, George O. and Mamie Morton, each sharing a half of his 2/9 or a one-ninth interest in his interest in the original estate of Oliver P. Morton. George O. Morton and Mamie Morton thus each share a 1/3 interest, and Carrie J. Littlebear a 1/3 interest in the original estate of Oliver P. Morton, as his sole and only heirs.

545 301 Mary Plumb heir. Mary Plumb at her death left her daughter, Minnie Plumb, as her sole and only heir, and she inherited her entire estate.

86 304 Clare Buffalohorn heir. Clara Buffalohorn at her death left her father, Thomas J. Buffalohorn, as her sole and only heir, and he inherits her entire estate.

259 305 John McKuk heirs. John McKuk at his death left his estate to his nephew, William Davenport, who shares a one-third interest; 125 to his niece, Nancy Davenport, who shares a one-third interest, and to his grand-nieces Nellie and Seba Davenport, each sharing a one-sixth interest, as his sole and only heirs.

125 318 Helen Starr heir. Helen Starr at her death left her entire estate to her son, Hiram Starr, who inherits the whole as the sole and only heir.

Sac & Fox – Shawnee Estates
1885-1910 Volume I

367 325 <u>Della Mathews heir.</u> Della Mathews at her death left her entire estate to her husband, Edward Mathews, who inherits the whole as the sole and only heir.

Incorrect

347 326 <u>Jefferson Davis heirs.</u> Jefferson Davis at his death left his wife, now Mary Hurr, who shares a one-third interest, and his children Robert and Orilla Davis, and Jane Johnson, each sharing 1/3 of 2/3 or 2/9 interest in the estate of Jefferson Davis. Jane Johnson died, leaving her 2/9 interest to her son, Orlando Johnson, as her sole and only heir at law. The heirs therefore are

    Mary Hurr, sharing 1/3 interest
    Robert Davis, " 2/9 "
    Orilla Davis " 2/9 "
    Orlando Johnson " 2/9 "

118 337 <u>Annie Nullake heir</u> Annie Nullake at her death left as her only heirs, her daughter, Ada Nullake, who inherited the entire estate. Ada Nullake at her death left her husband, Richard Duncan, and her daughter, Cossette Duncan, each sharing a half-interest;, Cosette Duncan died, leaving her half interest to her father, Richard Duncan as her sole and only heir, who thus inherits the whole of the said estate of Annie Nullake, deceased.

547 339 <u>Waw-ko-pah-she-toe</u> at his death left his mother, Mary Plumb, and his sister, Minnie Plumb, as his sole and only heirs, each sharing a half-interest in his estate. Mary Plumb died, leaving her half to her daughter Minnie Plumb, who thus inherits the whole of the original estate of Waw-ko-pah-she-toe as his sole and only surviving heir.

239 342 <u>Hiram Thorp</u> at his death left his wife, Julia Thorp, who share a one-third interest in his estate. He also left his children, Frank, George, Mary, James, Adaline, Edward, and Roscoe Thorp and Minnie Rider, each sharing 1/8 of 2/3 or 1/12 interest each in his estate. His wife and eight children are his sole and only heirs at law. inheriting this entire estate.

Incorrect

207 344 <u>James Wolf heir.</u> At his death he left George W. Pattock, a second cousin, and his sole and only heir at law, inheriting his entire estate.

208 345 <u>Jane Wolf heir.</u> Jane Wolf at her death left her husband, John Wolf, and her son, James Wolf, each sharing a half-interest in her estate as the sole and only heirs. John Wolf died, leaving his half interest to his son, James Wolf, as his only heir, who thus inherited the whole of the estate. James Wolf died, leaving George W. Pattock, a second cousin, as his sole and only heir at law, who thus inherit the whole of the original estate of Jane Wolf.

    We, the undersigned members of the Sac and Fox National Council hereby certify that the heirship determinations in the foregoing pages from page No.1 to page

Sac & Fox – Shawnee Estates
1885-1910 Volume I

No. 13, are true and correct determinations as they have been made by the council heretofore.

Witnesses:
Horace Guffin
Charles F Welles

his
Ulyses S. Grant   x mark
Alex Connelly

I hereby certify that the determinations of heirship cases shown in the foregoing pages (from page No. 1 to page No. 13) have been explain-[sic] to the persons signing and that they understood same.

Sac and Fox Agency, Okla.,　　　　　William Hurr
November 25, 1905.　　　　　　　　　Interpreter.

REFER IN REPLY TO THE FOLLOWING: **DEPARTMENT OF THE INTERIOR,**
Land.　　　　　　　　　**OFFICE OF INDIAN AFFAIRS,**
95920, 1905.　　　　　　**WASHINGTON,**
　　　　　　　　　　　　December 4, 1905.

The Superintendent,
　　Sac and Fox School,
　　　　Sac and Fox Agency, Oklahoma.

Sir:

Under date of November 29, 1905, the First Assistant Secretary of the Interior approved the enclosed deed from Richard Duncan and wife, and William Bear and wife, the sole heirs of Robert Duncan (Pah-kol-no-pe), a deceased Sac and Fox allottee, to Lee Patrick of Stroud, Oklahoma, conveying for $1,650.00 the NE/4 of Section 7, T 112 N, R 5 E, containing 160 acres. Attached you will find a certificate of deposit from the Stroud State Bank, Stroud, Oklahoma, dated July 13, 1905, for the full amount of the consideration, duly endorsed for deposit account of the grantors.

You will dispose of the deed and consideration in accordance with the amended rules and the instructions contained in Office letter of September 30, 1904, notifying you of their adoption. Forward to this Office the receipt for the deed and the deposit slips received from the bank. Copies are to be retained in the Agency files.

　　　　　　　　　　　Very respectfully,
　　　　　　　　　　　CF Larrabee
RMS-McC.　　　　　　Acting Commissioner.
　　　　　　　　**********

Sac & Fox – Shawnee Estates
1885-1910 Volume I

> Sac and Fox Agency, Oklahoma,
> January 6 1906.
> Received of W.C. Kohlenberg Supt. & Spl. Disb. Agt., at Sac and Fox Agency, Oklahoma, Warranty Deed from the heirs of Robert Duncan to Lee Patrick conveying the NE/4 of section 7-11-5 E for the consideration of $1650.00.
>
> Lee Patrick

****

> FIRST NATIONAL BANK,
>
> Stroud, Okla., Jany 8, 1906.
>
> W. D. Kohlenberg, Agt.,
> Sac and Fox Okla.
>
> Dear Sir:
>
> We credit Richard Duncan Acct. with $1237.50
> "   " William Bear,   "   "   412.50
> Total credited, ...$1650.00
>
> Yours Truly,
> Fred T. Bearley,
> Copy-   Cashier.

Supplemental Certificates of Heirship
To Accompany Voucher No.1, 3rd Quarter, 1906.

97 276   Beaver Falls   at his death left Samuel Falls, Grover Falls, and Annie Smith, his brother and sister, as his sole and only heirs at law, each sharing 1/3 interest in his estate.

Grover Falls died March 14, 1905, leaving his 1/3 interest to his brother and sister, Samuel falls[sic] and Annie Smith, each of whom shared shared[sic] a one-sixth interest through him of the original estate of Beaver Falls. Thus each of these (the brother and the sister) share 1/2 of the original estate of Beaver Falls.

Annie Smith died October 2, 1905, leaving her 1/2 interest to Frank Smith, her husband, and to her children, David and Sarah Smith, each

Sac & Fox – Shawnee Estates
1885-1910 Volume I

sharing 1/3 of her 1/2, or a one-sixth interest each in the original estate of Beaver Falls.

Sarah Smith died October 2, 1905, shortly after the death of her mother, leaving her one-sixth interest to her father, Frank Smith.

David Smith died November 15, 1905, leaving no mother, no brother and no sister; thus his one-sixth interest went to his father, Frank Smith, who thus secures 1/2 interest in the estate of Beaver Falls, who was his wife's brother.

The present heirs to the Beaver Falls allotment therefore are Samuel Falls, sharing 1/2 interest, and Frank Smith, sharing 1/2 interest.

98 271   Grover Falls at his death left his estate to his brother Samuel Falls and to his sister Annie Smith, each sharing 1/2 interest.

Annie Smith died October 2, 1905, leaving her half interest to her husband, Frank Smith, and to her children David and Sarah Smith, each sharing 1/3 of her 1/2, or a one-sixth interest each in the original estate of Grover Falls.

Sarah Smith died October 2, 1905, leaving her one-sixth interest to her father, Frank Smith.

David Smith died November 15, 1905, leaving his one-sixth interest to his father, Frank Smith, who thus shares 1/2 interest in the original estate of Grover Falls.

The present heirs therefore, are Samuel Falls and Frank Smith, each sharing 1/2 interest in the estate of Grover Falls.

262 76   Esau McCoy at his death left his entire estate to his father, Isaac McCoy, who inherits his entire estate as his sole and only heir at law.

284 176   Hiram Nullake at his death left his entire estate to his wife, Amanda Nullake, and to his son, Walter Nullake, each sharing 1/2 interest as his sole and only heirs at law.

357 20   Rufus Wakolle at his death left his entire estate to his wife, now Annie McKosito, and to his son, Grover Wakolle, each sharing a 1/2 interest as his sole and only heirs at law.

===============================

WE, the undersigned members of the Sac and Fox Council, and tribe of Indians, hereby certify that the above heirship determinations are correct.

Witnesses:	Chief McKosito his x mark
Harry L Elmslee	Wm Parkinson his x mark
Charles F Welles	Wm Pattequa x mark

Sac & Fox – Shawnee Estates
1885-1910 Volume I

RECEIVED
JAN 24 1906
SAC & FOX AGENCY,
OKLAHOMA.

Sac & Fox Agent
    Sir

Will you please advise me what to do about getting my share of Hiram Thorp's estate. Will you write and let me know what steps I will have to take to astablish[sic] my rights. Haram[sic] Thorp was my father.

        Yours truly   Chupko
        Fannie Grayson
           Okmulgee I.T.
        Jan. 18, 1906

REFER IN REPLY TO THE FOLLOWING:
Land.
1213-1906

RECEIVED
FEB 19 1906
SAC & FOX AGENCY,
OKLAHOMA.

DEPARTMENT OF THE INTERIOR,
OFFICE OF INDIAN AFFAIRS,
WASHINGTON,
February 15, 1906.

Superintendent in Charge, Sac and Fox Agency,
    Sac and Fox Agency,
        Oklahoma.

Sir:

    This Office is in receipt of your letter of January ?, 1906, giving the names of five Indians under our jurisdiction who have died, leaving on deposit to their credit money derived from the sale of inherited Indian lands, and saying that some persons to whom the deceased were indebted are attempting to have administrators appointed; that you have contended that this Office has charge if the selection of administrators, but the probate judges do as they please in the matter; that it is evident that something will have to be done with the accounts; and you request to be advised as to what action you will take in the matter.

    In answer you are advised that you should submit to this Office affidavits from all persons claiming to be heirs of these several Indians, stating that they are the sole heirs, and requesting that the money be transferred to their account in the bank. You will also accompany these affidavits with your recommendation in the premises, and you will then be given authority to call upon the bank to make the transfer as requested.

Sac & Fox – Shawnee Estates
1885-1910 Volume I

Very respectfully,
C.F. Larrabee
Acting Commissioner.

T.B.W:E.

SAMUEL SMITH, Probate Judge **O. C. LOWRY, Clerk**

- OFFICE OF -

PROBATE JUDGE

PAYNE COUNTY

Stillwater, Oklahoma,   Feb 15, 1906.

W. C. Kohlenberg,
    Sac and Fox Agency, Okla.

Dear Sir:-

In reply to yours of recent date relative to a susspposed[sic] deposit in payment of condemnation of a school cite, the property of the heirs of Townsend an Iowa Allottee, beg to advise you that there is no money in my hands owing said heirs, and the Clerk of the District Court has informed me that he has no such funds on deposit. Under our Statutes, covering the condemnation of lands for school purposes, the money when paid in is paid direct to the County Treasurer and by him turned over to the proper parties and he, the Treasurer has also informed me that there are no funds belonging to the said heirs. I am

Yours very truly,
Samuel Smith
Probate Judge.

[Letters below typed as given.]

Hiawatha Kans
March th[illegible] 1906

Mr. W.C. Kohlenburg
Dear Sir I have just recived a leter from the agent at the Kickpoo traning school in which he stated that land of my father and sisture can not bee least on acount of som of the hairs not willing I don't know who it is that is the kicker but I say that land should bee leased or sold so each one could get ther shair and one get it all I have nevr got but the $565 et which you sent me and my father has ben dead 12 years so

Sac & Fox – Shawnee Estates
1885-1910 Volume I

you see how much I get but I want that land leased and the rent equel divided or els sell the land and divide the same if it be convinet for you to see the hairs they are all down ther but my self I will sell or leas from

Eliza Morris

Yours Respectfuly

Direct to Hiawatha Kans   Rant no ome

****

Hiawatha Kans
March the 26 1906
R.F.D. One

Mr Kohlenburg Sir I have recived your leter of March the 6 Mr Kohlenburg what do you think this land is worth per acor I supose you have seen this land I am going to try som way to sell that land if it is posable I am som enclined to think she rents this land to som one and you dont no it she probly received the rent and dont say any thing to you in case you should find any one on this land or farming this land make him put up the rent or get off the land I think this land could be leased som wa or nother her part of the rent could be kept for her till she get ready to receive it it is foolish to keep this land and get nothing from it doo the best you can with if from Eliza Morris to Mr Kohlenburg

---

[Letter below typed as given]

RECEIVED
MAR 26 1906
SAC & FOX AGENCY,
OKLAHOMA.

Payson Okla 5-25-1906

US Indian Agent

Dear sir as Naomi Sullivan is dead what kind of a shape does that leave her place in will it be for rent or sale I am on the place [illegible] would like to have a chance at it if it will be for rent if it [illegible] will it be a [illegible ...] sale

Yours truly

Urich R Herndon

255

Sac & Fox – Shawnee Estates
1885-1910 Volume I

Abstract of Disbursements.
(Voucher No. 1---lease money)
3$\underline{rd}$ Qr 1906

Voucher Number	Allotment Number		
4	30	AUGRE	Augre at her death left her husband Tom Harticoo and her daughter Mary Small, each sharing a half interest in her estate as her sole and only heirs at law.
6 34	52	JOSEPHINE BROWN.	Josephine Brown at her death left her estate to John Brown, husband, sharing 1/3 interest; Thomas, Harry, Beulah, and Mary E. Brown, her children, each sharing a 1/6 interest, as her sole and only heirs.
14 38	86	CLARA BUFFALOHORN.	Clare Buffalohorn at her death left her father Thomas J Buffalohorn as her sole and only heir and he inherited her entire estate.
15	85	Out JENNIE BUFFALOHORN.	At her death Jennie Buffalohorn left her four children Margaret Bigwalker, George Appletree, Francis Martin and Julia Parkinson, as her only heirs, each sharing a 1/4 interest in her estate.
19 41	293	BENJAMIN BUTLER.	at his death Benjamin Butler left his three children as follows, as his sole and only heirs: Edward Butler, George Butler and Jane Butler, each sharing 1/3 interest.
46 8	45	LEVI BARKER.	At his death Levi Barker left his entire estate to his father, Andrew Barker, as his sole and only heir.
47 16	38	JIM BEAR.	Jim Bear died leaving his estate to his wife Mollie Bear (Butler) ---he left no children, father, mother, brother nor sister--. She died, leaving her estate to her children Edward Butler, George Butler and Jane Butler each sharing 1/3 interest.
33	214	Lucy Black	
62 56	380	JAY CONGER.	Jay Conger at his death left his son, Andrew Conger, as his sole and only surviving heir, and he inherits all of his estate.
63 57	386	HATTIE CONGER.	Andrew Conger is the sole heir of Hattie Conger, deceased, and inherits the whole of her estate as her only surviving brother.
65	467	Out CHARLES CRANE.	Charles Crane at his death, Dec. 18, 1903, left his wife, Mary L. Crane and his children, Carrie, John, Harry and Horace Crane as his sole ans[sic] only heirs at law. Mary E[sic]. Logan shared a 1/3 interest and each of the 4 children shared a 1/4 of 2/3 or 1/6 interest.

Sac & Fox – Shawnee Estates
1885-1910 Volume I

Mary E. Logan died Feb. 19, 1904, leaving her 1/3 interest to her children Carrie, John, Harry and Horace Crane and Theresa Logan, each sharing 1/5 of her 1/3 or 1/15 interest in the estate of Charles Crane.

Horace died Feb. 13, 1904 leaving his 1/6 and 1/15 (or 7/30) interest to his brothers John and Harry, and sister Carrie and half sister Theresa each sharing 1/4 of his 7/30 of 7/120 each.

Carrie Crane died Jan. 13, 1904 leaving her 1/3, 1904 leaving her 1/6 plus 1/15 plus 7/120 (total 35/120 or 21/72 to John and Harry Crane, her brothers, and Theresa Logan, her half-sister.

John Crane shares 7/18 interest.
Harry   "   "   7/18   "
Theresa Logan "   4/18   "

68 252 [Illegible] Davis
68 347 JEFFERSON DAVIS.
70
Jefferson Davis at his death left his wife now Mary Hurr, who shares 1/3 interest, and his children Robert and Orilla Davis and Jane Johnson, each sharing 1/3 of 2/3 and 2/9 interest.

Jane Johnson died, leaving her interest to her son Orlando Johnson as her sole and only heir at law. The heirs therefore are:

Mary Hurr   1/3
Robert Davis   2/9
Orilla Davis   2/9
Orlando Johnson   2/9

78 139 Out ROBERT DUNCAN at his death left his half-brother Richard Duncan and his sister Alive Duncan as his sole and only heirs each sharing 1/2 interest in his estate Alice Duncan died leaving her half to Richard Duncan, her brother, and William Bear, her husband, each sharing 1/2 of her half or 1/4 interest. Richard Duncan therefore inherits 3/4 and William Bear 1/4 interest in Robert Duncan's estate.

~~79~~ ~~119~~ Out ADA NULLAKE.
ADA DUNCAN (nee Nullake) at her death left her husband Richard Duncan and her daughter Cosette Duncan as her sole and only heirs, each sharing 1/2 interest.

Cosette Duncan died leaving her half interest to her father Richard Duncan as her sole and only heir, who thus inherits the whole estate of Ada Duncan, nee Nullake.

82 73 MARY DUPEE.
78
Mary Dupee at her death left her husband Victor Dupee and her children Mary Dupee, Dewey Dupee and Emily Murray as her sole and only heirs; Victor Dupee inherits 1/3 and each of the children inherit 2/9 interest in original estate of Mary Dupee.

90 26 JANE ELY.
88
At her death Jane Ely left her estate to the following persons:

257

Sac & Fox – Shawnee Estates
1885-1910 Volume I

  Mary Grant, mother, inherits 1/4 interest.
  Annie Nellie Grant, " 1/4 "
  Vestina Grant, niece " 1/4 "
   as daughter of Thomas Stanley Grnt[sic], deceased, who was brother of Jane Ely by right of representation.
  Frank Grant, Thelma Grant, Anna Grant, Ralph Green, Jefferson Green and Eva B. Morris, inherit 1/4 interest as the children of Wm. Green Grant, deceased, who was a brother of Jane Ely; each of these six children receives 1/6 or 1/4 or 1/24 interest in the original estate of Jane Ely, by right of representation.

97 276 Revise BEAVER FALLS. Frank Smith Revise
89 Revise Sam Falls and ~~Annie Smith~~ are the sole and only heirs of Beaver Falls, deceased, being the brother and sisdter and inheriting the whole of his estate.

98 271 Out GROVER FALLS.
  Grover Falls at his death left his estate to his sister Annie Smith and his brother Sam Falls, each sharing 1/2 interest as his sole and only heirs.

102 233 JOSEPH FOX.
360 Joseph Fox at his death left his wife Bettie Fox, sharing 1/2 interest, and Kate Ellis, Sargeant Ellis, Frank Ellis, Mary Papan and Sallie Ellis sharing the other 1/2 interest. Bettie Fox sold her half of the allotment of Jos. Fox, partitioned to her. Therefore the remainder—Lots 1&2 of NE/4 of 11-18-5-belong solely to the remaining heir, who share as follows:
  Frank Ellis, Sargeant Ellis, Sallie Ellis 2/9 each
  Kate Ellis and Mary Pappan[sic] 1/6 each

109 299 MOLLIE GUTHRIE
131 At her death she left her daughters Leona Grayeyes Shelah Guthrie and Kate Guthrie, each sharing 1/3 interest in her estate; Kate Guthrie died, leaving her 1/3 to her sister Leona Grayeyes and Shelah Guthrie, who each share 1/2 interest in the estate of Mollie Guthrie as her sole ad[sic] only surviving heirs.

110 302 KATE GUTHRIE.
130 Kate Guthrie at her death left her estate to her sister Leona Grayeyes and her half-sister Shelah Guthrie each sharing 1/2 interest in her estate as her sole and only heirs.

115 434 Revise CHARLOTTE GIVENS.
105 Revise At her death she left her mother Gertrude Givens, Lydia Grant, Lucy Thurman, Eveline Givens and Isaac Givens brothers and sisters, each sharing 1/5 interest in estate of Charlotte Givens. Gertrude Givens was killed in December, 1905 which leaves four heirs sharing in estate of Charlotte Givens---Lydia Grant, Lucy Thurman, Eveline and Isaac Givens (1/4) each. The name of Gertrude Givens should have been omitted from heirs on this item on this roll, and her share ($3) should have been divided equally among the other four heirs.

Sac & Fox – Shawnee Estates
1885-1910 Volume I

106 432   Gertrude Givens
125 25   THOMAS STANLEY GRANT.
121   At his death he left his estate to his wife, now Mary Harragara, and his daughter Vestina Grant, each sharing 1/2 interest in the estate as his only heirs ar law.
126 22   JOHN GRANT.
122   At his death John Grant left his wife, Mary Grant, who shaares 1/3 interest in the estate. He also left his daughter, Jane Ely, and Annie Nellie Grant, who share 1/6 interest each, and Mary Haragara and Vestina Grant, wife of daughter of deceased Thomas Stanly[sic] Grant, who each share half of 1/8 or 1/12 interest in his allotment.
          John Grant also left Mary Green Grant, wife, and Anna Frank and Thelma Grant, Eva B. Morris, Ralph and Jefferson Green, who inherit the 1/6 interest of William Green (Grant) deceased, who was a son of John Grant, deceased; Mary Green Grant [illegible] The sole and only heirs are:

Mary Grant, wife	1/3
Jane Ely heirs:	1/6
Annie Nellie Grant, daughter	1/6
Mary Harragara, dau. in law	1/12
Vestina Grant, gr.dau.	1/12
Mary Green Grant, dau. in law	1/18
Anna Grant, gr.dau	1/54
Frank Grant, gr.dau	1/54
Thelma Grat[sic], gr.dau	1/54
Eva B. Morris, gr.dau	1/54
Ralph Green, gr.son	1/54
Jefferson Green, gr.son	1/54

129 390   HIRAM GIBBS.
104   At his death Hiram Gibbs left his wife Dosh Gibbs, who shares 1/3 interest, and his children Amanda Scott, Gilbert Gibbs, Lindy Rogers, Alice Gibbs and Mary Black,xxxxxxxxxxxxx Lindy Rogers and Gilbert Gibbs, who each share 1/5 of 2/3 or 2/15 interest each.
138 65   Sold GRA-HA-ME-NE.
          At her death she left her estate to Lizzie Hallowell, her grand daughter (who was a child of Mary Roubideaux, her daughter,) and who inherits ther whole of the estate as sole and only heir.
142 471   RICHARD HAWK.
145   At his death he left Eunice Hawk, his mother, and Stella Hawk, minor daughter. ?
151 473   FRANCIS HARRIS.
          At his death he left his estate to his two children Mary and Moses Harris, who share the entire estate, he and his wife (Liza Martin) having been divorced.
          Liza Martin is the mother and natural guardian of the children.

Sac & Fox – Shawnee Estates
1885-1910 Volume I

152 105   JOSEPH HARRIS.
142   Liza Martin, Moses and Mary Harris, are the sole heirs of Jos. Harris, deceased, and inherit 1/3 interest each as wife and children.

154 41 Sold   IRENE HALLOWELL
           At her death she left her father, Benjamin Hallowell, as her sole and only heir, who inherits the entire estate.

155 40 Sold   HARRY HALLOWELL.
           At his death he left his entire estate to his father, Benjamin Hallowell, as his sole and only heir at law.

     69
158 70   HOT-CHI-SE & MUC-CUMPM-PE.
361
362   The funds on hand were derived equally from the rental of each alloment[sic]. The heirship is as follows:

Muc-cum-pem-pe died, leaving her daughter Mary Dupee (now deceased) and her husbad[sic] Hot-chi-se, each sharing 1/2 interest in her estate.

Hot-chise died, leaving his half interest to his nephews and nieces as follows:

Frank Nawanoway (Kent), Nellie Tohee, Mary Dupee and Maggie Lincoln, children of Nawanoway, a deceased brother of Hotchise, and Rachel McCreary, a daughter of Wag-sta-gay-me, a deceased sister of Hotchise, each sharing 1/5 interest of the 1/2 interest of Hotchise, or 1/10 interest in the estate of Muccumpempe. (Mary Dupee was a child of Muccumpempe, wife of Hotchise, by one of Hotchise's brothers, making her a niece as we as step-child.)

Mary Dupree's entire share in Muccumpempe's estate is her own half interest and the 1/10 received from Hotchise, or 6/10 interest. She died, leaving Victor Dupee (husband) sharing 1/3 of her estate or 1/5 interest in the estate of Muccumpempe, and Emily Murray, Dewey and Mary Dupee, each sharing 1/3 of the remaining 2/3 of Mary Dupee's estate or a 2/5 interest in the original estate of Muccumpempe.

Frank Nawanoway	1/10
Nellie Tohee	1/10
Maggie Lincoln	1/10
Rachel McCreary	1/10
Victor Dupee	1/ 5
Emily Murray	2/15
Dewey Dupee	2/15
Mary Dupee	2/15

Hotchise at his death left the following nephews and nieces, being the children of his deceased brother and sister ---Frank Nawanoway (Kent), Nellie Tohee, Maggie Lincoln, Rachel McCreary and Mary Dupee, each sharing 1/5 interest in his estate.

Mary Dupee died, leaving as her only heirs Victor Dupee (husband),

Sac & Fox - Shawnee Estates
1885-1910 Volume I

sharing 1/3 of her 1/5 or 1/15 interest in the estate of Hotchise, and her children Emily Murray, Mary and Dewey Dupee, each sharing 1/3 of 2/3 of her 1/5 or 2/15 each in the estate of Hot-chi-se.

162 509 Out ROBERT HUNTER.

At his death Robert Hunter left his five children Henry, Emma, Harrison, Gertrude and Daniel S. Hunter, each sharing 1/5 interest in the estate.

167 278 SARAH HALL.
139

At her death Sarah Hall left her husband Harry Hall (now deceased) who inherited 1/3 interest; also her children Fannie Bannister, Julia Brown, Benj. Harris, David Harris, and her nephew William H. Jefferson, who was a son of a deceased daughter of Sarah Hall, each sharing 2/15 interest.

Harry Hall died, leaving his 1/3 to his daughter Rachel Hall (1/6) and his wife, Jennie Hall (1/6). (Jennie Hall was not the mother of Rachel Hall) Jennie Hall died and left her mother, 5 sisters and a niece, each sharing 1/7 of Jennie Hall's 1/6 interest, or 1/42 each.

168 201 JENNIE HALL.
138

At her death she left her mother and sisters as follows:

Sarah Bigwalker, mother..............1/7
Esther Bigwalker, sister   1/7
Maude Bigwalker   "   1/7
Lelia Bigwaker[sic] "   1/7
Dollie McClellan,   "   1/7
Margaret Bigwaker[sic] "   1/7 died June 20/06
Mamie Morton, niece   1/7

169 287 HARRY HALL.
137

Harry Hall left his wife, Jennie Hall, and his daughter Rachel Hall, who each share 1/2 interest; Jennie Hall died, leaving her half to her mother and 6 sisters. Jennie Hall, deceased widow, was not the mother of Rachel Hall, therefore Rachel does not share from her.

Rachel Hall..................1/2
Sarah Bigwalker   1/14
Esther   "   1/14
Lelia   " "   1/14
Margaret   "   1/14   dead
Maude   "   1/14
Dollie McClellan.   1/14
Mamie Morton.   1/14

170 105 Out WILLIAM HAMILTON.

William Hamilton at his death left no wife, child or children, nor the sister of any deceased child or children, no father, no mother, no brother nor sister, nor the issue of any deceased brother or sister.

His father was Marga-he, deceased and his mother was Do-cha-che-gra-me (deceased); the latter left no brother or sister.

261

Sac & Fox – Shawnee Estates
1885-1910 Volume I

Marga-he had one brother no sister. The brother was Koshiway, now deceased, who was the father of Vana Koshiway, who is thus the first cousin and only heir at law of the said William Hamilton, deceased.

174 340 WILLIAM INGALLS.
159
At his death he left his estate to his mother Mattie Ingalls, and to his sister Sadie Ingalls, and his half brother Henry Ingalls, each sharing 1/3 interest as th sole and only heirs.

174 9 Ho[illegible] C Jones Jr heir

197 307 CHARLES KEOKUK.
183
Charles Keokuk at his death left his four children Frank, John, Peyton (or Robert) and Fannie Keokuk, as the sole and only heirs at law, each sharing 1/4 of his estate.

199 261 PHEOBE KEOKUK.
184
At her death Phoebe Keokuk left Marie Fear and Alice Lee, her sisters, each sharing 1/3 interest, and Moses Keokuk, her husband, sharing 1/3 interest. Moses Keokuk died, leaving his 1/3 to Mary A. Keokuk and Charles Keokuk, each sharing 1/2 of his 1/3 or 1/6 interest each. Charles Keokuk died, leaving his 1/6 interest to his 4 children John Earle, Peyton (or Robert)[,] Frank, and Fannie, each sharing 1/4 of 1/6 or 1/24 interest in original estate of Pheobe Keokuk.

205 258 CARRIE J. LITTLEBEAR.
191
Carrie J Littlebear at her death left her husband George Littlebear and her daughter Florien Littlebear as her sol ad[sic] only heirs at law, each sharing 1/2 interest in her estate.

209 332 Out MARY E. LOGAN.
At her death Feb. 19,, 1904, she left her estate to her children, Carrie, John, Horace and Harry Crane and Theresa Logan, each sharing 1/5 interest. Horace Crane died Feb. 23, 1904, leaving his 1/5 interest to his four brothers and half sister named above, each of whom share 1/4 of his 1/5 or 1/20 interest of Horace Crane.

192 330 John A Logan

[No other information given.]

[sic] share in Mary E. Logan's estate. The four surviving children therefore shared 1/5 plus 1/20 or 1/4 interest each in the estate of Mary E. Logan.
Carrie Crane died June 13, 1904, leaving her 1/4 interest to her brothers and half-sister, who each share 1/3 of her 1/4 or 1/12 interest each of her interest in the Mary E. Logan estate.
The three surviving children therefore share 1/4 plus 1/12 or 1/3 interest each in the original estate of Mary E. Logan as her sole and only heirs at law.
Mary E. Logan at her death was unmarried.

211 209 THOMAS LONG.
196
Thomas Long at his death left no wife, nor children, nor father nor

mother. He had one brother, Neno-quot, who died before him.

Neno-quot had one son who was the grandfather of David Pennock, who shares 1/3 interest. He also left a daughter who was the mother of M-jish-ke, who shares 1/3 interest. He also had a daughter who was the mother of Josephine Brown, who shared 1/3 interest. Josephine Brown died, leaving her 1/3 to John Brown, her husband, who shares 1/9 interest: Thomas, Harry, Beulah and Mary E. Brown who each share 1/18 interest in the oroginal[sic] estate of Thomas Long. The heirs therefore are:

David Pennock	1/3
John Brown	1/9
Thomas Brown	1/18
Harry Brown	1/18
Beulah Brown	1/18
Mary E Brown	1/18
M-jish-ke	1/3

212 210
195   AGNES LONG.

At her death Agnes Long left her husband, Thomas Long, and her brother George Manatowa, each sharing 1/2 interest in her estate. George Manatowa died leaving his half interest to his wife, now Laura Carter and his three children Elmer, Lorina, and Bertha Manatowa, each sharing 1/9 interest in the original estate of Agnes Long.

Thomas Long, husband of Agnes Long, died, leaving his half-interest to David Pennock, who was a grandson of his deceased brother, and who shares 1/6 interest, and to M-jish-ke, who is a grand daughter of a deceased brother, sharing 1/6 interest; the remaining 156 goes of John Brown, 1/18; Thomas, Harry, Mary E and Beulah Brown, each share 1/36 as husband and children of a deceased grand daughter of the brother to Thomas Long. The heirs are therefore:

~~each sharing 1/36 interest, as husband and the children of a deceased granddaughter of the brother to Thomas Long. The heirs are therefore:~~

Laura Carter	1/6
Elmer Manatowa	1/9
Lorina Manatowa	1/9
Bertha Mamatowa	1/9
John Brown	1/18
Thomas Brown	1/36
Harry Brown	1/36
Mary Brown	1/36
Beulah Brown	1/36
M-jish-ke	1/ 6
David Pennock	1/6

~~215 356   Maw-mello-haw~~

216 368   ROGER MATHEWS.
213
Rogers Mathews at his death left his wife, Maggie Mathews, and his

Sac & Fox – Shawnee Estates
1885-1910 Volume I

father, Edward Mathews, as his sole and only heirs, each sharing 1/2 interest in his estate.

221 367 DELLA MATHEWS.
211   At her death she left her husband, Edward Mathews, and her sons Roger Mathews and Walter Mathews, as her sole and only heirs, each sharing 1/3 interest in her estate. Roger Mathews died, leaving his 1/3 interest to his wife, Maggie Mathews, and to his father, Edward Mathews, as his sole and only heirs at law. Della Mathews heirship therefore stands as follows:

    Edward Mathews   1/2
    Walter Mathews   1/3
    Maggie Mathews   1/6

215 256 Maw mello haw (sheet 3)

223 373 ALMA MESSAWAT.
216   Linda Messawat is the sole heir of Alma Messawat, and inherits the whole of her estate as her only surviving sister.

224 372 JULIA MESSAWAT.
217   Linda Messawat is the sole and only heir of Julia Messawat, inheriting her entire estate as her daughter.

225 413 RUTH MILLER.
223   Ruth Miller at her death left her father, Henry Miller, who inherited her entire estate. Henry Miller died, leaving the entire estate to his wife, Mary Gokey (nee Miller) and to his daughter, Ida Miller, each sharing 1/2 interest in the original estate of Ruth Miller as the sole and only heirs.

242 303 OLIVER P. MORTON
236   At his death Oliver P. Morton left his wife (Carrie J. Littlebear, now deceased.) and his three children, Clifford H Morton, George O. Morton and Mamie Morton, as his sole heirs. Carrie J Littlebear's interest was 1/3, and that of Clifford, George O. and Mamie Morton 2/9 each. Clifford Morton died, leaving his 2/9 to his brother and sister, their share then being 1/3 each. Carrie J Littlebear died Nov. 5, 1905, leaving her 1/3 to be divided equally between her husband, Geo. Littlebear, and her daughter Florian Littlebear. The heirship stands as follows:

    George O. Morton   1/3
    Mamie Morton   1/3
    Carrie J Littlebear heirs 1/3

246 66 KERWIN MURRAY.
239   At his death he left wife, May Murray, and his son, Charles Murray, who each inherited 1/2 interest in his estate. May Murray Died, leaving her half interest to To-ne-go-ha, sister, and John Grant, half-brother, and Charles Murray, her nephew, son of her deceased sister (May Murray was not the mother of Charles Murray), each sharing 1/3 of her half, or 156[sic] interrest in the original estate of Kerwin Murray. The heirs, therefore, so far are

Sac & Fox – Shawnee Estates
1885-1910 Volume I

Charles Murray, 1/2 plus 1/6 or a 2/3 interest
~~To-ne-go-ha~~ Te-an-loo-hah   1/6   "
John Grant heirs   1/6   "

John Grant died, leaving his 1/6 to his wife, Mary Grant, who shares 1/3 of 1/6 or 1/18 interest; to his daughter, Jane Ely, who shared 1/4 of 2/3 of 1/6 or 1/36 interest; to his daughter, Annie Nellie Grant, who shares 1/4 of 2/3 of 1/6 or 1/36 interest, and to Mary Harragara, wife, and Vestina Grant, daughter of his deceased son, Thomas Stanley Grant, each 1/3 of 1/4 of 2/3 of 1/6, or 1/72 interest each and to Mary Green Grant, wife, and Anna Grant, Frank Grant, Thelma Grant, Eva B Morris, Ralph Green and Jefferson Green, children of the deceased son William Green Grant, his 1/4 of 2/3 of 1/6 (or 1/36 interest) each sharing as follows:
Mary Green Grant 1/3 of 1/36, or 1/108 interest
Anna, Frank, Thelma Grant; Eva B Morris, Ralph and Jefferson Green, each 1/6 of 2/3 of 1/36, or 1/324 each.

The entire heirship is therefore as follows:

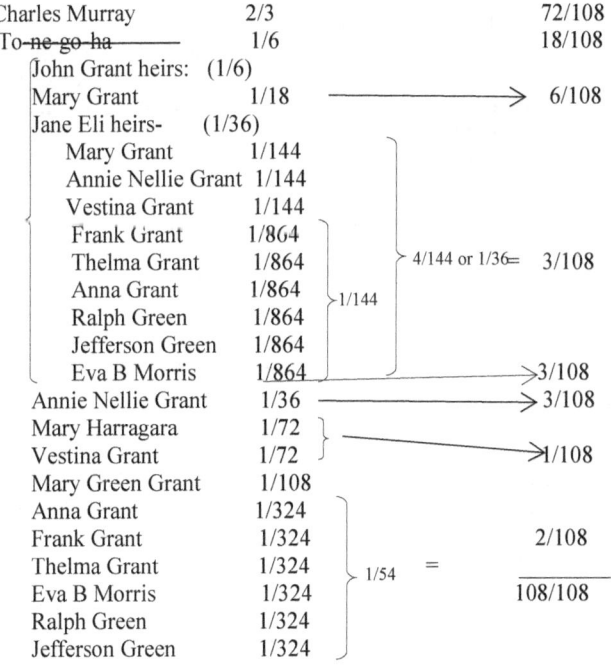

```
Charles Murray              2/3                            72/108
To-ne-go-ha                 1/6                            18/108
  John Grant heirs:  (1/6)
  Mary Grant                1/18        ———————→           6/108
  Jane Eli heirs-    (1/36)
      Mary Grant            1/144
      Annie Nellie Grant    1/144
      Vestina Grant         1/144
      Frank Grant           1/864
      Thelma Grant          1/864       4/144 or 1/36 =    3/108
      Anna Grant            1/864   ⎬1/144
      Ralph Green           1/864
      Jefferson Green       1/864
      Eva B Morris          1/864                         →3/108
  Annie Nellie Grant        1/36        ———————→           3/108
  Mary Harragara            1/72  ⎬
  Vestina Grant             1/72                          →1/108
  Mary Green Grant          1/108
  Anna Grant                1/324
  Frank Grant               1/324                          2/108
  Thelma Grant              1/324   ⎬1/54   =             ———————
  Eva B Morris              1/324                         108/108
  Ralph Green               1/324
  Jefferson Green           1/324
```

158   FLORA MOKOHOKO.
       At her death she left her daughter, Louisa Mack and her son Dickson Duncan as her sole and only heirs, each sharing 1/2 interest.

Sac & Fox – Shawnee Estates
1885-1910 Volume I

251 204	224	GEORGE MANATOWA. George Manatowa at his death left Laura Carter, his wife, sharing 1/3 interest; Elmer, Lorina, and Bertha Manatowa, his children, each sharing 2/9 interest in his estate as his sole heirs.
254 224	504	EGBERT MITCHELL. Minnie Plumb (now Minnie Barada) is the sister of Egbert Mitchell, deceased, and his sole and only heir at law, inheriting his entire estate.
256 200	27	MAH-TAH-PWA. Died Dec 8 1890 At his death he left his estate to his father Hugh Wakolle as his sole and only heir, who inherits the whole of the estate.
262 245	76	ESAU McCOY. Esau McCoy at his death left his father as his sole and only heir at law, inheriting the entire estate.
267-7 248	247	WILS. McKINNEY. At his death he left six children, as follows, each sharing 1/6 interest in his estate as the only heirs: Lucy O'Brien, Mary Connalis, Martha Connalis, Aaron McKinney, Lizzie McKinney, Annie Longshore.

271-2 250-51	102	BARBARA McKOSITO. At her death she left her husband, Chief McKosito, and a son, each inheriting 1/2 interest. This son died, leaving his half interest to Dickson Duncan and Allen G. Thurman, who each share 1/4 interest in the estate of Barbara McKosito. The heirship stands
		    Chief McKosito 1/2
		    Dickson Duncan 1/4
		    Allen G. Thurman 1/4

274 254	59	JOHN McKUK. John McKuk left his estate to Wm. Davenport, nephew, Nancy Davenport, niece, Nellie and Seba Davenport, grandnieces, who are his sole and only heirs. The niece and nephew each share 1/3 interest; the grandnieces 1/6. Nellie Davenport died March, 1905
285 263	118	ANNA NULLAKE. At her death she left as her only heirs her daughter Ada Nullake, who inherited her entire esatate. Ada Nullake died, leaving her husband, Richard Duncan and her daughter Cosette Duncan, each sharing 1/2 interest. Cosette Duncan died, leaving her half interest to her father, Richard Dunca[sic] as her sole and only heir, who thus inherits the whole of the said estate of Anna Nullake.
265-	176	Hiram Nullake. (sheet 4)
287 255	32	WILLIAM NAHMOSWE. At his death he left his entire estate to his daughter Lizzie Rice, as his sole heir. Lizzie Rice at her death left as her sole and only heirs her son Edward Rice and her daughter Cora Bear, each sharing 1/2 interest in the

Sac & Fox – Shawnee Estates
1885-1910 Volume I

original estate of William Nahmoswe.

293   133   (Out) MAMIE PATTEQUA.
At her death she left as her sole and only heirs Bertha and Addie Pattequa, her daughters, each sharing 1/2 interest in her estate.

295   482   (Out) WILLIAM PENNOCK.
At his death he left his estate to his son David Pennock as his sole and only heir at law, inheriting the entire estate.

299   545   MARY PLUMB.
278   Mary Plumb at her death left her daughter Minnie Plumb, as her sole and only heir. She inherits the entire estate.

300-1   229   LIZZIE RICE.
284-5   At her death Lizzie Rice left as her sole and only heirs her son, Edward Rice, and her daughter, Cora Bear, each sharing 1/2 interest in her estate.

315   216   (Out) HENRY SHAQUEQUOT.
Left his wife Grace Buffalohorn, and Kate Shaquequot, his daughter, each sharing a half-interest

321   451   Out HELEN STARR.
At her death Helen Starr left her son, Hiram Starr, as her sole and only heir, who thus inherits the whole of her estate.

327   107   LIZZIE SPRINGER.
218   Lizzie Springer at her death left William Springer, Elses[sic] Springer and John Deroin, her children, as her sole and only heirs, who each inherit 1/3 interest.

332   7   MAY SMALL.
297   At her death she left her estate to her three children Jack Lincoln, Charley Lightfoot and Edward Small, each sharing 1/3 interest in the estate as the only heirs.

310   331   Naomi Sullivan

335   239   HIRAM THORP.
357-   At his death Hiram Thorp left as his sole and only heirs the following:

Julia Thorp, his wife, sharing	1/3 interest	
Roscoe Thorp, son	"	1/15 "
Minnie Rider, daughter,	"	1/15 "
George Thorp, son,	"	1/15 "
Frank Thorp, "	"	1/15 "
Jim Thorp "	"	1/15 "
Mary Thorp, daughter	"	1/15 "
Adeline Thorp, "	"	1/15 "
Edward Thorp, son	"	1/15 "
Fannie Grayson, daughter,	"	1/15 "
William Lazley Thorp, son	"	1/15 "

Julia Thorp and the minor, Roscoe Thorp (who is an infant) do not

Sac & Fox – Shawnee Estates
1885-1910 Volume I

share in this rental, Mrs. Thorp having retained her interest by agreement with the other heirs, in land which she looks after herself; in other words, she retained 60 acres of land, being her and her child's interest, and the remaining land in cultiation was leased, from which the rental stated on this voucher was recveived.

349 64 TOWNSEND.
323
At his death he left his estate to his mother, Shar-tar-cher, and his half-sister, Maggie White, each sharing 1/2 interest. Maggie White died, leaving her 1/2 interest to her mother, Annie Perry, Jennie Lincoln and Farrah Roubideaux, each sharing 1/3 of 1/2 or 1/6 interest in the original estate of Townsend. These are his sole and only
~~to her mother, Annie Perry, Jennie Lincoln and Farrah Roubideaux, each sharing 1/3 of 1/2 or 1/6 interest in the original estate of Townsend.~~
Above are his sole and only heirs at law.

357 20 GEORGE WASHINGTON.
341
34
343
He left at his death no heirs excepting his granddaughter, Junitta Davis, by his deceased son Albert Washington, who was divorced from his wife, Deborah Rhodes. Deborah Rhodes receipts as natural guardian, she being the mother of Junitta Davis.

370 207 JAMES WOLF.
348
At his death he left George W. Pattock, a second cousin as his sole and only heir at law, he inheriting his entire estate.

373 208 JANE WOLF.
350
At her death she left her husband, John Wolf, and her son, James Wolf, each sharing 1/2 interest in her estate, as the sole and only heirs. John Wolf died, leaving his half-interest to his son, James Wolf, as his only heir, who thus inherited the whole of the estate. James Wolf died, leaving George W. Pattock as his sole and only heir at law, who thus inherit all the original estate of Jane Wolf.

374 206 John Wolf.
352
John Wolf at his death left his entire estate to his son, James Wolf, who died, leaving as his sole heir George W. Pattock, a second cousin, who inherits the whole estate of John Wolf.

378 ~~547~~ MARY WASHINGTON.
342 460
Mary Washington at her death left her estate to her son, George Washington, as her sole and only heir. George Washington died and left Junitta Davis, his granddaughter, (daughter of deceased son Albert) as his sole and only heir, inheriting the whole of the original estate of Mary Washington.

379 547 WAW-KO-PAH-SHE-TOE.
343
Waw-ko-pah-she-toe at his death left his mother, Mary Plumb and his sister, Minnie Plumb, as his sole and only heirs, each sharing 1/2 interest in his estate.
Mary Plumb died, leaving her half to her daughter, Minnie Plumb, who

Sac & Fox – Shawnee Estates
1885-1910 Volume I

inherits the whole estate of Waw-ko-pah-she-toe.

332 30   Wakolle- Rufus   sheet 7

DEPARTMENT OF THE INTERIOR
UNITED STATES INDIAN SERVICE.

CERTIFICATE OF HEIRSHIP NO. 3.

TERRITORY OF OKLAHOMA,
COUNTY OF POTTAWATOMIE, } SS

U. S. INDIAN AGENCY,
SHAWNEE, OKLA. MCH. 31, 1906.

WE, THOMAS W. ALFORD AND WALTER F. DICKENS, OF LAWFUL AGE BEING EACH DULY SWORN EACH FOR HIMSELF, DEPOSES AND SAYS THAT HE WAS WELL ACQUAINTED WITH CLARISSA SHINCIS, ABSENTEE SHAWNEE ALLOTTEE NO. 28, DURING HER LIFETIME; THAT SHE DIED DECEMBER 31, 1905, AT THE AGE OF 85 YEARS, AND LEFT AS HER ONLY SURVIVING HEIRS FRANK SHINCIS, SON AGE ABOUT 43 YEARS; LOUISE ALDAVA, DAUGHTER, AGE ABOUT 35 YEARS, AND ANNA CUELLAR, NEE BARONE; JOSEPHINE DURRAN, NEE BARONE AND CHARLEY BARONE, AGE 15 YEARS, SURVIVING CHILDREN OF JANE BARONE, DECEASED DAUGHTER OF THE SAID CLARISSA SHINCES[sic] .

WE FURTHER SWEAR THAT WE HAVE NO INTEREST WHATEVER IN THE ESTATE OF THE SAID CLARISSA SHINCES, AND THAT THE ABOVE STATEMENT IS TRUE TO THE BEST OF OUR KNOWLEDGE AND BELIEF.

Thomas W. Alford
Walter F Dickens

SUBSCRIBED TO IN MY PRESENCE AND SWORN TO BEFORE ME THIS 31ST DAY OF MARCH, 1906.

Frank A. Thackery
SUPT. & SPL. DISBURSING AGENT.

CERTIFICATE OF HEIRSHIP NO. 2.

U. S. Indian Agency,
Shawnee, Okla., **MARCH 31, 1906**

Territory of Oklahoma
County of Pottawatomie } SS.

Sac & Fox – Shawnee Estates
1885-1910 Volume I

We **Thomas W. Alford** and **Fannie Alford** being duly sworn each for himself deposes and says that he was well acquainted with **Elephant, Absentee Shawnee** allottee No **127** during **his** lifetime; that **he** died **January 24th, 1902** and left as **his** sole and only surviving heir **s at law, Sarah Elephant, wife, ager about 45 years, Lucy Elephant, age at time of death about 19 years, having died January 25, 1902, Henry Elephant, age 18 years and Gertrude Elephant, age 16 years.**

We further swear that we have no interest whatever in the attached lease nor in any manner in the estate of the deceased.

Witnesses

Thomas W. Alford
Fannie Alford

Subscribed and sworn to before me this **31** day of **March 1906** 190 .

Walter F. Dickens
Notary Public.
My commission expires **Jan. 1, 1908.** Certificate on File.

J.B. Charles, President   P.S. Hoffman, Vice President   H. Josey, Cashier   Lee Patrick, Asst. Cashier.

Stroud State Bank
DIRECTORS
J. B. CHARLES.   H. JOSEY.
P. S. HOFFMAN.   E. L. CONKLIN.
LEE PATRICK.

RECEIVED
APR 11 1906
SAC & FOX AGENCY,
OKLAHOMA.

Stroud Okla.   April 3rd 1906.

Hon. W. C. Kohlenberg,
  Supt. & $pl.[sic] Dis. Agent,
    Sac and Fox Agency, Oklahoma.

Dear sir :-

In compliance with your letter of the 28th ultimo, I return herewith the affidavits in the Mohee & Bain- McKinley matter, together with deeds from the additional heirs.

Sac & Fox – Shawnee Estates
1885-1910 Volume I

I also enclose three affidavits that I wish to have signed by at least two members of the Iowa tribe of Indians, same to be used in perfecting title as soon as the deeds are ready to be placed on record.

I did not have your form of blank or would have made one for you to use in forwarding the new deeds for approval provided you need anything further than the affidavits you already have.

As to the certificates of deposit, if you need new ones or want the consideration separanted,[sic] send the old certificates to me and I will issue new ones, one for the two heirs on first deed and one for the heirs on the second deed or one herewith submitted.

Please take the matter up at once and if there is anything further needed advise me and I will try and get it for you.

Thank you for past favors I am,

Very respectfully
Lee Patrick

****

Charles J. Wrightsman   *James B. Diggs*

RECEIVED   *Wrightsman & Diggs*
APR 20 1906
SAC & FOX AGENCY,   *Attorneys at Law*
OKLAHOMA.
                          Pawnee, Oklahoma   April 25, 1906.

Dear Sir:-

Kindly inform us what it the condition of the allotment made to Jane Ely, or Bassett. And to whom the allotment is rented- amount rented for, and what Indians your records show are the heirs of said Jane Ely, and among whom the lease money is distributed.

As we understand, Jane Ely died leaving as her sole heirs her mother Mrs. John Grant, her sister Nellie Grant, and the minor children of her brother, and we would like to know if these persons appear as heirs in your record of Jane Ely, and if any other persons are named as her heirs.

Yours Respectfully,
U. S. Indian Agent,   Wrightsman & Diggs
     Sac & Fox Agency,
        Oklahoma.
2-1-

****

Sac & Fox – Shawnee Estates
1885-1910 Volume I

WRIGHTSMAN & DIGGS
ATTORNEYS AT LAW
PAWNEE, OKLA.

CHARLES J. WRIGHTSMAN
JAMES B. DIGGS

RECEIVED
MAY 3 1906
SAC & FOX AGENCY,
Pawnee, Oklahoma, May 2, 1906.

Dear Sir:--

We are in receipt of your favor of the 30th giving us information concerning the allottment[sic] made to Jane Ely and the name of the lessee thereof. Please accept our thanks for your prompt kindness in furnishing us this information.

Yours respectfully,

Wrightsman and Diggs

Mr. M.[sic] C. Kahlenbug[sic],
Sac and Fox Agency, Oklahoma.
2/1

DEPARTMENT OF THE INTERIOR
UNITED STATES INDIAN SERVICE.

RECEIVED
SEP 27 1906
SAC & FOX AGENCY,
OKLAHOMA.

Potawatomi Agency.
Nadeau, Kansas, Sept. 25th, 1906.

Mr. W. C. Kohlenberg,
            Supt. & Spcl. Disb. Agt.
                    Sauk & Fox Agency,
                            Okl.

Dear Sir:-

M-jish-kee, was in the office to day making inquiry concerning the petition she signed for the sale of her interest in connection with other heirs to an estate under your jurisdiction, she desires to know if the land has been advertised, and if so when the time for the sale is set, or if it has passed.

Very respectfully,

JAS.   G L Williams
                    Supt. & Spcl. Disb. Agent

Sac & Fox – Shawnee Estates
1885-1910 Volume I

LOUIS S. WILSON. Wrightsman, Wilson & Johnson, VICTOR O. JOHNSON.
Successors to
Wilson & Johnson,
Attorneys and Counsellors at Law,
Pawnee, Oklahoma.

RECEIVED
OCT 18 1906
SAC & FOX AGENCY,
OKLAHOMA.

Oct. 17, 1906.

Dear Sir:-

We are writing you in behalf of William Atkins, concerning the estate of his wife, Nellie Grant. We understand from what he says that his wife at her death left surviving her himself, William Atkinson[sic], as husband and four children. From what he states to us, there seems to have been some misunderstanding on the part of some one in regard to whom this estate should descend to, as he is under the impression that certain children of deceased brothers and sisters of the decedent set up a claim to a portion of his estate. It is probably needless for us to tell you that they have no right whatever in the premises. We wish to cite you to running section 6895 of Wilson's 1903 statutes, and to the first division thereof, which states that the decedent leaving surviving a husband or wife and more than one child, or issue of a deceased child, one third shall go to the surviving husband or wife, and the remaining two-thirds in equal shares to the surviving children, or to the lawful issue of any deceased child, by right of representation.

Under our interpretation of this section, Mr. Atkins would be entitled in his own right to one-third of the estate left by his former wife, and the children of his wife should receive the remaining two-thirds between them. We trust that this will clear up any doubt, if any exists, in your mind in regard to the legal proposition involving the rights of the parties.

2.

How much money is there in your possession at this time belonging to the estate of the decedent?

Trusting we have not put you to too much trouble, we are,

Yours very respectfully,
Wrightsman, Wilson & Johnson
Per Wilson.

U. S. Indian Agent,
Sac & Fox Agency,
Oklahoma Territory.

****

Sac & Fox – Shawnee Estates
1885-1910 Volume I

WRIGHTSMAN, WILSON & JOHNSON
ATTORNEYS AND COUNSELORS AT LAW.

C. J. WRIGHTSMAN
LOUIS S. WILSON
VICTOR O. JOHNSON

2ND FLOOR PAWNEE NAT'L BLDG

PAWNEE, OKLAHOMA.

RECEIVED
MAY 17 1907
SAC & FOX AGENCY,
OKLAHOMA.

Pawnee, Oklahoma, May 16, 1907.

Dear Sir:-

  Mr. William Atkins, an Oto Indian, is in the office and states to us that he married Nellie Grant, an Iowa Indian, some years ago and that she died about 4 or 5 months ago leaving an allotment under control of your agency. Sometime previous a sister of hers, Jane Basset Ely also died leaving an allotment. At the time of the death of Jane Basset Ely she left living neither brother nor sister, except the said Nellie Grant, no father nor husband nor any issue, her sole heirs being her mother, Mary Grant and the said Nellie Grant.

  Under the laws of Oklahoma the said Nellite[sic] Grant Atkins would inherit an equal share with the mother, of the said estate of Jane Bassett Ely and at the death of said Nellie Grant Atkins her heirs, who are her husband William Atkins and their four children, would inherit this property together with the allotment of the said Nellie Grant Atkins.

  We would like to inquire the description of the property and likewise what, if anything, has been done in the way of transferring the title and the rents and profits of the land to Mr. Atkins and his four children whose names are Susie Atkins, 11 yrs. old, Clark Atkins and two other children whose english[sic] names the father cannot give at this time. Kindly write us giving us any facts in your possession pertaining to this matter and we will report the same to Mr. Atkins as soon as received.

  Thanking you in advance for any favors, we are,

    Very respectfully yours,

United States Indian Agent,
Sac & Fox, Okla.

Wrightsman, Wilson & Johnson
 Per Wilson.

RECEIVED
MAY 22 1906
SAC & FOX AGENCY,
OKLAHOMA.

Perkins Okla 5/2/1906

Dear Sir Mr. Kohlenberg,

I thought I would write a few lines to you in regard of that land of Charlie Mohee mother allotnee[sic] - My wife fall am heair to it When will she draw that 10^{\underline{00}}$ ten

dol. mounth[sic] I wish you write to me and tell me all about it I am going back to otoes[sic] you write to me at Red Rock, Okla.
    Oblige me   Your truly
                                          Joe Vetter

RECEIVED
DEPARTMENT OF THE INTERIOR MAY 8 1906
UNITED STATES INDIAN SERVICE. SAC & FOX AGENCY, OKLAHOMA.

                     Sac and Fox Agency, Oklahoma,
                              May 7, 1906.

Mr. W. R. Gulick,
        Chandler, O.T.
Dear Sir:
      I enclose herewith certificate similar to the one you sent in blank. I have made a little change in the wording. The wording says--"does hereby on oath certify. . . . .". I have omitted the words "on oath".

      Any time I can give you any assistance I will be glad to do so, but if any of these people want anything of this kind they will have to put up for notary fees, provided they want me to swear to these statements.
                              Very respectfully,
                              W.C. Kohlenberg
                              Supt. & Spl. Dis. Agent.

May 8th 1906.
  W   Encl.   *Well change or rewrite cert.*
      Ought not the Township to be Sixteen instead of Seventeen all of our papers show Township Sixteen. And sorry to trouble you in this but you have no idea of what we are up against in showing these Indian probate court proceedings and making the soles show in conformity to the Oklahoma statutes. We will appreciate your assistance and will sent Notary [illegible] when affidavits are required. Very truly yours W.R. Gulick

                                      ****

Sac & Fox – Shawnee Estates
1885-1910 Volume I

Lee Patrick, Pres.
S. W. Hoyt, Texas

F. B. [Illegible] Vice Pres.
Manager Insurance Dept.

W. R. Gulick
Manager, Abstract Dept.

The Abstract and Guaranty Company
of Lincoln County
Abstracts and Insurance
Chandler, Okla. May 4, 1906

Hon. W.C. Kohlenberg
Supt & Spc'l Disbursing Agent
Sac & Fox Agency
Okla Ty.

Dear Sir:-
   Would you kindly fill in the requirements of enclosed sheet as to the NW'4 7-16-6, the land was sold through the Indian office. The present owner is seeking a farm loan but company wishes the advertising of the sale more fully shown, hence this certificate. Thanking you in advance for this. I am

Very truly yours,
WR Gulick

****

TERRITORY OF OKLAHOMA,)
)   CERTIFICATE.
  Lincoln   COUNTY)

W.C. Kohlenberg, _____, Superintendent and Special Disbursing Agent at the **Sac and Fox** Indian Agency in said County, Oklahoma, does hereby ~~on oath~~ certify:
   THAT prior to the sale of the following described real estate:
   The Northwest quarter (NW 1/4) of section seven (7) township ~~seventeen~~ 16 (~~17~~) north of range six (6), east of the Indian meridian

being ~~a part of~~ the allotment of   **Bessie Ingalls** , application for the sale of which was made by the heirs of the said allottee, public notice of the sale of said lands by the heirs, and the guardian of the minor heirs, was made by posting in a conspicuous place in the office of the said Superintendent, in a clearly legible manner, for a period of 90 days, -a description of the land as above states. And that said notice was posted in

Sac & Fox – Shawnee Estates
1885-1910 Volume I

conformity with the rules and regulations of the Department of the Interior, dated October 2, 1902.

AND THAT, in addition thereto, a notice required under subdivision 11 of Section 1, of the said rules and regulations, was duly published in the following newspapers of general circulation, in the section of country in which said lands are located: **In the Chandler News, Chandler, Oklahoma**

DATED May 7,   190 6

Supt. & Spl. Disb. Agt.

DEPARTMENT OF THE INTERIOR
UNITED STATES INDIAN SERVICE.

Sac and Fox School, Iowa.
Toledo, May 9, 1906.

W. C. Kohlenberg,
Supt. & Spl. Disb. Agent.
Sac and Fox Agency, Okla.

Sir:-

Your favor of the 4th, instant, relative to the claim of Me-kah-taw and others is at hand, and will say, that I have called a meeting of the head men of the tribe together, and will present the case of the said Me-kah-taw, Sha-que-quot, and others to them, and will inform you of any information that may be elicited from them.

In the fourth paragraph of your letter you make this statement, "In my letter to you I asked you as to the death of certain parties. I have heard nothing from you, and the deed has been held up all this time." If I have been negligent in transmitting any intelligence to you which you have requested, I am sorry for the same, as I do not intentionally neglect business when confided to my ears.

I have gone over my files of letters for nearly two years, and do not find the letter to which you refer. If you will please give it immediate attention, and transmit the required information as soon as obtained, if perchance it be obtainable.

Nellie Davenport was foully murdered by some rascally miscreant on the night of March 4th, 1905. While I still believe we had the right person arrested for the dastardly crime, we could not connect him with the deed directly, and failed to secure a conviction.

Sac & Fox – Shawnee Estates
1885-1910 Volume I

Very respectfully,
W.G. Malin
Supt. & Spl. Disb. Agent

****

RECEIVED
DEPARTMENT OF THE INTERIOR MAY 26 1906
UNITED STATES INDIAN SERVICE.   SAC & FOX AGENCY, OKLAHOMA.

Sac and Fox School, Iowa.
Toledo, May 22, 1906.

W. C. Kohlenberg,
Supt. & Spl. Disb. Agent.
Sac and Fox Agency, Okla.

Sir:-

 I have had a meeting of the Business Committee, and others called, before whom I laid the Me-kah-tah matter, and questioned them closely relative to the relationship of the said Me-kah-tah to the persons named in your letter, but without any satisfactory evidence being elicited from them. I also sent word to the said woman, Me-kah-tah, and requested her presence and that of her husband at the said called meeting, but they absolutely refused to come, she stating that she did not want us to have anything to do in the matter.

 I think her attitude towards the Chief and his advisors has something to do towards closing their mouths, also, in making their memories defective &c. They claim to have no knowledge of the parties named in your letter. I then went to the home of Me-kah-tah with the tribal interpreter and had an interview with her, with about the same result. She states that she has no knowledge of Ne-ne-ma-ko-whah, but that her father's name was Wa-pe-ka-so, who was a full brother of the father of Maw-waw-she and herself were brother and sister, because their fathers were brothers. She professes to have no knowledge of Jay Conger, or any other person named in your letter.

 These people in their ignorance of business matters, are suspicious and will not trust those who are their best friends, and who are anxious to help them, but will go to some impecunious, irresponsible party who is seeking to despoil them of their property, and ask them to take charge of their business for them. I suspect something of the kind is in evidence in this case, and if parties from Montour should address you relative to this matter, please refer the same to me, as I want her interests protected. If deemed desirable, I will make further inquiries about this business, and try to unravel any mystery in which it may be enshrouded.

Sac & Fox – Shawnee Estates
1885-1910 Volume I

Very Respectfully,
W. G. Malin
Supt. & Spl. Disb. Agent.

"YOU GET ALL YOU BORROW."
OFFICE OF

THE DEMING INVESTMENT CO. RECEIVED
MAY 21 1906
MONEY TO LOAN ON IMPROVED FARMS
GOOD RATES • EASY TERMS • NO DELAY
SAC & FOX AGENCY, OKLAHOMA

ADDRESS ALL LETTERS TO THE COMPANY

OKLAHOMA CITY, OKLA.

May 16, 1906.

United States Indian Agent,
    Arlington, O. T.

Dear Sir:

    Can you furnish us a copy of the affidavit of the Business Committee in connection with the estate of John R. Moore to whom was allotted the North West quarter of Sec. 35 Twp. 18 Rng. 6 West?

    If it cannot be furnished from your files, kingly advise us about what the expense will be for obtaining a certified copy from Washington.

Yours very truly,
The Deming Investment Co.
By Miller.

****

L. W. CLAPP, President
J. S. HOPPING, Vice Prest.

A. D. KENNEDY, Cashier
H. E. KENNEDY, Asst. Cash.

Bank of Commerce.
Okmulgee, Ind. Ter.

5/18/'06.

W. C. Lohlenberg[sic]
    Sax[sic] & Fox, Okla.

Sac & Fox – Shawnee Estates
1885-1910 Volume I

Dear Sir:-

An Indian by the name of Davenport from Tana, Iowa claims to be one of three heirs to the South-west Quarter of 32-12-6. Claims this land was willed to him by the allottee. Will you kindly inform me how to proceed to buy this land?

Very truly, JS Hopping

P. O. CASSIDY   ED. O. CASSIDY

CASSIDY & CASSIDY
ATTORNEYS-AT-LAW
ROOM ONE, WALLACE BUILDING

Shawnee, Okla., 5/31/06.

Indian Agent,
    Sac & Fox Indians,
        Sac & Fox Agency, O.T.

Dear Sir:- Some time ago I called your attention to a claim held by our firm, Peyton & Traynor, against one "No-Ne-Qu-ah" deceased, for the sum of about $35.00 for merchandise, and with your assistance I tried to have the heirs of the deceased permit the payment of the debt out of the lease money derived from the land of the deceased, but with out success. At that time you advised me to probate the estate and have an administrator appointed in order that our debt could be collected by legal remedy, and I am about to act on that suggestion by making an application in the Probate court of this county for the appointment of an administrator. In order to do this I wish that you forward to me the following information.

1. Correct and full name of deceased:_____
2. Description of land and value:_____

---

3. Description and nature and amount of income derived from land:

---

4. Names of heirs: Ages: Placed of residence:

Lizzie Rice allotment

Sac & Fox – Shawnee Estates
1885-1910 Volume I

Respectfully,

J.T. Peyton

REFER IN REPLY TO THE FOLLOWING:

Land.
48862-1906.

DEPARTMENT OF THE INTERIOR
OFFICE OF INDIAN AFFAIRS,
WASHINGTON,

RECEIVED
JUN 22 1906
SAC & FOX AGENCY,

June 18, 1906.

Superintendent in Charge, Sac & Fox Agency,
 Sac and Fox Agency,
  Oklahoma.

Sir:

 This Office is in receipt of your letter of June 6, 1906, saying that Gertrude Givens (Brown) died December 10, 1905, leaving as her sole heir her husband John Brown and four children; that there is on deposit to her credit with the First National Bank of Stroud, Oklahoma, the sum of $363.34; and that these heirs are desirous of having this amount distributed in proper proportion.

 This Office is of the opinion that John Brown is the same man who was arrested on the charge of killing his wife, and desires to know what disposition was made of that case before taking any action as to the distribution of the estate.

    Very respectfully,
    CF Larrabee
T.B.W;E.   Acting Commissioner.

S. C. HUBER
ATTORNEY AT LAW,
TAMA, IOWA.

June 25th., 1906.

RECEIVED
JUN 27 1906
SAC & FOX AGENCY,
OKLAHOMA.

U.S. Indian Agent,
 Sac & Fox Agency, Okla.

Dear Sir:-

 John Allen, a member of the tribe of Sac & Fox Indians residing here requests me to inquire of you concerning his interest in certain lands which were

Sac & Fox – Shawnee Estates
1885-1910 Volume I

alloted[sic] to his daughter, Ma-ta-che who died sometime about a year ago. She died without issue and Allen is informed that these lands rightfully belong to him.

An Indian from your agency, named Me-she-pe-qua, who recently visited here informed Allen to that effect and can give you information as to the parties, if my letter is not sufficently[sic] clear, and I will admit that I am spelling by sound entirely.

Kindly advise me at your convenience and oblige.

Yours truly,

S.C. Huber

****

S. C. HUBER
ATTORNEY AT LAW,
TAMA, IOWA.

W.C. Kohlenberg,
   U.S. Indian Agent,
      Sac & Fox Agency,
         Oklahoma.

RECEIVED July 5-1906.
JUL 7 1906
SAC & FOX AGENCY,
OKLAHOMA.

My dear Sir:-

    Your favor of June 29th received a few days ago. John Allen came in this morning, I read the same to him. He states that Ma-ta-she[sic] (Ida White) was his daughter not by adoption but that he is her father and that at the time she was born, about 46 years ago, he was living in Kansas. Her mother was Ma-she-ta.

    I give you this added information at this time as it may help you in the further investigation that you said you would make.

Yours truly,

S.C. Huber

Per.S.

TRIPLICATE
DEPARTMENT OF THE INTERIOR
UNITED STATES INDIAN SERVICE.

U. S. INDIAN AGENCY,
SHAWNEE, OKLA. JUNE 30, 1908.

Sac & Fox – Shawnee Estates
1885-1910 Volume I

TERRITORY OF OKLAHOMA. (
                            (SS
COUNTY OF POTTAWATOMIE. (

WE, THOMAS W. ALFORD, AND THOMAS ROCK, OF LAWFUL AGE, EACH BEING DULY SWORN FORSHIMSELF[SIC] DEPOSES AND SAYS THAT HE WAS WELL ACQUAINTED WITH QUA-NO-THA, OR KATE FOREMAN, AB. SHAWNEE ALLOTEE[SIC] NO. 153, DURING HER LIFETIME, THAT SHE DIED JAN 4, 1906, AND LEFT AS HER ONLY SURVIVING HEIRS AT LAW;

FRANK FOREMAN, HUSBAND; MINNIE FOREMAN, DAUGHTER, AGE 8 YRS; TOMMY FOREMAN, SON, AGE 11 YRS.; ALBERT DEERE, SON AGE 18 YRS.; ANNIE HODJOE, DAUGHTER, JENNIE DIRT, DAUGHTER, AND CHESTER LOGAN SON.

WE FURTHER SWEAR THAT WE HAVE NO INTEREST WHATEVER IN THE ESTATE OF THE DECEASED.

WITNESSES.
W.F. Dickens   Thomas Rock his X mark
                                            Thomas W. Alford

SUBSCRIBED AND SWORN TO BEFORE ME THIS 30TH DAY OF JUNE 1906.

                                            Walter F. Dickens
                                            NOTARY PUBLIC.
MY COMMISSION EXPIRES JAN. 1, 1908.   CERTIFICATE ON FILE IN INDIAN OFFICE.

                                    Cushing Okla July 2nd 1906

RECEIVED
JUL 3 1906
SAC & FOX AGENCY, OKLAHOMA.

Hon. W.C. Kohlenberg
  Sac & Fox Agency Okla.
                         Dear Sir

The inclosed $40.00 are for rent due the Charles Ceokuk[sic] heirs for the use of S.W. 1/4 of Sec. 27 Township 16 R. 5 E

                       Respectfully yours
                       D.A. [Illegible]

                       Shawnee, Okla.,   **R E C E I V E D**
                                7/5/06.   JUL 7 1906
                                                    SAC & FOX AGENCY,
Supt. & Spl. Dis. Agent,   OKLAHOMA.
  Sac & Fox Agency, Okla.,

Sac & Fox – Shawnee Estates
1885-1910 Volume I

Dear Sir,- On June 5th we rec'd a letter from you in which you stated that you thought you could get the heirs of No-ne-quah to settle her acct. with us and you also stated you had sent them word to see us which they havn't[sic] come to see us in regard to the matter I herewith enclose you the amount due us and if you havn't paid them the lease money will ask you to present the bill and see what they say about it if it won't be to[sic] much trouble to you.

                          Yours Respectfully
                          Peyton & Traynor

Addr. J.T. Peyton
      Shawnee Okla.
R.R. #3, Box 70.

First National Bank,
Chandler, Okla.

CAPITAL. - - - $50,000.00
PROFITS & SURPLUS.   30,000.00

H. M. JOHNSON, President.
L. H. ROONEY, V. President.
J. A. McLAUGHLIN, Cashier.
E. C. LOVE, Ass't Cashier.

RECEIVED
AUG 13 1906
SAC & FOX AGENCY,
OKLAHOMA.

July 11, 1906.

Mr. W.C. Kohlenberg, Supt.,
    Sac & Fox Agency, Okla.

Dear Sir:-

    As requested in your favor of the 9th, we have transferred all the funds to the credit of Annie Smith to the credit of Frank Smith, subject to the conditions named in your letter.

                          Yours very truly,
                          EC Love
                          Ass't. Cashier.

                ****

REFER IN REPLY TO THE FOLLOWING:
Land.
59226-1906.

DEPARTMENT OF THE INTERIOR,
OFFICE OF INDIAN AFFAIRS,
WASHINGTON,

July 27, 1906

RECEIVED
JUL 31 1906
SAC & FOX AGENCY,
OKLAHOMA

Sac & Fox – Shawnee Estates
1885-1910 Volume I

Superintendent in Charge, Sac and Fox Agency,
    Sac and Fox Agency,
        Oklahoma.

Sir:

    This Office is in receipt of your letter of July 10, 1906, enclosing an affidavit from Frank Smith, a Sac & Fox Indian, setting forth that his wife Annie Smith died October 2, 1905, leaving two children, one of whom died October 2, and the other November 15, 1905, leaving said Frank Smith the sole heir of his wife.

    You say that Annie Smith had on deposit to her credit with the First National Bank, Chandler, Oklahoma, the sum of $760.20, derived from the sale of inherited Indian lands, and held under the amended rules, and ~~you~~ recommend that this money be transferred from her credit to that of Frank Smith as her sole heir.

    In accordance with your recommendation, you are hereby authorized to request the First National Bank of Chandler, Oklahoma, to transfer all funds to the credit of Annie Smith to the credit of Frank Smith on condition that they will be controlled by the rules governing the proceeds derived from the sale of inherited Indian lands.

                      Very respectfully,
                        CF Larrabee
T.B.W;E.   Acting Commissioner.

W.C. Kohlenberg-
    Sac & Fox Okla.

Dear Sir:-

    Is it possible for me to take my inheritance from the farm - in land? I speak of my mother's farm. John also would like his in land. Can this be arranged? I am anxious to know please.

    Don't you sometimes come to Sh[illegible]? We would like very much to have you call at the store and Mr. Banister can bring you out to the house. I should like so much to know you. I like the way you take hold [illegible] down there.

    Please let me hear from you.
                      Very truly
                      Fannie H Banister
July 8-06
        1004 Olive St
c/o [Illegible] & Weber [Illegible]

Sac & Fox – Shawnee Estates
1885-1910 Volume I

RECEIVED
JUL 28 1906
SAC & FOX AGENCY,
OKLAHOMA.

Sparks, Okla.
July 27, 1906.

Mr. W.C. Kohlenberg

Dear Sir,

I would like to know if the deeds come back yet to this hair land. I would like to know what I have to do about the rent on our part of the place. I tended our part myself. Would I have to give rent, or not? or keep it all myself. There is other work I could do on the place but I am afraid to go ahead. Seems like the rest of them are doing as they please with there[sic] part of the land please let me hear from you soon.

address to
Rout 2
Box 62

Yours Respect
Daniel O,Brien
Sparks,
Ok. Tery.

****

RECEIVED
JUL 28 1906
& FOX AGENCY,
  A.

Sparks, O.T.
July 27, 06

Mr. W.C. Kohlenberg
Dear Sir

I would like to know if I could extend the other 80 acres of my allotment or not   if I could I would like to extend it so let me know.

Rout 2
Box 62

Yours Respt
Lucy O'Brien
Sparks,
O.T.

MILTON BRYAN
ATTORNEY AT LAW

RECEIVED
AUG 14 1906
SAC & FOX AGENCY,
OKLAHOMA.

Shawnee, Okla., Aug

Hon. W.C. Kohlenberg, Supt.,
    Sac & Fox Agency

Sac & Fox – Shawnee Estates
1885-1910 Volume I

Dear Sir:-
      Have you on record or file in your office a copy of the business committee's certificate of heirship in the case of Charles Nullake to the southwest quarter of 5115, and if so, what will a certified copy of said certificate cost?
      I shall be pleased to hear from you at your earliest convenience.

                              Yours respectfully,
                                  Milton Bryan

Samuel Anderson

𝔉𝔯𝔢𝔡 𝔄. 𝔚𝔞𝔤𝔬𝔫𝔢𝔯,
𝔓𝔯𝔬𝔟𝔞𝔱𝔢 𝔍𝔲𝔡𝔤𝔢.

                                        RECEIVED
                                        AUG 22 1906

                                     SAC & FOX AGENCY,
                                          OKLAHOMA.
              ℭ𝔥𝔞𝔫𝔡𝔩𝔢𝔯, 𝔒𝔨𝔩𝔞𝔥𝔬𝔪𝔞.   August 21, 1906.

Mr. W. C. Kohlenberg,
      Sac and Fox Agency,
              Oklahoma.
Kind sir:
      You will find enclosed eight sets of notices of which you will please make copies of the same on the blank notices I send you in separate cover and deliver one of the notices to each of the relatives. You will also find on the back of one of each set an affidavit of which you will make your return on that you delivered the said notices to each of the relatives and return the same to this office.
                              Very respectfully,
                                  Oma Riner
                                      Probate Clerk

DEPARTMENT OF THE INTERIOR
UNITED STATES INDIAN SERVICE

              Quapaw Agency, I.T. 28, 1906.

Supt. F. A. Thackery,
      Shawnee Indian School, Oklahoma.
Sir:

287

Sac & Fox – Shawnee Estates
1885-1910 Volume I

Mrs. Rose Ann Kisco- Keyah, of this agency, is in this office making inquiry in regard to some lands under your jurisdiction to which she thinks she is an heir. She states that one Frank Back-ska (or some name like that) recently died at your agency and that she is his cousin and one of his heirs. Her father and his mother being brother and sister. She states that Frank left no widow or children and that his parents are also dead.

Please advise me on the subject for the information of Mrs. Keyah.

Very respectfully,

[Name Illegible]

Superintendent.

DEPARTMENT OF THE INTERIOR
UNITED STATES INDIAN SERVICE

Potawatomi Agency.
Nadeau, Kas. August 3rd, 1906.

RECEIVED SEP 6 1906 ANSD. 3 SEP 1906.

Frank A. Thackery,
Supr. & Spcl. Disb. Agent,
Shawnee, Okl.

Dear Sir:-

There is an Indian said to belong in the vicinity of your Agency by the name of Joe. Eteyan, who has been living with a member of this tribe for some time as husband, I have recently learned that he has a wife to whom he was legally married; I wish to obtain affidavits to this effect as the woman with whom he was living and claiming as his wife died a short time ago, and if it is a fact that he has a wife living to whom he is legally married he would have no claim to any part of the estate of the Kansas woman, and my object in procureing[sic] the affidavit is to protect the children of the dead woman from any claim he may set up.

Any information concerning this matter or assistance you can render will be appreciated.

Very respectfully,

JAS.

G.L. Williams
Supt. & S. D. A.
by J.A.S.

Sac & Fox – Shawnee Estates
1885-1910 Volume I

Peter Kah-dot-   James Kah-dot
Jane Curley   Annie Kah-dot nee

BYRON C. MITCHNER
LAWYER
ST. MARYS, KANSAS

St. Marys, Kansas, 14", Sept, 1906.

U.S. Indian Agent,
Shawnee, O.T.

Dear Sir: Will you kindly tell me if there is any one on the roll of Citizen Indians, (Pottawatomies.) as having land by the name of Francis Lafromboise. He was commonly called <u>Wabaunsee</u>. Wabaunsee or Lafromboise was married at the Mission at this place to Archangle, sometimes called daughter of compas[sic] and Nikas. Lafromboise was a citizen Indian, and his heirs are desirous to know if he had land in Okla., and if so what disposition has been made of it. Kindly write me at Mayetta, Kansas.

Yours truly,
David Pierson

DEPARTMENT OF THE INTERIOR
UNITED STATES INDIAN SERVICE.

Kiowa Indian Agency,
Anadarko, Oklahoma, September 3, 1906.

Mr. Frank A. Thackery, Supt.,
Shawnee Indian Agency,
Shawnee, Okla.

Sir:

Sac & Fox – Shawnee Estates
1885-1910 Volume I

Referring to your letter of the 28th instant, enclosing for delivery to Hah-mah-tom-se, a check on her inherited land funds for $10.00, you are informed that James Bob, Jr., to whom you have been sending checks on inherited land funds at your Agency, claims that he should continue receiving them, as he has only drawn $96.07 from the sale of his half borhter's[sic] allotment. Please advise me if this Indian has any more inherited land funds to his credit, and if so, what amount and when he can expect to receive further payments.

         Very respectfully,
         John P. Blackman
CLE   U.S. Indian Agent.

D. C. TILLOTSON,
LAWYER,
581 KANSAS AVENUE,
IND. PHONE 440.

RECEIVED
SEP 8 1906
SAC & FOX AGENCY
OKLAHOMA.

TOPEKA, KANSAS, 9-6-06

Maj. Kohlenberg
 Dear Sir:
  Some days ago I wrote asking you to give me the names; indian[sic] and English, of the Turner family to gether with a description of each allotment.
  On Aug. 27, '06 you wrote me that these lands were sold. I know that; but I am inquiring for another who claims to be an heir who was left out.
  So, if you will kindly furnish me the information it will be a great favor.

         Respectfully,
         D.C. Tillotson
     ****

Mollie Turner S.&S. allot. 531
 Lot 1 of SW/4 Sec 17
 Lots 1&2 & SW/4 if NE/4 Sec 20   A.J. Cain
 Lot 4 of NW/4 of Sec 21 0 186.   806

Fannie Turner   528   R.P. Carpenter
 NW/4 29-18-6   804

Sac & Fox – Shawnee Estates
1885-1910 Volume I

Earl Turner NW/4 20-18-6	530	R.P. Carpenter 804
Thomas Turner SW/4 20-18-6	529	R.P. Carpenter 804
Clarence Turner SW/4 20-18-6	527	R.P. Carpenter 900 All deeds app. Mar 23-05.

****

D. C. TILLOTSON,
LAWYER,
581 KANSAS AVENUE,
IND. PHONE 440.

RECEIVED
AUG 20 1906
SAC & FOX AGENCY,
OKLAHOMA.

TOPEKA, KANSAS, 8-17-06

Maj. Kallenberg[sic],
 Dear Sir:
  Some time ago I called at the Sac & Fox Agency and you kindly furnished the names, both indian[sic] and government, of the Turner family, with the discription[sic] of their several allotments. You may remember I appeared for Shipshe-wa-no, and of the heirs.
  Now, I need the above list as cannot find the one you furnished me. Will you kindly send me another?
  An early reply will be a personal favor.
      Respectfully,
      DC. Tillotson

****

DEPARTMENT OF THE INTERIOR
UNITED STATES INDIAN SERVICE.
Nadeau, Kansas,
September 14th, 1906.

RECEIVED
SEP 16 1906
SAC & FOX AGENCY,
OKLAHOMA.

W. C. Kohlenberg, Esqr.,
 Supt. & Spcl. Disb. Agent,
  Sac & Fox Agency, Okl.

Sac & Fox – Shawnee Estates
1885-1910 Volume I

Dear Sir:-

Ship-she-wahn-o, and Wish-ta-yah, asked me to write and request you to send them their monthly checks, due on the sale of their interest in the Turner estate. They ask that you send the checks begining[sic] with the date of their deposit, to the care of this office.

Very respectfully,
G. L. Williams
Supt. & Spcl. Dis. Agt.
by J.A. Scott
Leasing Clerk.

REFER IN REPLY TO THE FOLLOWING:
Land.
23435-1906.

DEPARTMENT OF THE INTERIOR,
OFFICE OF INDIAN AFFAIRS,
WASHINGTON,

RECEIVED
OCT 9 1906
SAC & FOX AGENCY,
OKLAHOMA.

October 5, 1906.

Superintendent in Charge, Sac & Fox Agency,
    Sac and Fox Agency,
        Oklahoma.

Sir:

Reference is hereby made to your letter of March 12, 1906, saying that George Manatowa died, leaving as his heirs Laura Manatowa, his wife (now Mrs. Carter), Bertha and Lorena, daughters, and Elmer, son; that Elmer is only 15 years of age and Lorena 11; that all of the heirs are allotted, except Lorena; that Mrs. Carter and the two older children are desirous of conveying their interests in the land allotted to George Manatowa to the younger child, Lorena, for a nominal consideration, for the reason that she has no allotment of her own; and you desire to know if there is any means by which this can be legally done.

In answer I have to say that there seems to be no means by which Elmer, a minor, can convey his interest in the allotment for a nominal consideration. Of course, there would be no difficulty in the adult heirs conveying their interest.

Very respectfully,
C.F. Larrabee,
Acting Commissioner.

T.B.W:E.

Sac & Fox – Shawnee Estates
1885-1910 Volume I

REFER IN REPLY TO THE FOLLOWING:
Land.
72121-1906.

DEPARTMENT OF THE INTERIOR,
OFFICE OF INDIAN AFFAIRS,
WASHINGTON,

RECEIVED
OCT 13 1906
SAC & FOX AGENCY,
OKLAHOMA.

October 8, 1906.

Superintendent in Charge, Sac & Fox Agency,
    Sac and Fox Agency,
        Oklahoma.

Sir:

    This Office is in receipt of your letter of August 17, 1906, in which you refer to four cases of deceased Indians where it is impossible for you to determine who are the legal heirs to the estates. You recommend that these cases be referred to the Probate Court to settle the question in dispute in regard to heirship.

    In answer you are advised that if this land is to be sold or if there is any immediate necessity for determining the question of heirship, the Office has no objection to your referring it to the Probate Court for proper action.

                    Very respectfully,
                    C.F. Larrabee,
T.B.W:E.   Acting Commissioner.

REFER IN REPLY TO THE FOLLOWING:
Land.
69572-1906.

DEPARTMENT OF THE INTERIOR,
OFFICE OF INDIAN AFFAIRS,
WASHINGTON,

October 5, 1906.

Superintendent in Charge, Sac & Fox Agency,
    Sac and Fox Agency,
        Oklahoma.

Sir:

    Reference is hereby made to your letter of March 12, 1906; saying that George Manatowa died, leaving as his heirs Laura Manatowa, his wife (now Mrs. Carter), Bertha and Lorena, daughters, and Elmer, son; that Elmer is only 15 years of age and Lorena 11; that all of the heirs are allotted, except Lorena; that Mrs. Carter and the two older children are desirous of conveying their interests in the land allotted to George Manatowa to the younger child, Lorena, for a nominal consideration, for the

Sac & Fox – Shawnee Estates
1885-1910 Volume I

reason that she has no allotment of her own; and you desire to know if there is any means by which this can be legally done.

In answer I have to say that there seems to be no means by which Elmer, a minor, can convey his interest in the allotment for a nominal consideration. Of course, there would be no difficulty in the adult heirs conveying their interest.

Very respectfully,
C.F. Larrabee,

T.B.W:E.   Acting Commissioner.

REFER IN REPLY TO THE FOLLOWING:
Land.
72121-1906.

DEPARTMENT OF THE INTERIOR,
OFFICE OF INDIAN AFFAIRS,
WASHINGTON,

October 8, 1906.

Superintendent in Charge, Sac & Fox Agency,
   Sac and Fox Agency,
      Oklahoma.

Sir:

This Office is in receipt of your letter of August 17, 1906, in which you refer to four cases of deceased Indians where it is impossible for you to determine who are the legal heirs to the estates. You recommend that these cases be referred to the Probate Court to settle the question in dispute in regard to heirship.

In answer you are advised that if this land is to be sold or if there is any immediate necessity for determining the question of heirship, the Office has no objection to your referring it to the Probate Court for proper action.

Very respectfully,
C.F. Larrabee,

T.B.W:E.   Acting Commissioner.

POTTAWATOMIE COUNTY COURT	REGULAR TERMS BEGIN ON THE FIRST MONDAY IN JANUARY, APRIL, JULY AND OCTOBER
E.D. REASOR, JUDGE R.C. GREEN, CLERK NANNIE E. SAXON, STENOGRAPHER	CONCURRENT JURISDICT[ION WITH THE DISTRICT] COURT IN CIVIL MATTERS TO B[E ILLEGIBLE ...] ALL CRIMINAL OTHER TH[AN ILLEGIBLE...]

RECEIVED
OCT 24 1906
SAC & FOX AGENCY,
OKLAHOMA.

Tecumseh, Okla. Oct. 20th, 1906

Sac & Fox – Shawnee Estates
1885-1910 Volume I

Mr. W. C. Kohlenberg,
Sac & Fox Agency, Oklahoma.

Dear Sir:-

In regard to the matter of THOMAS BROWN et al, Minors, heirs of the Estate of JOSEPHINE BROWN, Deceased. On the 13th day of June, 1906, J. E. SIMPSON of this City was appointed Guardian of said Minors by my predecessor in this office. During this time there has been an accumulation of costs and Attorney's Fees to the amount of $26.55, and I understand these Minors have some money in your hands belonging to them. Kindly mail me a check of this amount to cover these items, and oblige.

       Yours respectfully,
       E.D. Reasor
       County Judge.

EDR/NES

WESTERN DEPARTMENT
CHICAGO.

WALTER H. SAGE,
MANAGER
JOHN C. INGRAM,
ASST. MANAGER
WILLIAM L. LERCH,
2ND ASST. MANAGER

[FIRE]

German American
Insurance Company
New York

Perkins, Oct. 25th 1906
W.C. Kohlenberg
       Dear Sir

A few days ago when John Arnold was here he gathered the Indians all in and they signed a Petition to the Probate Judge asking my appointment as Administrator of the Charley Murray = Estate. i[sic] sent said petition to the Judge and he writes me that an Attorney must also be retained to look after this matter = now you will see at a glance that the result would be that what little money Charley's check and his cotton money would bring in would be consumed by Court and Attorney fees. it[sic] seems to be that this matter could be settled up without so much expense I would like to hear from you in this matter at once.
      Yours Respt
      A G Williams
P.S. Robert Small keeps asking me about some lease Refers that were to be sent here

     ****

Sac & Fox – Shawnee Estates
1885-1910 Volume I

SAMUEL SMITH, Probate Judge

- OFFICE OF -

PROBATE JUDGE

O. C. LOWRY, Clerk

RECEIVED
NOV 3 1906
SAC & FOX AGENCY,
OKLAHOMA.

PAYNE COUNTY
Stillwater, Oklahoma, Nov. 2, 1906.

W. C. Kohlenberg,
    Sac and Fox Agcy, Okla.,

Dear Sir:-

    I beg to advise you that A. G. Williams of Perkins, has this day filed a petition asking for letters of asministration[sic] on the estate of one Charles Murray, Deceased, a member of the Iowa tribe of Indians.

Yours very truly,
Samuel Smith
Probate Judge.

DEPARTMENT OF THE INTERIOR
UNITED STATES INDIAN SERVICE.

Sac and Fox Agency, Iowa.
Toledo, October 27, 1906.

RECEIVED
NOV 1 1906
SAC & FOX AGENCY,
OKLAHOMA.

W.C. Kohlenberg,
    Superintendent, &c.
        Sac and Fox Agency, Okla.

Sir:-

    I have the honor to herewith return accomplished receipts for checks delivered to Minnie Barker, Stella Barker, Emma Hunter, and Allen G. Thurman. I have not yet succeeded in having an Administrator appointed for the estate of Lucy Thurman, deceased, but will try and have that work accomplished during the coming week. There seems to arise a question of jurisdiction, in the minds of some of our attorneys in the case, which I will try and have solved in the near future.

Very respectfully,
Wm G. Malin
Supt. & Spl. Disb. Agent.

Sac & Fox – Shawnee Estates
1885-1910 Volume I

****

Department of the Interior
UNITED STATES INDIAN SERVICE.

RECEIVED
NOV 3 1906
SAC & FOX AGENCY,
OKLAHOMA.

Sac and Fox Agency, Iowa.
Toledo, November 1st, 1906.

W.C. Kohlenberg,
    Supt. & Spl. Disb. Agent,
        Sac and Fox Agency, Okla.

Sir:-

    The work confided to me in having an administrator appointed for the estate of Lucy Thurman, has been unavoidably delayed, because of the fact, that I was summoned to appear as a witness in some whisky cases, before the U.S. District Court at Cedar Rapids, Iowa, and the time lost has been hard to make up, as work in the office has accumulated to such a degree, that it has been impossible for me to take time for other work, until that which demands immediate attention is dispatched. There being no clerk allowed for this office, everything devolves upon me, including writing all communications &c.

    I will look after this matter to-day if possible, and forward to you the information required.

    Jim Scott, (No-ka-ka,) Lucy Thurman's husband is making anxious inquiries as to whether his children, (aside from Allen G. Thurman) are included in the distribution of the $50,000, released by act of Congress. There are three or four other children here who belong to his family.

    Pone-way-tah is also making inquiries about her interests in come inherited lands, which she petitioned to have sole, some months ago.

    any[sic] information relative to these matters which you may impart, will in turn, be given to the interested parties.   Wm G. Malin

        Very respectfully,   Supt. & Spl. Disb. Agt

Sac & Fox – Shawnee Estates
1885-1910 Volume I

[Letter below typed as given]

Hiawatha   RFD
Kans
Nov 10th 1906

Mr. W.C. Kohlenburg[sic]

Sir My sister was up here a few day a go and you had sent apertiton for the sale of the Jefferson Whitecloud land I saw the agent and he said he no such papers if you have the papers send them direct to me for I want my sheer

Mr Kohlenburg will you bee kind enough to give me Jak Poole age when he was put on the rale as ther is a desput over his age and I no that I am right

Yours Respectfuly
from
Eliza Morris

****

JACOB PUCKETT, President.
C. W. CARPENTER, Vice-President.
JOHN FOSTER, Cashier.

DIRECTORS:
JACOB PUCKETT.   L. B. HAY.
C. W. CARPENTER.   J. B. CHARLES.
JOHN FOSTER.   E. L. CONKLIN.
P. S. HOFFMAN.

FIRST NATIONAL BANK
OF CUSHING.
CAPITAL STOCK, $25,000.00

Cushing, Okla. Nov 9   1906

W. C. Kohlenberg-
   Sac & Fox, Okla.

Dear Sir:-
   Enclosed please find the petition, which we have started. I would like to suggest that you have the other heirs sign during their payment. Mr. Banister will take a course of study in Stillwater this winter. So please write us there.

Very truly
Fannie H Banister

Sac & Fox – Shawnee Estates
1885-1910 Volume I

Department of the Interior
UNITED STATES INDIAN SERVICE.
Sac and Fox Agency, Okla.,
November 3, 1906.

Frank A. Thackery, Supt. & Spl. Dis. Agt.,
Shawnee, Okla.

Dear Sir:

There are two small balances on our lease rolls standing to the credit of the heirs of Pope and Mattie Stanley, which I am desirous of paying off. Of these the following are under the jurisdiction of your agency---Stella Little Ax, James Littlebear, Jesse Chisholm, George Littlebear, Florien Littlebear and Shoney Littlebear. I am enclosing receipts covering the shares of these persons in the balances mentioned. The other heirs are Eliza Littlebear (Mrs. Eli Ellis,) to whom I have sent receipts at Tulsa, I.T., and Lilly Neal, Lucy Logan, Thos. J. Buffalohorn and Maggie Tyner, whose shares will be paid at this office. The balance on the Popo Stanley account is $14.84 and on the Mattie Stanley $11.33.

Very respectfully,
W.C. Kohlenberg
Supt. & Spl. Dis. Agent.

Fred A. Wagoner,
Probate Judge.

Chandler, Oklahoma.   Dec. 1   1906.

Mr. W. C. Kohlenberg,
Sac & Fox Agency, O. T.

RECEIVED
SAC & FOX AGENCY,
OKLAHOMA.

Dear Sir:-

The second year of my term of office is about to come to a close and it is necessary that all fees earned since the first of January, 1905, be paid as I am required to make a settlement with the County Commissioners on the first day of January next and pay to the County Treasurer all fees earned belonging to the county. It is impossible for me to make that settlement unless those who owe fees are prompt in payment.

Sac & Fox – Shawnee Estates
1885-1910 Volume I

    I am enclosing herein a card which shows the total amount of fees due and owing by you to this date which amount you will either call personally and settle or mail to me a check, draft or postoffice money order on or before December the 20th, 1906. In making remittance either personally or by letter please bring or mail the within card. A compliance with this request will be a great favor to me.

    Trusting that you will give this matter your prompt attention and settle the same by the above mentioned date, I remain

Your Obedient Servant,
Fred A. Wagoner.
Probate Judge.

****

[The above letter is given again but the stamped date is Dec 5 1906]

Index

[ILLEGIBLE]
Elizabeth 7
Florien B 84
Frederick F 16
Mary.. 2
WILLIAM................................129
ABLE, Agent.............................24
ACTON, Zora............................72
ADAMS, Ernest W 67
AHK-NAH 43
AH-KO-SEE 197
AH-LAY-MAH-WA-SE 83
AH-NA-KA-WA 105
AH-NA-WIT.............................220
AH-NO-WA-TA 108
AH-QUAH-SAH.......................248
AH-QUAW-SAW......................183
AH-SQUAH-SUP-PIT 108
AH-SQUA-SA-PE-TA 105,106
AH-SQUA-SA-PI-TA..................105
AH-SQUA-SUP-PIT....103,105,106, 148
AHT-SE......................................33
ALDAVA, Louise......................269
ALFORD
Betsy......................................37
David.....................................28
Fannie..................................270
Gertrude................................56
James................................67,68
Maimie..................................28
T W 15,53
Thomas W........37,83,269,270,283
Thos W..................................28
ALLEN.................................35,282
John 104,105,112,281,282
AM-NA-ANE............................... 3
AN-A-WA-TA 107
ANDERSON
Hester.................................153
Lidda..................................102
Samuel 163
ANTOINE, Mary 67,68,126,127,131, 132,135,139,141,168,172,181,195
APPLETREE, George 245,256
AP-TAS-KA, Joseph...............23,24
ARCHANGLE............................289
ARMSTRONG, Franklin..............8,9

ARNOLD, John 295
ASBURY, Calvin........................16
ASHER, W R........................13,14
ATKINS
Clark...................................274
J D C....................................... 6
Mr.......................................273
Nellie Grant........................274
Nellite Grant.......................274
Susie...................................274
William..........................273,274
ATKINSON, William................273
AUGRE....................................256
AW-KO-SEE 184
AX, John..........................56,67,68
AXE
James.................................... 56
John...................................... 63
BACK-SKA, Frank...................288
BAIN.......................................270
BANISTER
Fannie.................................247
Fannie H......................285,298
Mr................................285,298
Mrs Fannie..........................170
BANNISTER, Fannie.................261
BARADA, Minnie 266
BARKER
Andrew........140,141,142,247,256
Levi..............................247,256
Minnie 296
Sarah...................................142
Stella...................................296
BARNES
Mary............................42,192,193
May..................195,196,218,219
Mrs 194
BARONE
Anna...................................269
Charley...............................269
Jane....................................269
Josephine 269
BASHAM, H A............................65
BASSETT, Jane.........................271
BATES, William H 59
BAYLIS, Wm C..........................72
BEAR
Cora..................246,247,266,267

Index

Jack 116
Jim 241,256
Joe 241
Mollie 241,256
Sarah 85
William 246,250,251,257
BEARLEY, Fred T 251
BEASON, C J 45
BEAVER
   Caesar 87
   Charlie 23
BENNETT, Mary 55
BENSON, C J 60,63
BENTLEY, M J 66
BERTRAND
   Adelaide 85
   B B 85
   John 22
   Lawrence 85
   Lawrence J 85
   Mary 85
   R R 21,22,85
BIG EAR, Theresa 38
BIGWAKER
   Lelia 261
   Margaret 261
BIGWALKER
   Esther 243,244,247,261
   Jennie 247
   Lelia 243,244,247,261
   Margaret 243,244,245,247, 256,261
   Maud 243,244,247
   Maude 261
   Sarah 243,244,247,261
BLACK
   Amos 3,4,130,132,202
   James 2,3,202,220
   Leda 142
   Lucy 2,3,256
   Mary 130,246,259
BLACK HAWK WOMAN 198
BLACK WING 177,178
BLACKHAWK 202
BLACKHAWK WOMAN 203
BLACKMAN, John P 290
BLUE COAT 9,10,13,14,15
BLUECOAT 10,11,12,13

Stella 56,67,68
BOB
   George 72
   James, Jr 290
   Susan 57,58,69,72
BOBB
   Charley 221
   Nannie 220
BOGGS, Frank W 63
BOYER
   Annie 60
   W C 52
BRIGGS, William E 49
BROWN
   Beulah 244,246,256,263
   Eva 110,130,131
   Gertrude 183,281
   Harry 243,244,246,256,263
   John 243,244,246,256,263,281
   Josephine 244,246,256,263,295
   Julia 247,261
   Mary 243
   Mary E 244,246,256,263
   Mary N 244
   Mr 74
   Mrs Julia 170
   Samuel L 130,132
   Thomas . 243,244,246,256,263,295
   W H 73
BRUNT, Mr H C 189
BRYAN, Milton 286,287
BUCKHEART, Jacob 64
BUFFALO-HORN, Thomas J 143, 144
BUFFALOHORN
   Clara 143,256
   Clare 248
   Grace 151,267
   Jennie 245,256
   Mamie 151
   Thomas J 151,248,256
   Thomas Jefferson 151,152
   Thos J 299
BULL FROG, Anna 46
BULLFROG
   Ben 63
   Billy 17
   Ellen 17

Index

Jennie 17
Jim 17
Thomas 17
BURKLEO, Eli 47,48
BURKLOO, Eli 47
BUTLER
   Benjamin 256
   Edward 241,256
   George 241,256
   H H 29,30
   Jane 241,256
   Mollie 256
   Mr 31
CADE, C H 73,81
CAIN, A J 290
CAMPBELL, C M 59
CANOE, John 111,240
CARDE, C M 117
CARLISLE, John G 174,175
CARPENTER
   C W 136,137,139,144,147,298
   C C W 143
   H P 197
   R P 119,120,290,291
CARTER
   Bertha 266
   Elmer 266
   Frank 1,4,138,139
   Jesse 173
   Jessie 174
   Laura 138,243,263,266
   Lorina 266
   Martha 138
   Mrs 292,293
CASSIDY
   Ed O 280
   P O 280
CASSIDY & CASSIDY 280
CEOKUK, Charles 283
CHA-KA-TA-CO-SEE 197
CHALCRAFT
   E L 123,125,128,130,132,144
   Edwin 124
   Edwin L 125,126,127,129
CHALORAFT, Supervisor ... 165
CHARLES, J B 270
CHARLEY
   Joe 57,58,69,72

Nancy 57,58
CHEESMAN, D G 8
CHEROKEE, William 66
CHE-WE-QUAY 32,33,34,35
CHIEF 104,105
CHISHOLM, Jesse 299
CHRISTHER, F W 93
CHRISTNER, F W 93,95
CHUCK-E-QUAH 148,165
CLAPP, L W 116,117,279
CLARDY
   B J 60
   Carrie B 60
   A H 60
   Isabella 59
   Joshua 60
   Lucy I 60
   Mattie J 86
   William 60
CLARK
   Lucy 121,195,218,219
   Miss 194
CLARY, L E 168
CLEGHORN
   James 102
   Jim 102
CLEGHORNE, James 49
CLEVENGER, O B 86
CLOTHIER, Mary 192,193
CLUTHER, Mary 42
CLUTHIER, May 218
COLLINS, William W 70
COMPAS 289
CONGER 167
   Andrew 243,256
   Hattie 243,256
   Jay 256,278
   May 119,120
CONKLIN
   E L 113,174,175,183
   Mr 113
CONNALIS
   Cedro 226,229,230,231,233, 234,236,237
   Joe 228,229,230,231,233,234, 236,237
   Martha . 224,225,227,228,229,230, 231,233,234,236,237,241,246,266

Index

Martha McKinney 224,225
Mary 224,225,226,228,229, 230,231,233,234,236,237,241,246, 266
Mary McKinney 224,225
CONNELLY, Alex 250
CONNOLLY
   Alex .. 1,2,3,4,141,159,163,187,241
   Alexander 90,91
COOMBS, C W 79
CORDELL, S A 77,121
COVNEY, Wm 123
CRANE
   Carrie 256,257,262
   Charles 119,121,256,257
   Charlie 119,120
   Harry 256,257,262
   Horace 256,257,262
   John 256,257
   Mary E 119
   Mary L 256
CUELLAR, Anna 269
CUPPAWHE, Mary 3,4,19
CURLEY, Jane 289
CURLY
   Andy 75
   Wezo 75
CURTIS
   Fannie 168
   James 168
CUSTIS, J S 167
DANIEL, R E L 67,68
DAUGHERTY, J H 9,10,11,12, 13,15
DAVENPORT 118,280
   Nancy 248,266
   Nellie 248,266,277
   Seba 248,266
   William 118,248
   Wm 266
DAVIS
   Flora 207
   Frank 208,210,216
   Frank B 210,216
   Harry 210,216
   Henry 114,115,198
   Jefferson 249,257
   Juintta 156

Junitta 152,153,156,206,215, 248,268
Orilla 249,257
Robert 249,257
DAY
   Sam 66
   Sampson 66
DE PUE, William B 156
DEEN, J B 60
DEERE
   Albert 283
   Amos 84
   Douglas 84
DEERR
   Bob 70
   Tilda 70
DELAWARE
   Ellen 22,75,76
   Jane 22
DELEWARE
   Ellen 53
   Jane 53,54
DEPUE
   Mr 153,157
   W B 153,156
   William B 152
DEROIN
   Birdie 217
   John 267
DESHANE, Caleb 69
DICKENS
   W A 179
   W F 283
   Walter F 269,270
DIGGS, James B 271
DILL, William H 87
DIRT, Jennie 283
DO-CHA-CHE-GRA-ME 261
DOLE, Willie 50,61
DOLLEY, J N 91,92
DONNELL
   H R 102
   W R 110,111,113
DOUD
   Grace 72,73
   Leroy P 73
   Leroy Palmer 72,73
   Zora 72

Index

DOW, Lorenzo 8
DUNCA, Richard 266
DUNCAN
  Ada 93,94,257
  Alice 246,257
  Cosette 257,266
  Cossette 249
  Dickson 245,246,248,265,266
  McKinley 95
  Richard 93,94,95,246,249,250, 251,257,266
  Robert 246,250,251,257
DUNN
  Albert 93,94,95
  Caroline 93
  Ralph 19,93,94
DUNWORTH, C M 219
DUPEE
  Dewey 257,260,261
  Mary 257,260,261
  Victor 257,260
DUPUIS
  John 128
  Lydia 128,129
DURRAN, Josephine 269
EASON 79
EASTON 79
EATON
  Cassle 8,181,182
  Cassie, Jr 8,26,27
  John C 26,27
  Mrs 8
  Mrs Cassie 8,26,27
EDWARDS
  Mr 205
  O C 198,204,211,213,214
  Superintendent 211
ELEPHANT
  Gertrude 270
  Henry 270
  Lucy 270
  Sarah 270
ELI, Jane 265
ELLIE, Katie 244
ELLIS
  Dick 67,68
  Frank 245,258
  Kate 245,258

  Katie 66,244
  Mabel 147
  Mrs Eli 299
  Sallie 258
  Sarah 147,244
  Sargeant 258
  Sargent 245
ELMSLEE
  H L 155,158,176,179,186
  Harry L 161,217,252
ELY
  Albert 48,49
  Jane 49,257,258,259,265, 271,272
  Jane Basset 274
  Samuel 48,49
EMBRY, John 65,194
ES-QUA-SA-PI-TA 107,108,109
ETEYAN, Joe 288
EWING, Frank 198
EZELL, Victoria 239
FAGAN, W E 91,92
FALLOON
  James 211
  Jas 212
FALLS
  Beaver 245,251,252,258
  David 160,162
  Edna 162,183
  Grover ... 161,162,246,251,252,258
  Sam 258
  Samuel .. 161,162,245,246,251,252
FALOON, Jas 213
FEAR, Marie 244,262
FLYNN, D T 87
FORD 199
  John 198
FOREMAN
  Frank 283
  Kate 283
  Minnie 283
  Scott 51
  Tommy 283
FORMAN
  Betsy 37
  Eli 37
  Ellen 37
  Frank 37

James 37
John 37
Mary 37
Sallie 37
Susie 37
Tiney 37
FOSTER
Geo W 67
John 130,131,132,145,173,206, 208,210,215,217,298
FOWLERS, William B 63
FOX
Bettie 245,258
Jas 258
Joseph 18,245,258
FRANK, Anna 259
FRANKLIN
Benjamin 36,202
Leona 3,4,202
FRIEND, Howard 79
FULLEN, Jefferson P 63
GALICK, W N 82
GARDINER
Albert 151
Albert F 164
Albert T 153,154
GARDNER
Albert 163
John F 163
GE-HE-QUA 83
GIBBS
Alice 246,259
Dosh 246,259
Gilbert 246,259
Hiram 246,259
GIBSON
Betsy 46
Fannie 46
Mary 83
Mrs 46
GILBERT
Fannie 202,203
Judith 203,204
Mr 72
GIST, G H 23
GIVENS
Charlotte 246,258
Evelina 183

Eveline 246,248,258
Gertrude 246,248,258,259,281
Isaac 183,246,248,258
GOKEY
Leo 123,124
Lizzie 123,124
Mary 246,264
Mary Miller 200
Paul 200
Ruth 200
GOODBOO
Frank 6,222
Hannah 6
Josie 222
Lewis 6
Mary 222
Thomas 6,221,222
GOODELL
Isaac 168
Mary 168
GOODNER, [Illegible] 44,45
GRA-HA-ME-NE 259
GRANT
Anna 258,259,265
Annie Nellie 258,259,265
Charles 19
Elwood Oldman 67
Frank 258,259,265
John 259,264,265
Lydia 183,246,248,258
Mary 258,259,265,274
Mary Green 259,265
Mrs 67
Mrs John 271
Nellie 271,273,274
Thelma 258,259,265
Thomas Stanley 259,265
Thomas Stanly 259
Ulyses S 2,3,241,250
Vestina 258,259,265
William 259
William Green 265
Wm Green 258
GRASS
George 159
Mary 159,160
Silas 159,160
GRAT, Thelma 259

Index

GRAYEYES, Leona 247,258
GRAYSON, Fannie 253,267
GREEN
   Christena 92
   Christina Eliza 92
   Ernest Ray 91
   Herbert Reinhart 92
   Jefferson 258,259,265
   John 91,92
   R C 294
   Ralph 258,259,265
   William 259
GRIFFIN, Ross 115
GRIM, A, Jr 210
GRIMM
   A, Jr 210
   P C 33,34,35
   Phil C 33,34,35
GRNT, Thomas Stanley 258
GUFFIN
   Horace 124,126,127,131,132,
   133,134,135,137,139,151,155,158,
   159,161,163,164,169,171,172,174,
   181,186,187,208,217,241,250
   Horace K 140,141
   Ross ... 88,90,102,103,104,105,106,
   108,109,110,111,112,113,114,115,
   116,117,118,119,122,140,141,142,
   183
GULICK, W R 78,83,88,275,276
GUTHRIE
   Kate 247,258
   Shela 247
   Shelah 258
HAH-MAH-TOM-SE 290
HAHN-KA-WEP-EA-SE 54
HALL
   Eudora 192
   Harry 192,244,247,261
   Henry 170
   Jennie 170,192,243,244,247,261
   Rachel 170,244,247,261
   Rufus 191,192
   Sarah 246,247,261
HALLOWELL
   Benjamin 260
   Harry 260
   Irene 260

   Lizzie 259
HAMBLIN, Frank W 42,193
HAMILTON, William 261,262
HAMMONDS, A E 66
HAND, J W 77
HA-NE-KA-WA 108
HARAGARA, Mary 259
HARDIN, Hannah 6
HARRAGARA, Mary 259,265
HARRIS
   Benj 261
   Benjamin 247
   David 247,261
   Francis 245,259
   Irene 247
   Joseph 4,243,260
   Liza 243
   Mary 4,243,245,259,260
   Moses 4,243,245,259,260
   Sarah 247
HARRISON
   Benjamin 3,4,202
   Stephen 3,4,202
   Thomas 5
HARRY, J H 73,81
HARTICOO, Tom 256
HARVEY, W L 18,19,20
HAWK
   Eunice 245,259
   James 245
   Richard 245,259
   Samuel 245
   Silas 245
   Stella 245,259
HAWKINS
   Charles 58
   G A 87
HAYDEN, R F 92
HAY-WE-COO-LAH 38
HERNDON, Urich R 255
HICKS
   Mr 212
   R W 115,212
HIGGINBOTHAM, Ethel 52
HILL, Frank 46
HILLIS
   William 102
   Wm 102

Index

HODGE, Mary 160
HODJOE, Annie 283
HOER, F R 219
HOFFMAN
  P S 77,78,152,153,156,206, 215,270,298
  Roy 65,128,129,194
HOFFMAN & EMBRY 65
HOOD
  Boletha 53,54
  Ellen 17
  George 54
HOOKER, J W 59
HOPPING, J S 279,280
HORTON
  Lawrence 58
  Rose 87
HOT-CHI-SE 260,261
HOT-CHISE 260
HOTCHISE 260,261
HOUSTON, Judith 172
HOWARD
  J B 128
  John B 128
HOYT, S W 276
HUBER, S C 102,112,281,282
HUNTER
  Bertha 148,165
  Daniel S 247,261
  Emma 247,261,296
  Gertrude 247,261
  Harrison 247,261
  Henry 148,164,165,183,247,261
  Robert 247,261
HURD, Mary E 61
HURR
  Mary 249,257
  William .. 56,124,131,132,133,134, 135,137,151,159,161,164,171,172, 176,179,241,250
INGALLS
  Bessie 20,197,276
  Hattie 247
  Henry 247,262
  Horace 175,176,177
  John I 187
  John J 166,179,180,190
  Lucille 197
  Mattie 176,179,180,197,262
  Sadie 176,180,190,247,262
  William 190,197,247,262
INGLES, Horace 176
INGRAM, John C 295
JACOBS, John A 69,70
JAMES
  Geo W 24
  George W 25
JEFFERSON, William H 247,261
JENNINGS, J D F 58
JENSEN, J 217
JOBE
  Mr 47
  A T 47,48
JOHN, Doctor 51
JOHNSON
  Arthur R 149
  Emma 84
  H M 284
  Jane 249,257
  Maggie 24
  Miss Maggie 20
  Mrs 42,193
  Orlando 249,257
  Susan Morris 24
  Victor O 274
  William 33
  Willie 24
  Wm 20
JOHNSTON, Willard 73,74,81,82
JONES
  A B 80
  Emilie 155
  H C 155
  Henry 199
  Henry C 155
  Ho[illegible] C, Jr 262
  Levi W 199
  Melissa 155
  W A 27,32,35,47,48,58,60,69, 71,74,76,87,90,113,114,124,125,128, 130,133,134,137,138,140,145,182, 197,198
  William 104,108
JOSEY, H 166,176,180,185,186, 187,270
KAH-DOT

Index

Annie..................................289
James.................................289
Peter..................................289
KAHDOT, Etienne.........................74
KAHLENBUG, M C 272
KAKAQUE
  Jesse..................................244
  Maud.................................244
KA-KE-PA-NO 184
KALLENBERG, Maj..................291
KAN-KEH-O-QUA-HIT 189
KASHENAY
  Ida......................................102
  Mrs....................................102
KAW-TOPE 90,91
KEE-WAN-MO-QUA 188
KENNEDY
  A D.....................................279
  H E.....................................279
KEN-NO-QUA 44
KENT
  Emma................................167
  Frank..........................167,260
KEN-WA-THE 44
KENWORTHY, Albert...............207
KEOKUK 193
  Alice................................29,30
  Charles........... 42,116,169,193,241,
  244,262
  Fannie......................241,244,262
  Frank.......................241,244,262
  John................................29,262
  John Earle 241,244,262
  Mary A.......................169,244,262
  Moses........29,30,31,42,90,91,114,
  115,116,168,169,193,198,211,212,
  213,244,262
  Peyton......................241,244,262
  Pheobe...............................262
  Phoebe..................29,30,31,244
  Robert 262
KERKER
  C F.....................................151
  Charles F 153,154,164
  J F......................................151
  John F.......................153,154,164
KETCH KUM EE 123
  Francis...............................123

KETCH-KUM-EE
  Arthur 122
  Francis 122
KEWA CHE WAH NO QUA 55
KE-WA-PE-KA-SO 184
KEYAH, Mrs............................ 288
KIDNEY, Estelle E...................... 36
KING
  Anna 70
  J C........................ 10,11,13,14,15
  John C................................. 83
KING & ASHER 13
KINN-ME-QUA, Keth................. 22
KIRKER
  C F..................................... 151
  Chas F................................ 163
  J F..................................... 151
KISCO-KEYAH, Mrs Rose Ann 288
KIT-TOE.................................. 145
KOHLENBERG 254
  Maj 290
  Mr..................................... 274
  W C 85,120,124,131,132,133,
  134,136,137,139,141,142,144,145,
  146,147,148,150,151,152,153,154,
  155,156,157,158,159,160,161,162,
  163,164,165,166,167,168,169,170,
  171,172,173,174,175,176,179,180,
  181,182,184,185,186,187,188,189,
  190,191,192,194,195,196,197,198,
  199,200,201,202,203,204,206,207,
  208,209,210,211,213,214,215,217,
  218,219,222,226,228,229,231,233,
  234,236,237,240,241,251,270,272,
  275,276,277,278,282,283,284,285,
  286,287,291,295,296,297,298,299
  William C 134,135,136,143
  Wm C 140
KOHLENBURG
  Mr..................................... 255
  W C 254,298
KO-NAW-PAW-KAH......... 112,240
KOSHIWAY 262
  Vana 262
KOTTOE, Fannie......................... 3
LAFALIER, Sophia 222
LAFROMBOISE, Francis.......... 289
LARACY, John 37,38,81

Index

LARGENT, A M 155
LARRABEE, C F .. 201,202,205,207,
209,211,213,215,216,217,219,220,221,
242,250,254,281,285,292,293,294
LATHAM, Geo D 79
LATHAM & COOMBS 79
LAWRENCE, Mrs 81
LEAVES, John 150
LECLAIR 44
   Ahk-nah 43
   Silas 43
LEE 81
   Alice 31,244,262
   Bessie 9,134,136
   Jessie 134
   Mrs Alice 29,30
   Philip 134,135
LEECH, Edw 135
LERCH, William L 295
LEUPP, F E 223
LEWIS
   Debbie 47
   Jim 47,48
LINCOLN
   Abraham 116
   Fullwood 116
   Jennie 268
   Maggie 116,260
   Thomas 116
LITTLE AX
   Stella 299
   Switch 56
   William 56
LITTLE BEAR
   Carrie J 143
   Charley 83
   Eliza 83
   George 83
   James 81,83
   Lilly 83
   Lucy 83
   Mattie 83
   Shoney 83
   Stella 83
LITTLE BIRD 61
LITTLE CAPTAIN 17
   Betsey 17
   Betsy 17

   Martha 17
   Martin 17
LITTLEAX
   Polly 55
   Switch 56,67,68
   William 56,67,68
LITTLEBEAR 82
   Carrie J 248,262,264
   Eliza 299
   Florian 264
   Florien 262,299
   Geo 264
   George 262,299
   James 299
   Janie 82
   Lillie 82
   Lucy 82
   Shoney 299
LOGAN
   Carrie 262
   Chester 283
   John 262
   John A 262
   Lucy 299
   Mary E 256,257,262
   Theresa 257,262
LOHLENBERG, W C 279
LONG
   Agnes 243,263
   Arthur 178
   Thomas 243,244,262,263
LONGMAN, John 54
LONGSHORE
   Anna 224,225,226,228,229,230,
   231,233,235,236,237
   Anna McKinney 224,225
   Annie 222,241,266
   Chas 226,228,229,230,231,
   236,237
   Wilson 246
LOVE, E C 284
LOWRY, O C 254,296
LUCINDA 65
LUSK, F B 118
MACK
   Edgar 116,172,209
   Louisa 245,248,265
MADISON, Susan 18

Index

MAH-AKE-NA............ 2
MAHAW-TAW-WAW-PAH-WAH
..93
MAH-MAH-KE-AH 112
MAH-MAW-KAW-SHE 95
MAH-NE-PAM-DOSH 21
MAH-QUE-QUAH 16
MAH-TAH-PWA 248,266
MAH-TAW-WAW-PAH-WAH ...94
MA-KA-SO-PE-AT 146
MA-KE-SO-PE-AT 122
MAKE-SO-PE-AT 247
MALIN
   Agent............... 104,112
   W G.... 80,89,103,150,240,278,279
   Wm G.......... 107,108,109,111,118,
   122,146,148,185,197,296,297
MALLICOAT
   W H.............76
   Wm H.............76
MA-MA-NA-WA 107,109
MA-MA-WA 108
MA-MA-WAH 105
MA-NA-KA-WA 185
MANATOWA
   Bertha............243,263,292,293
   Elmer...........243,263,292,293,294
   George..........243,263,266,292,293
   Laura............292,293
   Lorena............292,293
   Lorina............243,263
MANSUR
   Betsey 217
   Ida 217,245
MARGA-HE 261,262
MARGRAVE
   Mr 205,212
   Mrs Margaret 110
   W A 25,204,205,213,214,215
   Wm A 25
MARSHALL, Gabriel 166
MARTIN
   Francis 245,256
   Liza 4,259,260
MARTWAS 43
MA-SHE-TA 282
MASON
   Edith 130,131
   Gracie 130,131
   Nellie 191
MA-SQUA-TA 184
MA-TA-CHE 282
MA-TA-SE-MO 32,33,34
MA-TA-SHE 282
MATCH KE, Mary 21
MATCH-KE 22
MATCH-KE, Mah-ne 21
MATCHKE, Mary 21
MATHEWS
   Della 249,264
   Edward 249,264
   Maggie 263,264
   Roger 263,264
   Walter 264
MATTHEWS
   Ann 136
   Edward 136,137
MAW MELLO HAW 264
MAW-MAW-KAW-SHE 94
MAW-MEL-LO-HAW 244
MAW-WAS-SHE 184
MAW-WAW-SHE 184,278
MAXEY
   J F, Jr 143,144,145
   J H 134,135,136,157,158,
   171,172,173
   J H, Jr 181,182
MAZHE 22
MC,CLELLAN, Flora 207
MC.KUCK, John 118
MCALLISTER
   M 24
   R 24
MCALLISTER, Robert 20
MCCLANAHAN, Pierre B 70
MCCLELLAN
   Dollie 243,247,261
   Edward 210
   John 144,210
   Rebecca 139,144,210
MCCLELLN, Dollie 244
MCCOY
   Esau 252,266
   Isaac 126,127,252
   Jacob 126
   Jennie 54

Index

Mary 126,127
MCCREARY, Rachel 260
MCGUIRE, Mr 50
MCKINLEY 270
MCKINNEY, Lizzie 225
MCKINNEY
   Aaron 224,225,226,228,229,
   230,231,233,234,236,237,241,266
   Annie 222
   Emma 226,228,229,230,231,
   233,234,236,237
   Jefferson 128,224,225,229,232,
   233,235
   Lizzie 224,225,226,228,229,
   230,231,233,234,236,238,241,246,
   266
   Wils 266
   Wilson .. 127,222,224,225,227,228,
   236,238,241,246
MCKOSITO 90
   Annie 241,244,246,252
   Barbara 246,266
   Chief 171,172,209,246,252,266
   Moses 208,209
MCKUK, John 248,266
MCLAUGHLIN
   J A 284
   J T 25
MCMILLAN, A T 160,161
MCMILLEN, A T 162
MCPHERSON 27
   Albert 193
ME JASH KEE 146
MEAD
   Harry 208,209
   Mr 189
MEEDE, Cyrus 193
MEEK, David N 126,127
ME-GAH 22
ME-KAH-TAH 278
ME-KAH-TAW 277
ME-KA-TAW 184
MENO-QUOT 244
ME-SAW-WHAT 163
MESH SHAWCHE 120
ME-SHE-PE-QUA 282
MESH-SHAW-CHE 119
MESSAWAT

Alma 243,264
Julia 246,264
Linda 243,246,264
ME-WA-PE-KA-SO 184
MILES-SE-SO-TAY-SE 221
MILES-SE-SO-TY-SE 220
MILLER
   C W 74,75,242
   E W 75
   Henry 200,201,246,264
   Ida 200,246,264
   Mary 246,264
   R L 123
   Ruth 200,246,264
   W L 204
MIS NO QUA 22
MITCHELL
   Amelia 123,124
   Egbert 245,266
MITCHNER, Byron C 289
M-JISH-KE 243,244,263
M-JISH-KEE 272
MK-IT-AO-KO 21
MKIT-AO-KO 21
M-NIS-NON-SE, Bazil 37
M-NIS-NON-SE, Bazil 38
MO-CHO-WIN 61
MOCK-E-NAW 167
MOHEE 270
   Charlie 274
MOKOHOKO, Flora 245,248,265
MONTGOMERY, Hunter ... 125,126
MOOK-KUT-TAH-O-SO-QUE 130
MOON, A M 81
MOORE
   Jane 103
   John R 279
MOOSE
   Jos 23
   Joseph 24,62,189
   Peter 22
MORGAN, James 104,105
MORRIS
   Eliza 53,255,298
   Eva B 258,259,265
   Harriet 19
MORTON 65
   Clifford 248

Index

Clifford H 264
George O 248,264
Mamie ... 243,244,247,248,261,264
Oliver P 143,248,264
MOSKOCHAKEN 24,25
MS-COP-GO, Louise 122,123
MTCH-KE 22
MUC-CUM-PEM-PE 260
MUCCUMPEMPE 260
MURRAY
  Charles 264,265,296
  Charley 295
  Emily 257,260,261
  Kerwin 264
  May 264
MYERS, H A 73
NADEAD, Eli 44
NAG, Lucy 28
NA-HA-PA-NO-QUA 105,108
NAH-AW-KE-TE 144
NAHMOSWE, William 247,266, 267
NAH-SO-PEA-SE 220
NAH-WAH-LAH-PEA-SE 56,67, 68
NAK NASH KUK 22
NA-KNA-CHKUK, Joseph 80
NA-NA-AH-PA-MA-QUA ... 107,109
NA-NA-GRA-WAY-HE-SE-KA .. 23
NA-SA-PA-PHIA 108
NA-SA-PE-PHIA 105
NA-SAQ-PA-PHIA 104
NA-SHE-TA 122
NA-SHE-TAH 146
NAVARRE
  A F 7
  Isadore 7
  Jerome 7
NAWANOWAY, Frank 260
NEAL
  Isadore 173
  Lilly 299
  Mary 103,174
  Moses 6,44
  Victor 173
NE-BAH-QUAH 113
NEE-PASH-NEE-WIN-KAR 202
NE-MA-KO-WA 184

NE-NE-MA-KO-WHAH 278
NENO-QUOT 263
NE-PAU-SA-QUA 146
NE-PAU-SE-QUA 247
NE-PO-PE 156
NEP-PETH-SKE 44
NICHOLS, William R 32
NICKEL, W K 138,139
NIKAS 289
NIKIT-A-O KO 21
NIKITA-O-KO 21,22
NO-KA-KA 297
NO-NE-QU-AH 280
NO-NE-QUAH 284
NO-TO-KAH 112
NULLAKE
  Ada 249,257,266
  Amanda 185,187,252
  Amania 245
  Anna 266
  Annie 249
  Charles 153,163,164,287
  Henry 185,186,187
  Hiram 245,252,266
  Walter 185,187,245,252
NUZUM, George 204
O SE DEAD 117
O,BRIEN, Daniel 286
O'BRIEN
  Daniel 226,228,229,233, 234,236,237
  Lucy 224,225,226,228,229,232, 233,234,236,237,241,246,266,286
  Lucy McKinney 224,225
OGEE, L N 222
O-GIH-MAH-QUAH 113
OGLESBY, John T 26
OLD BOB DEER 69
ONAWAT, James 104,148
ON-A-WA-TA 104,106
ON-A-WOT 103,105,106,107, 108,109
ONE WHITE HORSE 67
ON-NA-KA-WA-NA 111
ORR, R J 38
O-SHA-KE 136
OTHA-KE-SE 46
OTWAS, Mrs. 242

Index

OUTCELT, G A 65
O-ZHA-OCK-PEESE 143,144
PA KSH KAH, Frank 81
PAH QUA SKLAH 24
PAH TE KO TA 89
PAH-KOL-NO-PE 250
PAH-PAS-KO-KUCK 160
PAH-SHE-KO-KAW 123
PAH-SHE-PAW-HO 152
PAH-SHE-SHA-SHE 175
PAH-SH-RAH, Frank 62
PAK-SH-KAH
   Frank 50
   Mnes-no-que 62
PA-ME-KA-WO 112
PA-NAH-WEP-EA-SE 54
PA-NAU-SEE 122
PANTHER, Eliza 46
PAPAN, Mary 258
PA-PHIA,NAW 247
PA-PHIA-NA 122,146
PAPPAN, Mary 245,258
PA-QUA-SKLAH 25
PARKINSON
   Julia 245,256
   Maggie 4
   Mamie 2
   William 2,202
   Wm 252
PA-SA-SHA-SHE-HA 122
PAS-CA-WE, Frank 37
PA-TAY-QUAH-COM-SE 83
PATRIC, Lee 57
PATRICK 65,149
   Agent 76,193
   Col 7
   A E 159,160
   Lee 25,26,27,28,30,31,35,36,38, 39,40,42,43,46,47,48,49,50,51,52,53, 55,57,58,59,60,61,62,63,64,65,66, 67,68,69,70,71,72,73,74,75,77,78,79, 80,81,84,85,86,87,89,116,148,164, 166,168,169,175,176,177,179,180, 193,200,201,218,222,250,251,270, 271,276
   Mr 74,82,116,117,150
   S L 7
   Samuel L 8

PATTEQUA
   Addie 1,247,267
   Bertha 1,85,247,267
   Mamie 1,247,267
   William 90,91
   Wm 252
PATTOCK, George W. 245,247,248, 249,268
PAU-AU-CHE-QUA 111,240
PAW DOSH, Mah-ne 21
PAWDOSH, Mah-ne 21,22
PE-AD-WA-DAH 21,22
PEANNA, Mary 63
PEARCE, Justice Joh 81
PECAN
   Bin-mik 46
   Lucy 66
PEN-AH-THO 45
PE-NA-SHE 145
   Tom 145,202
PENASHE
   Thomas 200
   Tom 3,4
PENDLETON, W S 52,93,94,95
PENNOCK
   David 243,244,263,267
   William 267
PEP-KA-WA 63
PERRY, Annie 268
PERSON, Ash-nick 241
PE-SHAW-KAW 177
PE-TAH-WEP-EA-SE 54
PETER THE GREAT 43,44
PE-TO-KE-MO 112
PE-WAH-TAH 16
PEYTON, J T 281,284
PEYTON & TRAYNOR 280,284
PICKARD
   Joseph 166,185,186
   Mr 167
PICKET, Maggie 80
PICKETT
   Caroline 3,4
   Maggie 88,89
PIERCE, Thomas 84
PIERSON, David 289
PLUMB
   Mary 248,249,267,268

Index

Minnie ... 245,248,249,266,267,268
PO KO HOM 113
PO KO HOM-A-WAY 111
PO-KO-HOM-A-WAY 110
PONE-WAH-TAH 247
POOLE, Jak 298
POWERS
   F V 43,192,193,195,196,218
   George 42,193
   Jennie V 42,193
   Mr 193
   Mrs 32,193,194
   Mrs F V 31
PRICE, Mr H D 63
PSHUCK-TO-QUA 23
PUCKETT, Jacob 29,31,127,173, 174,298
PUSH-E-TO-NEKE-QUA ... 104,105
PUSH-E-TO-NEKE-QUE 108
QUA-CHE-WE 197
QUAH-PEA-SE 83
QUAH-QUAH-CHE 143
QUA-NO-THA 283
QUA-SQUA-WA 184
QUIN-E-PAH 185
QUINTARD
   James B 36
   Maddie F 36
RAH-SH-ITAH, Frank 50
RANDALL
   Fannie 3,145
   Paul 3,4
RANDELL, Paul 202
RAY 28
RAZEY, Mr. 116
REASOR, E D 294,295
REDROCK
   Abbey 240
   Abby 112,240
REEVES, John R S 5
REGGLES, W A 75
REID, J H 72
RHODD, Edd 86
RHODES, Deborah 268
RICE
   Edward 246,247,266,267
   F M 123,124
   Lizzie 246,247,266,267,280

RIDER, Minnie 249,267
RIDGE, Jesse 136,137
RIGAS, Mr J W 76
RIGGS, W J 208,209
RILEH KUMEE, William 123
RIMER, Mrs Piercie 61
RINER, Oma 287
ROBERTSON, J B A 220
ROBINSON 80
   W C 177,179
   William C 178
ROCK
   James 54,75,76
   Thomas 54,283
RODD, Charley 73
ROGERS
   Linda 246
   Lindy 259
ROONEY, L H 284
ROSE, Geo L 50,79
ROSS
   Mary 77
   A T 87
ROUBIDEAUX
   Antoine 204,205
   Farrah 204,205,268
   Ida 134,135
   Jennie 204,205
   Joseph 204,205
   Maggie 204,205
   Mary 259
   Sarah 204
ROUBIDOUX
   Antoine 214
   Ida 9
   Joe 214
   Joseph 214
   Maggie 214
   Old Mr 214
   Sarah 213,214
   Tecumseh 9
RUBIDOUX, John 16
RUFFALOHORN, Thomas J 139
RUGGLE, W A 22,23
RUGGLES, W A 220,221
RYAN, Thos 91,101
SAGE, Walter H 295
SAM 84

Index

SANACHEZ, Fred 117
SAXON, Nannie E. 294
SCHOCH, W F 92
SCOTT 190
  Amanda 246,259
  Ellen 24
  J A 292
  Jim 297
  L A 123
  Mrs Ella 20
  S J 7
SEGAR, Jennie 70
SENACHE, Anna 208,209
SESAQUA 24
SHAFFER, Mr 71
SHANTEY, Mattie 82
SHA-QUE-QUOT 277
  Cora 247
SHAQUEQUOT
  Henry 267
  Kate 267
SHA-QUIN, Henry 198
SHAQUIN, Henry 115
SHAQUINE, Henry 114,213
SHA-QUI-NEE, Henry 115
SHAR-TAR-CHER 268
SHA-WA-NA-QUA-HK 104
SHA-WA-NA-QUA-HUK 105
SHA-WAS-[??]-HUCK 3
SHAWNEE
  Mr 71
  Mrs 71
  Walter H 32,33,34,35
  Wm 71
SHAWNEE LITTLE BEAR 82
SHAWNINGO
  John 69,70
  Stella 69,70
SHAZQUEQUOT, Cora 247
SHERMAN
  Lucy Anderson 143
  Tecumseh 134,135
SHINCES, Clarissa 269
SHINCIS
  Clarissa 269
  Frank 269
SHIP-SHE-WAHN-O 190,292
SHIP-SHE-WA-NO 291

SHOFFNER, Geo T 132,133
SIME-HA-THLE 55
SIMPSON, J E 295
SIZE-HA-THLE 67,68
SMALL
  Charley Lightfoot 267
  Edward 267
  Jack Lincoln 267
  Julia 188
  Mary 256
  May 267
  Robert 188,295
SMITH
  Alexander 132,133
  Annie 161,162,245,246,251,
  252,258,284,285
  David 251,252
  Frank 162,217,251,252,258,
  284,285
  H A 67
  Horace A 67
  Ida 185,186
  Jane 53,54
  Mrs Millie A 18
  Samuel 254,296
  Sarah 251,252
  Thos P 21
  Webster 132,133,156,185,
  186,215
SOUTHGATE, Geo M 72
SPEAR, Dennis Numott 55
SPEED, Horace 188,190
SPENCER, D W 23
SPITTO, M 122,123
SPOON
  Jim 68
  John 68
SPRINGER
  Elses 267
  Frank Falk 206,215
  Joe 128
  Josie 128,129
  Lizzie 38,267
  William 267
SPYBUCK
  Cinda Emma 28
  Frank 52
  John 52

Index

Maimie 28
Mrs Sallie 52
Sallie 52
STANLEY
   Mattie 299
   Pope 299
STARR
   Helen 248,267
   Hiram 248,267
STUART, Wm I 115
STUDHOLME, John 178
STUMP
   Ferdinand M 31
   Mr 32
   Mrs 32
SULLIVAN, Naomi 255,267
SWITCH, Chas 64
TA TA LA KO 117
TA-CO-SE-NE-NE 109
TAGGART, Agent 42,46
TAH-PAW-SHE-PAH-ME-HOT 185
TAH-TAW-SHE-PAH-ME-HOT
 186,187
TAH-TUP-PUCK-KO 174,175
TANKSLEY 165
   J A 147
   J S 149
   Mr 36
TAPSEY 188,189
TA-TA-PAU-GO 122
TAU-TA-PAU-GO 150
TAYLOR
   E F 24
   Isaac A 5
TE-AN-LOO-HAH 265
TENWAS, Joseph 62
TESSON, Peter 74
THACKERY
   F A 220,221,287
   Frank A 45,82,84,122,177,178,
   179,221,269,288,289
   Frank H 299
   Superintendent 113
THACKRY, Frank A 239
THAH-KE-WE-LAY-SE-CA 54
THOMAS 22
   Agent 24
   E L 21

Edw 13,18
Edw L 23
Edward L 8,15,16,24,31
Edward S 21
Genera 31
THOMPSON, Sallie 51
THORP
   Adaline 244,249
   Adeline 267
   Charlote 244
   Charlotte 157,244
   Edward 244,249,267
   Frank 249,267
   George 157,158,249,267
   Haram 253
   Hiram 157,158,249,253,267
   James 244,249
   Jim 267
   Julia 157,249,267
   Mary 244,249,267
   Mrs 268
   Roscoe 249,267
   William Lazley 267
THORPE
   Charles 125
   Charlotte 158
   Hiram 125,126
   Julia 125,126
   Martin 140,141,142
THREADGILL, Dr 71
THRIFT, William 77,78
THROPE, Martin 141
THURMAN
   Allen C 246
   Allen G 266,296,297
   Lucy 183,246,248,258,296,297
TILLMAN, C H 24
TILLOTSON, D C 290,291
TIP-KAW-WE 179
TOHEE
   Daniel 188
   Julia 215
   Millie 188,215
   Nellie 260
   Robert 188
TO-NE-GO-HA 264,265
TONEY, James M 71
TONNER

Index

A C.... 27,30,31,36,37,38,40,41,43,
51,52,55,57,59,62,88,101,105,110,
119,127,129,142,144,147,150,152,
153,154,155,157,158,160,162,164,
166,167,168,170,173,174,175,177,
185,188,191,192,194,199
A D..181
TOWNSEND......................254,268
TRIBBLE, Cassie 181,182
TRIGER, Cassie 26
TROMBLA, Louis......................179
TURNER............................290,292
   Clarence................................291
   Earl...291
   Fannie 290
   M L 219
   Mollie.....................................290
   Thomas 291
TYNER
   Charley...............................17,56
   Charlie..............................56,67,68
   Claude..............................56,67,68
   Maggie 299
   Ross..17
URIBES, Wiley..........................209
VENLEE...................................189
VETTER
   Fred..216
   Joe..275
   Lucy.......................................216
   Mary.......................................216
VIEUX, Mary...............................25
VILLINES, Joseph N...................79
WAB SHAW..............................123
WABAHAW..............................122
WABAUNSEE...........................289
WA-CO-AW-NA-NE 107
WA-CO-SE-NE-NE 107
WADLE, Mr 18
WAGONER, Fred A......287,299,300
WAG-STA-GAY-ME.................260
WAH KO LE, David 20
WAH-KAH-SOE..........................23
WAH-KO-QUA............................44
WAH-PAH-NE-SE.....................247
WAH-SE[?]-SE-QUAH 110
WAH-THAH-PEA-SE 46
WA-KAH-SOE 23

WAKOLLE
   David................................. 171,172
   Grover.......................... 241,246,252
   Hugh...................................248,266
   Rufus................... 241,246,252,269
WALKER
   Ben.....................................209,241
   Elmer..................................209,241
   Guy.....................................209,241
   I H..75
   Ira.......................................209,241
   Leo......................................209,241
   Lidie 241
WALL, Susan Morris....................24
WALLACE, Chas A......................61
WA-NE-CE-WA-HA 111
WA-PA-NA-SEE.......................146
WA-PE-KA-SO.........................278
WA-PELLU-KA 105,108
WA-PELLUKA..........................104
WAP-PE-KO-[?]-AH.................110
WARD
   A B 192
   Cora 167
   Susan 36
WARRIED
   Charles...................................... 15
   Chas.. 15
   Mrs Nellie................................. 15
WASHINGTON
   Albert................................ 156,268
   Caesar 14
   Ceasar 9,10
   Ceaser 15
   George 19,152,248,268
   James 9,10,14,15,56,67,68
   Jesse................................. 56,67,68
   Mary.............................. 248,268
   Nellie............................. 11,12,13
   Peter................................ 56,67,68
   Thomas 68
WA-SO-SA 213
WA-TA-TO-WAH 80
WA-THA-THA 212
WA-THO-THA 115,116
WATKINS, Angeline 25
WA-TO-TA-WA 88
WA-TO-TA-WAH 88

Index

WAU-MA-KEE 89
WA-WA-CO 108,109
WA-WA-TO-SA 106
WA-WA-TO-SAH 107,108
WA-WA-TO-SEE ... 106,107,108,109
WAW-KO-MO 166
WAW-KO-PAH-SHE-TOE 249
WAW-KO-PAH-SHE-TOW 268
WAW-ME-KETCH-THO-KO ... 162
WAW-SAH-QUE 147
WAW-WAW-KO 107
WAW-WAW-SHE 153
WAY-HO-NEE-MIE 128,129
WE-KE-AH 174
WELLES, Charles F ... 5,241,250,252
WE-PAU-SA-QUA 122
WE-PE-LU-KA 112
WE-SHO-WA 105,108
WES-KEN-NO, Marry 61
WE-SKO-SAH 115
WHEELER, Eva 171,172,173
WHISTLER
   Marie 29,30,31
   Marie A 29
WHITACRE, N 226,228,233,234, 236,237
WHITE
   Galbert 42
   Gilbert 193
   Ida 200,201,282
   Mabel 64
   Maggie 268
   Mrs Bob 64
   Rhoda 64
   Roda 64
   Talbert 18
WHITE CLOUD 53
   James Chief 53
WHITE TURKEY 32,59
   Ellen 37
   Tena Foreman 59
   Tiney 37
WHITECLOUD, Jefferson 298
WHITEWATER, Nettie 217
WILLIAMS
   A G 295,296
   G L 146,190,272,288,292
   Mary C 75,76

W I 189
WILSON
   [Illegible] 177
   Estelle 75
   Jeptha 67,68
   Louis S 274
   Nancy 74
   Naura 178
   Spanish 73
   Susie 37
WISH-TA-YAH 292
WISH-TE-YAH 189,190
WOLF
   James 245,247,248,249,268
   Jane 248,249,268
   John 247,248,249,268
WOOD
   Mr J D 26
   R E 189
WORTHER, Tonley 64
WRIGHT, A D 120,121
WRIGHTSMAN
   C J 274
   Charles I 271
WRIGHTSMAN & DIGGS 271,272
WRIGHTSMAN, WILSON & JOHNSON 273,274
WYMAN, Bertha 148,164,165
ZAH-JAH-NO 79

www.ingramcontent.com/pod-product-compliance
Lightning Source LLC
Chambersburg PA
CBHW020245030426
42336CB00010B/619